Ethics, Ethnocentrism and Social Science Research

This book addresses the ethical and methodological issues that researchers face while conducting cross-cultural social research.

With globalization and advanced means of communication and transportation, many researchers conduct research in cross-cultural, multicultural, and transnational settings. Through a range of case studies and drawing on a range of disciplinary expertise, this book addresses the ethics, errors, and ethnocentrism of conducting law and crime-related research in settings where power differences, as well as stereotypes, may come into play. Including chapters from scholars across cultures and settings – including Greece, Canada, Vienna, South Africa, India, and the United States – this book provides an invaluable survey of the issues attending cross-cultural social justice research today.

Engaging issues confronted by all cross-cultural researchers, this book will be invaluable to those working across the social sciences as well as professionals in criminal justice and social work.

Divya Sharma is a Professor of Justice and Law Administration at the Western Connecticut State University. She holds a PhD in Sociology and Master's degrees in Sociology and Criminal Justice. Her research focuses on topics related to informal banking systems, money laundering; immigration, globalization, and ethnic identity; and white-collar crimes.

Ethics, Ethnocentrism and Social Science Research

Edited by Divya Sharma

Routledge
Taylor & Francis Group
a GlassHouse Book

First published 2021
by Routledge
2 Park Square, Milton Park, Abingdon, Oxon OX14 4RN

and by Routledge
605 Third Avenue, New York, NY 10017

First issued in paperback 2022

a GlassHouse book

Routledge is an imprint of the Taylor & Francis Group, an informa business

Publisher's Note
The publisher has gone to great lengths to ensure the quality of this reprint but points out that some imperfections in the original copies may be apparent.

British Library Cataloguing-in-Publication Data
A catalogue record for this book is available from the British Library

Library of Congress Cataloging-in-Publication Data
A catalog record has been requested for this book

ISBN 13: 978-0-367-64447-5 (pbk)
ISBN 13: 978-0-367-20106-7 (hbk)
ISBN 13: 978-0-429-27026-0 (ebk)

DOI: 10.4324/9780429270260

Typeset in Bembo
by Deanta Global Publishing Services, Chennai, India

Contents

Editor and contributor

Divya Sharma is a Professor of Justice and Law Administration at the Western Connecticut State University. She holds a PhD in Sociology, and Master's degrees in Sociology and Criminal Justice. Her research focuses on topics related to informal banking systems, money laundering; immigration, globalization, and ethnic identity; and white-collar crimes. She has published several peer-reviewed journal articles, book chapters, submitted technical reports, and written a criminology textbook. She has expertise in conducting field research, survey research, and program and policy evaluation. Her recent projects include evaluation of the Y.D.U. program at Garner Correctional Institution in Newtown, CT, and the G.R.E.A.T. program at Bridgeport Police Department's Community Services Division; outsourced service sector, routine activities, and crime in Delhi, India; and refugees and forced migrants in western India. She has also conducted Research Methods Workshops for graduate students. She is further researching in the field of visual criminology, including photo essays, media narratives, and documentaries.

Contributors

Gordon Alley-Young, PhD, is the Chairperson for the Department of Communications and Performing Arts at Kingsborough Community College (KCC) – City University of New York (CUNY) where he is a Professor of Speech Communication. His research explores intercultural communication, popular culture, and critical socio-cultural perspectives on teaching/learning, identity, ethnicity/race, gender, class, and sexuality. His research appears in several peer-reviewed journal articles including, "(The) Earl Had to Die: Teaching Popular Ballads and Oral Traditions in a Performance Studies Class" in *JCSTAND*, 2014/2015, as well as chapters in several edited books including, "The Ties that (Un)Bind: Whiteness and the Racialization of Jewish Bodies in the film *School Ties*" in Dr. Janice D. Hamlet's *Films as Rhetorical Texts: Cultivating Discussions about Race, Racism, and Race Relations* from Lexington Books, 2020. Selected pieces of Dr. Alley-Young's research, previously published in English, appear in works that have been translated into Spanish and Turkish.

Shahid Alvi is a Professor in the Faculty of Social Science and Humanities at the University of Ontario Institute of Technology (UOIT), Oshawa, Canada. He has worked mostly in the areas of the political economy of crime, violence against women, and youth crime. His recent research focuses on the relationships between online technologies, violence and aggression, the political economy of technology in education, and online subcultures. He is currently researching for a book on online harms in contemporary society. Dr. Alvi earned a BA and MA in Sociology from the University of Saskatchewan, and a PhD in Sociology from Carleton University. He has received numerous awards for community service and was also the 2002 recipient of the Critical Criminologist of the Year award from the American Society of Criminology's Critical Criminology Division.

Vasiliki Artinopoulou is full Professor in Criminology in the Sociology Department of Panteion University of Social and Political Sciences (Athens, Greece), Head of the Department (2016–present), and the former Vice Rector of the University (2009–2011). She is also the Director of the "Restorative

Justice and Mediation Lab" at Panteion University of Athens. She participates in the Core Management Committee of the EU COST Action on "Cultures of Victimology." She is the Head of the Crime and Criminal Justice Unit and the Gender Issues Unit in the European Public Law Organisation (EPLO, EU). Professor Artinopoulou is an international expert and has carried out research on human rights and violence (women's and children abuse), the rule of law and aspects of injustice, victimology, gender equality and sexual harassment at workplaces, and trafficking. Professor Artinopoulou is the author of nine books, and almost 70 publications in peer review journals and collective volumes in English, French, and Greek languages.

Aneesa A. Baboolal is an Assistant Professor in the Department of Crime and Justice Studies at the University of Massachusetts – Dartmouth. Her research interests include gender-based violence across intersecting identities including race/ethnicity, immigrant, and religious minority status. Her recent work examines how Muslim people across various social identities experience and respond to gendered and racialized violence in the United States.

Ryan Bachman is a Doctoral Candidate in the History of American Civilization Program at the University of Delaware. He is a graduate of Western Connecticut State University and James Madison University. Bachman's work focuses on issues of race, colonialism, and public culture in the early American republic. He is currently in the early stages of dissertation research. Bachman's dissertation examines the role that ethnographic wax figures played in normalizing racism and colonial expansion in the early United States. His previous work includes digital humanities projects done in collaboration with the Shenandoah Valley Black Heritage Project in Harrisonburg, Virginia, and with the George Read II House and Gardens in New Castle, Delaware. Originally from Connecticut, he currently resides in the Shenandoah Valley.

Lisa V. Blitz, PhD, LCSW-R is an Associate Professor, Department of Social Work, Binghamton University, State University of New York, USA. Lisa uses community-engaged participatory research to develop approaches designed to enhance the school climate and has authored multiple publications on culturally responsive trauma-informed approaches for schools. She comes to this work following a 20-year career as a social worker. Lisa is the Co-Editor of the books, *Racism and Racial Identity: Reflections on Urban Practice in Mental Health and Social Services*, and *Knowledge Pathing: Multi-, Inter- and Trans-Disciplining in Social Sciences Series Volume 1: Issues Around Aligning Theory, Research and Practice in Social Work Education*. In addition, she leads a community-engaged research and asset-based community development project in Malawi. Lisa received her bachelor's degree from California State University, Los Angeles, and completed her Master's of Science and

Doctor of Philosophy degrees at Columbia University School of Social Work.

Reena Mary George was born in Mumbai, India. She completed her doctorate (interdisciplinary Sociology and Law) from the University of Vienna in 2014. Presently, she is based in Vienna and works with the United Nations Office on Drugs and Crime. She is also a Guest Lecturer at the Department of International Development, University of Vienna. She teaches/has taught courses on human rights, sustainable development, gender, ethics, and methodology in prison research and on conducting fact-finding in cases of custodial death and torture at the University of Vienna and the University of Mumbai. She has worked in programs and managerial capacity in programs on the rehabilitation of prisoners, children in conflict with the law, and on prevention of dropouts among girls. She also worked as the Project Head at the Resource Cell for Juvenile Justice, a Field-Action Project of Tata Institute of Social Sciences. Her topics of interest include prison research, ethical concerns in research, human rights, and gender.

Vamsee Juluri is a Professor of Media Studies at the University of San Francisco and the author of *Becoming a Global Audience: Longing and Belonging in Indian Music Television* (Peter Lang, 2003), *Bollywood Nation; India through its Cinema* (Penguin India, 2013), and several other books. His articles have been published in *Critical Studies in Media Communication*, *European Journal of Cultural Studies*, *Television and New Media*, *Communication Theory*, *Foreign Affairs*, and numerous newspapers and blogs including *The Huffington Post* and the *Times of India*. His current projects include a study of Hindu representation in American media, and an ongoing fictional trilogy set in the pre-Anthropocene era entitled *The Kishkindha Chronicles* (Westland, 2017 and 2020).

Mogomme Alpheus Masoga is a Professor and Dean of Arts faculty at the University of Zululand, South Africa. He holds a doctoral degree in African Orality from Free State University (UFS), South Africa. Mogomme's research in African Indigenous research and Decoloniality follows 25 years of research and teaching experience. He has developed Afro-sensed approaches and frames for conducting research in and with local communities. Pushing for a strong place of local communities in research and challenging researchers to "negotiate space" in their work. He has widely published in peer-reviewed journals and book chapters. He is the book Series Editor of the series publication, *Knowledge Pathing: Multi-, Inter- and Trans-Disciplining in Social Sciences* published by AOSIS.

Sheetal Ranjan is full Professor in the Department of Sociology and Criminal Justice at William Paterson University, USA. She serves on the Policy Committee of the *American Society of Criminology* and is a board member of *The Crime and Justice Research Alliance*. She is the immediate past Chair of the *Division on Women & Crime* of the *American Society of Criminology*. Her research interests include violence prevention and intervention with a primary focus on applied research. She has received Federal funding from the Department of Justice, Office on Violence Against Women ($600,000) to establish William Paterson University's *Campus Violence Prevention Program*. Her most recent award in partnership with Jersey Shore University Medical Center ($2.4 million) uses federal funds from the Victims of Crime Act (VOCA) to establish a hospital-based violence intervention program.

Allucia Lulu Shokane is Professor of Social Work and head of the Department of Social Work at the University of Zululand, South Africa. She holds a doctoral degree in social work from the University of Johannesburg (UJ), South Africa. Her research interests include, among others: the broad field of social work and community development; critical and radical social work, decolonized methodologies, Indigenous knowledge and practices within the context of community development; poverty alleviation strategies; and asset-oriented community-led development (ABCD) – thus specific to social work education. She is lead Co-Editor of the book project, *Knowledge Pathing: Multi-, Inter- and Trans-Disciplining in Social Sciences Series Volume 1: Issues Around Aligning Theory, Research and Practice in Social Work Education* published by AOSIS. She is currently serving as the Vice-President of the Association of South African Social Work Education Institutions (ASASWEI).

Acknowledgments

I thank the contributors for making this volume possible and their commitment and patience in its completion. The initial idea for this project came about at a panel where topics of ethnocentrism, decolonization of social science, field research in foreign and cross-cultural settings, and vulnerable subjects and ethics were discussed. As I reached out to various experts and scholars, I was received with enthusiasm and excitement, and the diverse group of contributors has helped to bring about rich narratives and intellectually challenging insights about social science research. I appreciate the time and effort that they have taken to collaborate and write.

I am greatly thankful to Dr. Colin Perrin, the commissioning editor at Routledge, for his patience and guidance throughout this process. The volume would not have materialized without his knowledge, support, and vision.

On a personal note, I am also extremely grateful to my sister and mother for putting up with me as I traveled between the United States and India multiple times carrying suitcases full of books and papers. Their love and encouragement keep me going.

Introduction

This volume focuses on the ethical and methodological issues that researchers face while conducting social science research. These dilemmas and challenges are more pronounced in studying vulnerable populations including victims, minorities, and respondents in settings that are not easily accessible. With increased globalization and ease of travel, there is also concern about helicopter researchers, especially when presenting information to the audience that is largely unfamiliar with the topic and the setting.

The volume also addresses topics of ethics, gaps in information, gatekeepers and access, and the significance of recognizing power equations – including between researcher and respondent – as well as stereotypes rooted in religion, race, culture, and so on. These may come into play while exploring contemporary topics of crime, justice, victimization, and even while conducting a historical analysis of the same. With a gradual but constant recognition of the need to decolonize higher education, this volume serves as a valuable means to advance that dialogue, while providing critical information about what concerns may arise and how and why to address them.

The ethical dilemmas, ethnocentrism, prejudices, and power hierarchies are not new; however, as the field of higher education largely remains insular, many of these limitations receive little scrutiny. With the flattening of the world through social media, these issues are addressed in the news and popular media, but academia still lags, yet at the same time, there is a real danger of social media muddling news and academic spaces if researchers are uncritical of the information they receive and are not careful about the limitations of the methods of data collection they use.

With globalization and advanced means of communication and transportation, many social scientists collect data on topics that were previously rare or considered out of reach. Many researchers in cross-cultural, multicultural, and transnational settings are using qualitative methods to conduct exploratory research. However, limited or lack of hypothesis testing necessitates observing phenomena in as much detail as possible without overgeneralizing and being mindful of gaps in information. This volume presents a rich insight into a wide range of topics about collecting data from refugees, prisoners, victims of domestic violence, and religious and ethnic minorities. It also explores the biased, prejudiced, or poorly informed manner in which ethnic, religious, and racial groups may be portrayed in the media. By highlighting these topics, it is hoped that future researchers, including those involved in field research, will be less likely to commit the same errors. It also attempts to recognize the toll that field research may take on researchers studying sensitive topics.

Chapter 1 discusses ethical challenges and limited generalizability while using qualitative research methods to study sensitive behaviors. It also includes a brief discussion on the growing concern about uncritical acceptance of news and social media narratives by scholars in the field of crime, justice, and victimization, and the related ideological pitfalls, biases, and stereotypes that could potentially contaminate the academic space in criminology and criminal justice. It explains these challenges while using data collected from refugees in Jodhpur, India, as a case study. It examines ethical dilemmas about the use of intensive interviews and focus groups while collecting data on topics related to violence, displacement, loss, and trauma. It addresses topics of access, reliability of the data, and generalizability in qualitative research. The field research often generates rich individual narratives that carry strong internal validity, but these need to be presented critically and carefully to avoid overgeneralization.

Chapter 2 is on the topic of (in)visibility of emotions and ethical concerns in prison research. It is based on four empirical prison research studies conducted from 2005 to 2014 in 22 different prisons in various states in India. The research participants included children of recidivists, women prisoners, families of prisoners, and prisoners on death row. This chapter attempts to present many layers of prison research, including the application of ethical principles. It further addresses some of the methodological limitations in prison research as well as challenges one faces as a researcher, specifically from a woman researcher's perspective in a male-dominated setting. The chapter culls out its "stories" and examples from the above 22 prisons in India and discusses the complex nature of criminological research leading to certain peculiarities in prison research. It elaborates on the value conflicts and emotions of such research studies, and some suggest ways to better equip oneself for prison research studies, thereby contributing to the discourse on (in)visibility of the emotional functions and ethical concerns in prison research.

Research in prison settings is especially challenging due to ethical dilemmas, an extremely restricted environment, and the emotional toll that it may take on the researcher. While collecting data from prisoners, the researcher has to manage not just the physical movement, or lack thereof, but also the core human emotions with objective data collection.

Chapter 3 provides an overview of some fundamental methodological and ethical challenges confronting those doing social science research in Canada. It introduces some of the key aspects of the Canadian context. The importance of understanding context, both historical and contemporary, is discussed, as is the question of the ultimate purpose of social science research. The chapter stresses the role of neoliberalism, the experiences of Indigenous peoples, and the increasing importance of digital technologies in shaping contemporary social science research in Canada. In particular, the chapter highlights the importance of paying attention to old and emerging ethical issues, the legacy of colonialism, ongoing questions regarding the implications for privacy and the welfare of research subjects, and the potential of digital technologies to enhance our understanding of social problems. Some limitations of conventional positivist stances on research are reviewed, and readers are encouraged to consider the power and privilege accorded to researchers in the research enterprise.

Chapter 4 recognizes that the research and knowledge production can no longer be conducted with Indigenous communities as if their views do not count or their lives and personal experiences, including their experiences of the research process, are of no significance. Nor can their experiences be interpreted and voices heard filtered through Western scientific epistemology alone. In the absence or marginalization of the African voice, Western epistemology, including its methods, paradigms, and production and dissemination of knowledge, amounts to imperialism in the guise of modern scientific knowledge. The starting point for the production, recording, and dissemination of knowledge should be the community involved in the research process along with the researcher. Drawing upon their experiences of engaging in participatory research with communities in South Africa and Malawi, and offering a critical examination of Western epistemology, the authors explore Afro-sensed frameworks and Indigenous knowledge. The chapter concludes with recommendations to promote Indigenous approaches and participatory research methods.

Chapter 5 explores issues relevant to conducting criminal justice research in Greece. The authors note that conducting criminal justice research in any foreign country requires an understanding of the structure of the criminal justice system within it as well as the nuances and practices of the interactions between various governmental, non-governmental, and academic institutions; knowledge of the official language and/or ability to work with interpreters; knowledge of the agencies responsible for ensuring ethical research practices within the country and the procedures to obtain approvals including nuances associated with the same; an understanding of the social and cultural practices that may apply to the research questions being investigated; and sample characteristics and legal norms. This chapter draws on the first-hand experiences of the authors in conducting domestic violence-related research in Greece. It highlights the challenges and successes so far and also provides a roadmap of best practices that future researchers can draw on as they embark on similar projects in international settings.

Chapter 6 highlights a common but often overlooked problem of imposing Western sensibilities and expectations in non-Western settings. In February 2011, Western journalists began reporting on Syrian women's/LGBTQ+ rights activist Amina Abdallah Arraf al Omari's blog *A Gay Girl in Damascus* (*AGGiD*). In June 2011, Amina was revealed to be a hoax perpetrated by

Scotland-based, US graduate student Tom McMaster who apologized and deleted *AGGiD*. The media blamed McMaster and amended and potentially redacted its *AGGiD* related reports. This case study argues that *AGGiD* was accepted as real because it reflects Western fantasies of Muslims/the Middle East and LGBTQ+ people, facilitated safe reporting on Syria, and offered a first-person perspective that news audiences increasingly seek. This critical cultural case study of *AGGiD* will examine the ideological blind spots in Western reporting about the Middle East and marginalized cultural groups, will consider the challenges of confirming reports by first-person citizen journalists in dangerous contexts with limited field access, and suggests potential sources of information used in the creation of *AGGiD*.

Topics of feminism, social justice, gender justice, equality, and so on are multilayered and non-linear, and often defined by the cultures where they are experienced, evolved, and explored. It is imperative to resist the idea of force-fitting Western understanding and expectations on other cultures around the world. This chapter presents a clear analysis of these topics and also identifies the gaps that commonly exist due to limited first-hand information and field access.

Chapter 7 provides a detailed analysis of Hinduphobia in not only the entertainment media in the West but also in mainstream news platforms, including when presenting news about crime and victimization. The normalization of Hinduphobia in the West is largely underexplored, and the author provides a comprehensive framework in identifying and addressing it. In 2017, two cases of media misrepresentation brought out strong protests from the Indian community in the United States. The first was the CNN series on religion called *Believer*, hosted by the author Reza Aslan, which featured a travelogue showcasing caste and cannibalism in India. The second was the acclaimed documentary *The Problem with Apu* by comedian Hari Kondabolu. The difference in these two cases of contestation though was the name under which critics and protestors raised their voices; CNN was accused of Hinduphobia and the misrepresentation of Hinduism and Hindus. *The Simpsons* was accused of bias along racial/ethnic lines ("Brownvoice," similar to "Blackface"), and the question of Apu's depiction as a Hindu character was completely ignored in *The Problem with Apu* and in the extensive press coverage that followed. In this chapter, the author argues that this polarization needs to be addressed to decolonize the field of media research from the use of categories of analysis originating in the Western academy such as "Hindu nationalism" as a way of denying emerging categories of self-representation and agency for Hindus in the United States such as the term "Hinduphobia." The author notes that Hinduphobia needs to be recognized by scholars, journalists, and activists as a valid category of intervention in media (and in talking about real-life concerns about terrorism and violence faced by Hindus), and proposes a media content analysis methodology to study Hinduphobia along with examples from his ongoing study for the benefit of future researchers.

After the 9/11 terrorist attacks, there were increased Islamophobia and hate crimes in the United States that necessitated addressing it at policy and academic levels. Similarly, increased crimes against Sikhs prompted the Federal Bureau of Investigation to collect specific data on hate crimes against Sikhs as a separate category under hate crimes. In that regard, it would be relevant to study how mainstreaming of Hinduphobia has put Hindus at risk of ridicule, abuse, or worse violent victimization as well as underreporting and nonreporting of that victimization. Unless it is systematically reported, documented, and studied, there cannot be any reasonable policy response to it.

Chapter 8 presents an in-depth discussion on conducting ethical interviews with Muslim international and Muslim American students in the Trump era. Muslim people from diverse backgrounds experienced discrimination and violence leading up to, and months after, the 2016 US presidential election, yet, the Muslim student experience is unique as a result of the intersectional nature of Islamophobic sentiment in subtle on-campus interactions and more overtly in public spaces off-campus. These incidents mimic the experiences of the Muslim community after 9/11 where Muslim people were increasingly subject to unique threats of discrimination, suspicion, and harassment. Reflections and observations in this chapter emerge from an exploratory qualitative study that examines the perceptions of Muslim undergraduate and graduate students (n = 50), across gender, race/ethnicity, and immigrant identity in the months after the 2016 US presidential election. Methodological issues related to obtaining entry into the Muslim community and utilizing insider/outsider identity, as well as the complexity of utilizing the researcher's own intersecting identities, to build trust and facilitate access are examined in relation to subject safety and vulnerability in cross-cultural interviewing contexts.

Chapter 9 emphasizes the importance of identifying ethnocentric narratives surrounding the representation of Native American history and culture as showcased in American museums for the audience. These institutions, invariably owned and operated by white men, used Indigenous material culture to advance popular notions of Indian "primitiveness" and racial inferiority – notions that helped justify contemporary policies of national expansion at the expense of Native people. Although such viewpoints were found in numerous popular culture mediums, they enjoyed an appearance of scientific legitimacy through their placement in museums. By the second decade of the nineteenth century, Native people were exhibiting their own histories and cultures within American museums. These demonstrations helped complicate established, ethnocentric museum interpretation. This chapter examines one such exhibition and uses it as a vehicle to explore how Native people exercised a degree of input over how their respective societies were represented in early American museums.

In studying any culture and society, it is critical to see how its attitudes have evolved and shaped over time, and whether orientalist and ethnocentric views may influence the continued treatment of certain populations.

Chapter 1

Ethics and generalizability in qualitative research

Collecting data from refugees and forced migrants, a case study

Divya Sharma

Introduction

Qualitative research has been an essential part of criminology, victimology, and penology. It presents meaningful insight into events and processes from the perspective of the people that shape and influence them and vice versa. Using qualitative methods in cross-cultural and multicultural settings present many methodological and ethical challenges. This chapter examines some of these challenges while using data collection from refugees in Jodhpur, India, as a case study. It begins with a brief literature review of the key topics in qualitative research. It also includes a short discussion on the growing concern about uncritical acceptance of news and social media narratives by scholars in the field of crime, justice, and victimization, and the related ideological pitfalls, biases, and stereotypes that could potentially impair the academic space in criminology and criminal justice. It is followed by a description of push factors that have forced refugee migration from Pakistan to India and then explains the setting where the data was collected. Thereafter, it examines ethical dilemmas about intensive interviews and focus groups, while collecting data about violence, displacement, trauma, and loss. It concludes with a discussion on reliability and generalizability in qualitative research.

Literature review

Qualitative research is contextual research that provides an in-depth understanding of setting, people, and processes. It is particularly useful while using the exploratory approach. In their study of Vietnamese refugees, Haines, Rutherford, and Thomas (1981) observed that "exploratory fieldwork approach furnishes useful conceptual contributions to the more general field of refugee studies" (p. 98). It helps explain the framework within which various behaviors, attitudes, causal relations, and perceptions are shaped. It reveals the individual and subjective nature of information (Heyink and Tymstra, 1993; Jones, 2004) that may be unique to each individual. As a result, there is limited generalizability. Nonetheless, the knowledge that it provides cannot be accessed as easily through other means. For many cross-cultural and transnational topics in victimology, the inductive approach of data collection and production of knowledge may be the only possible starting points. Hence, grounded theory rooted in data becomes a significant part of research (Glaser and Strauss, 1967; Strauss and Corbin, 1990). However, even the inductive research of developing grounded theory may lead to revising and developing general hypotheses that can be then tested, making it resemble deductive research (Ambert, Adler, Adler, and Detzner, 1995; Bogdan and Biklen, 1992; Campbell, 1979).

With an increase in global mobility among researchers, sometimes the findings based on small sample sizes and non-probability methods are presented without any caveat about their generalizability. Qualitative methods often help in giving a face to a story. That very fact may raise concerns about objectivity being lost in analyzing and presenting such findings. However, at times, researchers and policymakers need to cater to human emotion to convey that people affected by issues of crime and justice are more than mere statistics. They live in complex, multiple overlapping, and shared realities (Berger and Luckmann, 1966) that can be explained a lot better by using qualitative research. According to Blumer (1969), these realities are not static; there is a continuous process of interaction and interpretation. That is, social behaviors and systems evolve, and the researchers must be mindful of the period in which they are collecting and interpreting data. It necessitates dating qualitative data, especially if used in policymaking as some of the populations are transient and many issues evolve. It is true for the quantitative methods as well, but it needs a closer analysis of qualitative methods due to the exploratory, individual, and subjective approach.

A growing concern with qualitative research is that of helicopter researchers that access complex, multicultural, and cross-cultural settings one time only. They fly in and out of settings, take data, leave, and give nothing back (Struthers, Lauderdale, Nichols, Tom-Orme, and Strickland, 2005). Their access to a setting is also impacted by religious, cultural, economic, and linguistic factors. That is, their access is determined and defined by the local contacts that may present a filtered view. Concerning measurement reliability, it is important not to be consistently wrong. While presenting findings, these concerns should be spelled out. Some researchers almost romanticize with the findings in their description, analysis, and presentation that may include the use of props.[1] These dramatized presentations at times become the focal point of how the findings are consumed and minimize the significance of the topic and critical scrutiny of the findings. In his study on extreme violence and suicide terrorism, Thrift (2007) notes that news is increasingly presented in conflation with entertainment at a local and global level.

Orientalism, ethnocentrism, errors, and gaps in information

While researching in cross-cultural settings, it is important to guard against orientalism, cultural appropriation, and preset biases. Some studies (Clarke, 1997; Erchak, 1992) have noted that it is not uncommon for many in the West or Europe to have a self-image of superiority, while having a stereotypical understanding of the East, even viewing it as inferior (Rosen, 2000). For example, since the 9/11 terrorist attacks in the United States, many researchers have started to study informal banking systems that allow people to transfer money either without going through formal banks, without following formal procedures, or both. Many such systems have existed around the world and even predate the Western banking systems. Some of the more commonly known systems are Hundi[2] in the Indian subcontinent, Hawala[3] in South Asia and the Middle East, Undiyal in Sri Lanka, and fei ch'ien in China, casa de cambio (stash house), phoe kuan (message houses), Chop Shop, and Chits, etc. (Sharma, 2008; Sharma, 2006). In her research on Hawala, Edwina Thompson (2007) states that there is "the tendency in current Indian literature on hawala to dissociate local financial practices there from those that are tainted with the brush of terrorism in neighboring Pakistan and Afghanistan" (p. 289). The passage that Thompson refers to explains Hawala practices in India *before the 1940s*, while Pakistan was created in 1947: she overlooks a simple historical fact and attributes that there must be country-related bias. Additionally, over time, many Hawala practices in India have served the same purpose as the Hundis did for hundreds of years. The work that Thompson refers to contains interviews with Hawala brokers in India, not the Middle East, Pakistan, or Afghanistan. While many may use Hawala as part of the Islamic banking system, many Hawala brokers brokers in India have *nothing* to do with Islam or Islamic banking system; that is, many non-Muslims also use it and and use the use the terms Hawala and Hundi interchangeably. Thompson overlooks these historical and cultural factors and assigns bias to "current Indian literature." Any investigator, police officer, scholar, or researcher from that part of the world would have shared this information, had Thompson approached the topic perhaps without preconceived notions about India and Pakistan, or worse, Hindus and Muslims. She repeats the same assumption about Indian researchers in another article in 2008 (Thompson, 2008) while citing the same material. It is only one example of misconstrued realities and should not be overgeneralized to reflect upon the majority of researchers working in cross-cultural, multicultural, and transnational settings. However, it highlights the need to conduct closer scrutiny of research in diverse settings, especially as some research works are difficult to replicate.

Whether it is a genuine misunderstanding about the larger context, naiveté about India or Pakistan, or an example of inherent bias, it highlights the problem of creating facts by repetition. It also underlines the problem of looking at India and Pakistan in perpetually conflictual and religious terms, while almost bullying non-Western researchers to subscribe to a Eurocentric perspective. It is a reductionist approach that makes qualitative research come across as crude and unscientific. It also takes away from the seriousness of the problem that leads to either no policy response or poor policy response.

While using qualitative methods, it is all the more important to understand historical, cultural, and religious contexts, and not give in to sensationalism and rigid schemata. The audience that is served these works through journal articles, books, or conferences has few options for authenticating these accounts. With the globalization of information, such errors in the news media are somewhat easy to identify, but the relative insularity of the academic community gives certain faulty or biased narratives a longer shelf-life. The motivation of such an approach can be anyone's guess, but academically, the creation of facts by repetition and tautological errors pose hurdles when trying to conduct a fact-based analysis of topics of crime, justice, and victimization.

In another instance, Qadri (2017), writing for the *New York Times* attempted to relate the use of *saree* (commonly worn by women all across South Asia) with Hindu nationalism, because of the right-wing party that came to power in India in the 2014 elections. It is a seemingly harmless, nonetheless, faulty assumption and reflects a certain phobia in mainstream media. Journalists, including left-wing and those highly censorious of the Indian government, as well as many voices from the Muslim-majority countries of Pakistan, Bangladesh, and so on, were equally critical of such assumptions about *sarees* (Dutt, 2017; "Love for sarees," 2017). It reflects a troubling approach of not only assigning caste and religion in spaces where they did not exist but also perhaps befouling these spaces going forward.

India faces problems rooted in caste and religion, but to assign everything to these factors is, at the very least, intellectually dishonest and generally lethargic. For example, various Indian governments have taken steps to identify money laundering through shell companies and bogus organizations, and have transparency about the source of funding that various non-government and religious organizations receive in India; many such measures are criticized as anti-Muslim, anti-Christian, anti-national, or even anti-democracy depending on the source of money or organization that is being questioned. The power dynamic is such that the Western and European academics have far greater control over the narrative about the rest of the world: Voices from different cultures and places, thus, need to decolonize academia and reclaim their spaces and stories by identifying and addressing orientalism and ethnocentrism. However, in doing so, many fear being labeled and bullied, especially due to the herd mentality most prominently manifested across social media, and some sections of academia. It is also a concern if academics misrepresent facts and then repeat their work, as proof of their argument, and thus committing tautological errors.

While explaining terrorism in India, Martin (2015) notes that "Nationalists declared independence of Khalistan in 1987, but 500,000 Indian troops violently occupied Punjab, causing an estimated 250,000 Sikh deaths between

1984 and 1992" (p. 146). Martin does not cite any source for this information. In their work, Singh and Kim (2018) note that the official number of deaths during the insurgency was 30,000. Martin's numbers are closest to the estimates given by the Council of Khalistan (Kumar, 2008), an anti-India organization (Purewal, 2011) that supported the militancy that resulted in extensive violence and killings of civilians, public officials, and police and army personnel. It does not imply that Martin cannot use these numbers, but that as an academic, he should cite the source and perhaps even acknowledge the different estimates, and a lack of corroboration. Additionally, the victims included Sikhs, Hindus, civilians, army, and police personnel. The textbook where Martin writes this has already had at least five editions. It is not difficult to imagine that the same numbers could have been repeated in journals, newspapers, conferences, and other forums. Both misinformation and skewed information are problematic in trying to assess the extent of any problem. As criminologists conduct research in cross-cultural settings or conduct historical analysis about topics on which they do not have first-hand information, it is all the more important to recognize limitations of access to information, language barriers, intent and ideological blocs and compulsions of the gatekeepers providing that information, and the resultant gaps.

In the age of global communication, journalists often serve as gatekeepers or first responders in providing an account of crime and victimization in various parts of the world. This is not a new development, but the speed of information and the need to give the "breaking news" puts hurdles in checking the veracity of the information or getting complete information before it has traveled half the world away; misinformation cuts across the ideological divide ("When in 2012," 2019; Fox, 2018; Gray, 2017). The stereotypes about India are not limited only to caste and religion, but also sex crimes and the news about rape is often presented as an Indian male mentality. It got accentuated after the horrific Nirbhaya gangrape where a young woman was raped and killed by five men and a teenager in Delhi in December 2012. A British filmmaker made a documentary about it, but just before the worldwide release, the BBC edited the number of rapes across the world listed in the end credits ("BBC cut out," 2015). Indeed, even one rape is one far too many, but it is a global problem, yet increasingly the news about rape in India is related to religion (despite no formal recording of victims and offenders by religion) and culture. To their credit, Indian news channels cover the news of rape and sexual assault almost every day, while in many Western countries, it does not hit the headlines unless an athlete or a judge is accused of such crimes. The direct comparisons across countries are not possible due to underreporting and conviction rates on the one hand, and the social support or lack thereof, for the victims on the other. But to build narratives that it is an exclusively India problem is disingenuous and especially troubling for researchers and academics. In one instance, a professor at Germany's Leipzig University refused an internship to an Indian student stating that she does not accept any Indian male students as interns due to India's rape problem (Osborne, 2015). Though the German Ambassador to India rebuked the professor in an open letter, it is emblematic of the possible risks that such stereotyping creates for Indians in India and abroad, including in the academic sphere.

On the one hand, there is a sociopolitical and cultural movement to not associate religion with a crime, reduce racism and xenophobia, not associate individual behaviors to stereotypes or negatively label cultures, countries, regions, religions, and so on, and yet in the case of India, there seems to be a movement to associate every negative stereotype with its people. In another example, the Hindu–Muslim and Muslim–Hindu riots in February 2020 were wrongly covered as a "pogrom" in many Indian (primarily English), Western, and Western-backed newspapers and channels (Merchant, 2020). Among others, a case was filed against *The Wall Street Journal* for misreporting the facts about the gruesome murder of the Intelligence Bureau officer, Ankit Sharma (Karthikeyan, 2020), who had 51 injuries on his body – including 12 stabbings (Sharma, 2020) – and whose body was dumped in a garbage drain. Another victim, Dilbar Negi's arms and legs were chopped by a sword and he was burnt to death in the shop where he worked ("The Wire once," 2020). Many such victims (in this instance, Hindus) were acknowledged primarily, though not exclusively, on social media and right-wing news outlets. The underreporting and non-reporting of certain victims based on religion, caste, and so on, and thus, their shorter existence in the mainstream news, also shape broader narratives about criminology in academic and policy analysis. It is similar to the issue of ethics of funding where some topics receive more funding, and thus, more visibility than others. It is as though the mainstream media has been divided along the sharpest ever ideological lines, and each group covers news about violence and victimization as per its preferred editorial position rather than objective principles and ethics. When journalists and even some academics posting on social media were called out for their bias, many failed to recognize that the criticism was not about reporting on the Muslim victims of violence, but about non-reporting and underreporting of the Hindu victims of violence. The bias, therefore, is also reflected in the omission of certain information, commonly called selective observation in social science research. To some extent then, the little to no systematic reporting of the persecuted minorities from Pakistan struggling to resettle in India could be attributed to preset hierarchies of victims and editorial preferences.

Further, the value-association with professions as a means to legitimize or delegitimize victimization is another problem. For example, in the brutal murder of Mohammed Akhlaq in 2015, one of the leading journalists in India Barkha Dutt, framed the "legitimacy" of the victim by asking his son how he felt given that his *patriotism* could never be questioned as he worked in the Indian Air Force. Through a substantial coverage of the case, she kept talking about patriotism with reference to the victim's son's profession – if the son had any other career, would the victimization be any less severe?

Similar religious, caste, professional, and class tropes are used while covering news about crime and victimization. In some incidents, the caste and religion are mentioned without either element having any role in the crime, while in some they are omitted if they do not fit the narrative of the preferred victim and the perpetrator. It is anyone's guess what motivates media personnel to frame the narratives in the way that they do – for instance, the *Washington Post* headlined Baghdadi as an "austere religious scholar" ("Washington Post criticized," 2019); *Reuters India* called Naikoo, commander of the terrorist group Hizbul Mujahideen, a "maths teacher turned rebel" (Reuters, 2020) – clearly these are not their claims to infamy. The marker or a trait used to highlight one's persona could be a clickbait to get a reaction, an attempt at softening or hardening an image or just making it palatable enough for the target audience – as noted earlier, the news is presented in conflation with entertainment (Thrift, 2007). On the contrary, many of the same mainstream news outlets use pejorative terms to refer to democratically elected politicians, misreport facts, and weaponize every narrative – it is one thing to criticize policies based on logic and facts, but it is another to delegitimize democratically elected leaders in other countries based on the personal or editorial ideological drive while romanticizing terrorists, dictators, theocratic, and totalitarian regimes.

Given the umpteen sources of information, the role of news media is perhaps more important than ever, but if the money, ideology, or social media fame/infamy[4] begin to debase it, it would have a contagion effect and hurt the legitimacy of many institutions, including academia. The larger concern, therefore, is that in an increasingly globalized world, many of these media narratives shape the scholarly and academic framing of societies and cultures to which Westerners have limited direct access. It creates a community of like-minded people that feed off each other and often talk in silos, thus, lacking the ability to fact-check, explore the larger context, learn the opposing view, admit mistakes, or conduct critical and non-ideological analysis; one is almost obligated to go with the view of the gatekeepers – the journalists that provide virtual access to foreign settings or validate the preset notions about the setting and its people. It also creates a hierarchy of what is worth studying and how.

Armstrong (2002) wrote about colonization resulting in creating an inferiority complex and almost disdain for one's own culture, language, and values among people in the Middle East; the same can be applied to the way some Western scholars tend to study topics about other cultures, histories, and societies. These are important elements to take into account to understand the framing of various narratives that end up in academic sources and spaces. If scholars and consumers are driven by social media trends, likes, and shares, it would lead to distortions, faulty assumptions, and skewed perceptions about cultures and countries – a movement of anti-intellectualism. It also means that the victims that are not up on the hierarchy of social and news media, and academics, would struggle to enter the psyche of policymakers or receive the needed assistance as has been the case of Hindu refugees from Pakistan.

There is also the challenge of ethics of funding – some topics are funded easily; there is a large amount of money available to study them, and as a result, one may be able to access umpteen journals, books, technical and agency reports, and scholarly sources, while the rest remains underexplored and creating a perception about the significance of the topic. For example, after the 9/11 terrorist attacks, there was a lot of money available to study the criminal aspects of various informal banking systems, while millions around the world use these systems for non-criminal purposes. Even for the topic of discussion in this chapter, before entering the field, I had to rely on social media and news sources (and thus the limited insight about the setting and the people ahead of time) rather than academic journals. It felt like a disadvantage as refugee studies have been dominating the scholarly and academic space for the good part of the past two decades, but not many have focused on this group of refugees. Therefore, with very limited information available about the setting and respondents, one has to rely on the qualitative approach rather than quantitative; one does not know what to expect in the field and cannot frame every question ahead of time.

On the one hand, qualitative research can showcase personalized content, and on the other hand, it faces the challenge of being shared in a manner that should go beyond a trip to an exotic part of the world, an adventure in the wilderness or a conflict zone. It is not to suggest that there is any method without bias or error, but that the research should be conducted in a systematic manner instead of impressionistic (Eisenhardt, 1989; Miles and Huberman, 1984). It might take conducting multiple studies on the same topic to extrapolate logic, patterns, and themes, and eventually lead to a theory (Smith and Geoffrey, 1968). Qualitative research is not a mere description but often includes interpretation and evaluation as well. However, others have argued (Wehlage, 1981) that description remains the most fundamental goal, though it does not mean abandoning generalizations that may lead to a theory. However, many researchers conducting qualitative research shy from generalizations (Sharma, 2011; Dillon, 1989; Merriam, 1988).

As qualitative research presents many unanticipated events and situations, the use of software programs has become common when processing large quantities of such data. It makes it easy to present these findings, but the researcher still needs to guard against generalizations. Ambert et al. (1995) note that "qualitative research seeks depth rather than breadth" (p. 880). The use of unstructured and semi-structured interviews provides an incredible opportunity to "conduct [a] trustworthy inquiry in a world of complex and interwoven constructed realities" (Bradley, 1993, p. 432). The sampling methods and the context and nature of data must be kept in mind while organizing, analyzing, and presenting the information.

The case study: Refugees and forced migrants

The push factors: Religious persecution and economic struggles

In 1947, the British colonizers partitioned India into India, Pakistan, and East Pakistan (Bangladesh since1971). There is an extensive body of knowledge about the partition, the immediate migration, massacres, and resettlements. However, there is a limited systematic study of the continued displacement of Hindu minorities from Pakistan that are seeking refuge in India due to religious persecution and economic struggles. Though other religious minorities are also persecuted, Hindus being the largest minority in Pakistan are the most "visibly" displaced.

In 1965, approximately 10,000 refugees sought shelter in India, followed by another 90,000 that came to India in 1971. Following the 1971 India-Pakistan war, about 55,000 of these refugees were resettled in Barmer District in Rajasthan, India, in 1977–1978 (Sodha,[5] personal communication). Since then, the ebb and flow of migrants have continued and escalated after the 1999 Kargil war.

The year 2009 witnessed increased violence in the Swat Valley. More than 6000 Pakistani Hindus migrated to India in the months before March 2009 ("Human Rights in," 2012). According to Khan (2009), the Taliban imposed sharia in the North-West Frontier Province region that required even non-Muslims to wear a burqa, and Hindus and Sikhs were required to either leave or pay *jizya* (Islamic tax for religious minorities in exchange of protection). With little recourse available against the Taliban from the state machinery, many Sikhs and Hindus have been displaced within Pakistan as well. In 2014, "Pakistan Muslim League (N) parliamentarian Ramesh Kumar Vanwani told the national assembly that around 5,000 Pakistani Hindus were migrating to India every year" (Shakil, 2017, para.6).

Sindh province: Forced conversions, kidnappings, rapes, and murders

The Sindh province is home to about 94 percent of Pakistan's Hindu community ("Populations of Hindus," n.d. as cited in Yusuf and Hasan, 2015) that overall makes up less than 2 percent of the total population. Many activists, independent bloggers, and journalists in Pakistan have been reporting about violence and forced conversions.[6] According to Yusuf and Hasan (2015), "Religious and sectarian leaders offer prompt dispute resolution in matters ranging from water-sharing to marriage and law-enforcement issues" (p. 19). The duo further report that extremist organizations and seminaries are increasingly involved in dispute resolution and also serve as moneylenders (p. 19). It has driven many Hindu moneylenders away, and that puts poor Hindus further at the mercy of extremist elements. In 2012, Azra Fazl, a member of the Pakistan People's Party, told the National Assembly that the Hindus in Sindh were facing a lot of challenges and the state should address the problem of forced conversions (Gishkori, 2012). In a handful of cases where victims have been produced before the court and asked of their "choice" or "free will," many have criticized the courts for not even addressing the problem of fear, threats, abuse, and duress.

According to Shakil (2017), the politicians in Sindh drafted legislation to address abductions, forced conversions, and rapes of Hindu girls and boys. However, The Council of Islamic Ideology declared the bill un-Islamic (Ackerman, 2018). It dashed hopes of many minorities that were seeking protection within the realm of the law, especially those in the lower-income groups and having little social capital. Yusufzai (2014) notes that the true extent of the problem cannot be estimated due to the dearth of press coverage and reluctance of the police to investigate such cases. Indeed, the news coverage, as well as social media trending of the Hindu victims in Pakistan, has been episodic at best, and researchers and academics have generally been reluctant to study it.

Forced marriages and bonded labor are the most common tools of abuse and conversion. "Most bonded laborers in Sindh belong to the Hindu minorities, mainly belonging to the Scheduled Castes … Working in agriculture, brick kilns, tanning, and carpet industries, they are usually submitted to physical and/or sexual violence" ("Forced Conversion of," 2017, p. 5). This modern-day slavery puts Hindu boys working as bonded laborers at a very high risk of exploitation (including sexual abuse) in the Sindh province where they have little financial, political, religious, or legal clout. Though Pakistan had passed the Bonded Labor (Abolition Act) in 1992, and despite the human rights activists on the ground, little progress has been made, especially in the case of Hindu bonded laborers.[7]

Many Hindus and Sikhs are forced to bury their dead or travel long distances as most cremation grounds have disappeared (Sehgal, 2014; Khan, 2016; "The long road," 2017). Sehgal (2014) quotes Amritsar-based Sikh historian Surinder Kochhar who states that in the city of Lahore, before independence, there were almost a dozen cremation grounds, but now it does not even have one. According to Sehgal, Hindus traveling long distances also risk getting robbed as they carry money for cremation; the families are stopped at every checkpoint and asked to show no-objection certificates, and many have to wait for hours to find a district magistrate to issue it. In the past, many Hindus and Sikhs were allowed to perform cremation near their temples, but most temples and the surrounding land have been encroached upon by land mafia (Sehgal, 2014).

Fear of negative labels

Despite the growing and clear evidence of religious persecution, activists and journalists with the greatest reach seem uninterested in the topic, and for the most part, academics have stayed away as well. The reasons for such indifference are unexplored, but some of it could be rooted in the concern about being incorrectly labeled as a racist or Islamophobe (Scruton, 2014). For example, in the infamous Rotherham scandal, where predominantly British-Pakistani men (Kurdish and Kosovan men were also involved [Jay, 2014]) targeted teenagers for sexual grooming and raped them, the sexual victimization was ignored for years as:

a) the police did not want to come across as xenophobic, racist, or Islamophobic when the victims were white teens; and
b) though most of the victims were white girls, the police were accused of normalizing these acts of sexual abuse and violence as part of "their culture" when the victims were South Asian teens. Many families of British-Asian victims did not report the abuse due to a distorted sense of "family honor" and shame.

The principle of relativism is important in understanding the cultural, religious, and political framework within which certain behavior is constructed or deconstructed; however, it is troubling to see that very principle being used to normalize crime or overlook victimization. Islamophobia is a real challenge and must be dealt with, however, calling out crimes committed by anyone who happens to practice Islam should not be automatically termed Islamophobic, just as calling out crimes committed by anyone who happens to be a Hindu cannot be termed Hinduphobic, and so on. It would be incorrect labeling as in doing so the actual religion is misconstrued as sanctioning of these criminal acts. Even when crimes are committed in the name of *any* religion, there should be no hesitation in calling out those crimes as that is the only way to not legitimize crime and criminality in the name of religion, whichever religion it may be.

Naila Inayat (2019) writes that the "forced conversion and marriage under duress of these helpless victims has become a cause *célebre* in pre-election India [referring to the rise of nationalist cause during elections] and post-election Naya Pakistan" (para.1). A few of the victims that Inayat mentions in her article are listed in the endnotes.[8] She also refers to the problem of people being labeled by one or the other group and notes that the activists who work to help the victims are often labeled as "kafirs" or traitors. As for those forcefully converted, she notes that "Handed over to her new 'household', she turns into—who knows?—a sex slave, a glorified domestic worker, a compliant wife cut off forever from her roots and her maternal home" (Inayat, 2019, para.12). Hadi (2015) also refers to a secondary source that interviewed Bherulal Balani, a former legislator, according to whom, "Once the girls are converted, they are then sold to other people or are forced into illegal and immoral activities" (p. 12).

Kali Beri settlement: Setting for field research

About 200 Hindu families displaced from Pakistan have made Kali Beri their home approximately since 1999/2000. It is government-owned land located approximately 18 kilometers (11 miles) from Jodhpur in the state of Rajasthan, India. Locals also call it "Bhil Basti."[9] Most of these settlements are nothing more than tents made out of bedsheets, thatch, and tarp where refugees live for an undetermined time while being exposed to all kinds of elements. There are also some more stable settlements where people have made huts out of mud, brick, and clay. There are many such settlement camps across Rajasthan state (in cities like Jaisalmer, Bikaner, Barmer, and Ganganagar) and across India (in Punjab, Haryana, Gujarat, Delhi, etc.). The terms "refugee" and "migrant" are used interchangeably by volunteers, media, and the affected people themselves due to a lack of clarity about their status and options; some of them have a visa, some do not; some have applied for Indian citizenship; some have violated the terms of their visas; a few have even received citizenship but have been waiting for other documents such as caste and Below Poverty Line (BPL) certificates, and so on. Below is an excerpt from a Photo Essay on the refugees (Sharma, 2015):

> The refugees in the settlement struggle to meet their daily needs. A local member of the Legislative Assembly arranged for water a few years ago, but most people struggle to have access to electricity, sanitation facilities, and other basic infrastructure. The huts and other structures where people live often leak during the rainy season and they are exposed to the elements, including snakes. There is a school (till fifth grade) in the settlement; the only teacher who is employed there struggles to get chalk, books, stationery, etc. Under the Government of India's Midday Meal Scheme, children in the school receive free lunch on weekdays, and for many, it may be their only meal of the day. Without proper roads, the food cannot be delivered at the school and the children have to run to the main road to get their meals. The children of the more recent refugees who live in makeshift tents across the state have it far worse. From being pulled out of schools in Pakistan, they are practically left on the road in India with no structure or access to education in a new country – as expected, their families need to first find a roof over their heads and arrange for food. The people in Kali Beri have built a small temple. The refugees express deep sadness that many could only bring their faith with them; faith is especially important in a community where many have lost family members and friends to violence and poverty. Many of them remain hopeful and lean on their faith for strength. The refugees also hope that the land where they have settled would become their permanent home, but feared being displaced by the mining in the area. Over the years, politicians of all stripes have visited these families, received letters and petitions on their behalf, and made promises to resettle them. But their stories remain untold and their victimization remains underreported and nonreported. Most refugees complained about the tedious, expensive, and long process of acquiring Indian citizenship. Many of them did not know how to follow up on the

> status of their case. Even after meeting the eligibility requirement, many applicants continued to wait for up to 14 years.

In the above setting, the data collection presented numerous methodological and ethical challenges. The data was collected using focus groups, field observations, and intensive interviews. The primary focus group was organized in the Kali Beri settlement. It consisted of ten men whose ages ranged from 22 years to over 80 years. They were asked questions about their family composition, the work that they did in Pakistan, reasons for coming to India, visa or citizenship application status, work in India, living conditions, immediate needs and concerns, hurdles in obtaining BPL certificates, access to basic utilities such as water, electricity, and sanitation, and the assistance provided by the UJAS. They were also asked about access to education and healthcare.

The respondents narrated their experiences one by one, while also at times engaging in a group conversation building on one another's account. I had to interject to get them to add their basic introduction, including age, the year when they came to India, and the number of family members. I also interacted with approximately five to seven women while walking around the settlement. They shared information about the lack of safety from the elements, water clogging, and lack of basic amenities. The data was also collected during a visit to two camps in and around the city of Jodhpur, where additional respondents engaged in informal conversations. They were more recent migrants (some had been in India for less than four weeks) and did not have very detailed accounts of the challenges about resettlement in India. They generally talked about the problems that they had faced in Pakistan that forced them to migrate to India. Five intensive interviews were conducted in the office of the UJAS. Additional information on various aspects of the displacement and resettlement of refugees was collected from Sodha, other volunteers at the UJAS, and independent activists in Delhi. The emails and letters sent to the government officials in Delhi went unanswered.

The respondents shared experiences about kidnappings, rapes, murders, and forced religious conversions. In Pakistan, most of them lived in extreme poverty, and their financial situation is not much better in India either. They talked about a lack of legal, financial, and social recourse in Pakistan, and were forced to move to India. However, getting visas for India is extremely challenging and many of them reported having to pay bribes to middlemen or agents. The travel to the embassy, lodging, and waiting time for visas created more uncertainty and financial burden. Additionally, some members of a family may get visas while others have to stay back, thus splitting families. Those who are left behind, face the further risk of abuse and persecution. The visas issued to them are often for specific districts in India that may split families even after reaching India. To search for work, get in contact with friends and family members, and to attend any social or familial gatherings, they may have to travel outside the designated districts. To do so, they have to report to the local police station where they may have to pay bribes, spend time in jail, and so on. While in the field, I had to drop the idea of interviewing refugees that were locked up in jail. The decision was strictly due to the time constraint. If I had prior information about it, I would have set aside more time for the data collection. It is not uncommon for researchers to run out of time during field research, but it further conveys that the sample in qualitative research may not represent the population as sometimes one learns about the population while in the field.

Most families in Kali Beri that have acquired Indian citizenship do not necessarily have their caste and BPL certificates that could afford them subsidized food and education. Many refugees in Jodhpur also struggle to break perceptions of looking at them through the absolutist view of either Pakistanis or Hindus only. Though they complain about being persecuted in the name of religion and economic status, they want policymakers and researchers to see them as human beings – men, women, and children – who deserve basic rights and dignity. As one respondent put it, for the left activists, they are "too Hindu," and for some of the right activists, they are "too Pakistani." For researchers, academics, and policymakers, it is important to avoid these ideological perils and inveiglements.

Access, language, culture, and data collection

Due to the extremely limited information available on this group, it was better to use qualitative methods. Though there are numerous studies on refugee populations around the world, and many similar strands run across such populations, yet each group is shaped by a particular set of cultural, geographical, historical, and sociopolitical factors relevant to it. Therefore, it was reasoned best to use an inductive approach and select data collection as the starting point. There were a handful of news articles, blogs, and a short news program on refugees from Pakistan. There were also a few YouTube videos. These were analyzed to gain a preliminary understanding of the location, people, and the setting. The initial emails were exchanged with a journalist who has first informed me about the topic. This was followed by email and phone conversations with Sodha. Contacting the gatekeepers is essential in understanding and planning for field research, gaining trust and cultural competence, and improving accuracy (Smith, 2009). After meeting with the journalist in Delhi, I traveled to Jodhpur to meet with Sodha. The initial meeting lasted over two hours that helped in gaining a deeper understanding of the historical, religious, and economic factors. It was immediately evident that I would need to rely on open-ended questions and a semi-structured approach to let the respondents explain their concerns in detail.

Sodha informed me that the refugees were generally skeptical of outsiders, and he too was wary of people using this group to advance their agendas. He noted that at least one researcher in the past had written about the group from her personal Eurocentric view of politics and religion in India and Pakistan, rather than the actual accounts shared by the refugees. At the start and during the process of data collection in my study, respondents were reminded that they were free to not answer any questions, refuse to share their names, decline to be in photographs and videos, and could stop taking part in the study at any time.

As previously mentioned, the data was collected by using focus groups, field observations, and intensive interviews. The focus group in Kali Beri consisted of ten men, but a few additional men joined while the focus group discussions were in progress. Most of them were daily wage earners and had to miss their work to participate in the study. This financial loss was not compensated, yet after the initial reluctance to talk to a stranger, they were keen on sharing their plight. Many struggled to control their emotions as they talked about their painful journeys and an uncertain future in India. Most respondents shared their own experiences, while a few also talked about what had happened to their friends or someone in their community. Their loss of income weighed heavily on my mind as I tried to remain focused on data collection. In many research projects, coupons and money are often used as incentives to encourage participation. I did not want to do so in Kali Beri as I felt that given their extreme economic vulnerability, it may almost compel them to participate and dilute the voluntary nature of participation.

In Kali Beri, the women were eager to show their living spaces, get their pictures taken, and also share their struggles. These were more informal interactions while walking around the settlement. Most women are married at a young age due to cultural, economic, and safety reasons. The children in Kali Beri were also keen on getting their pictures taken.[10] The majority of them were shy, but their school teacher shared concerns about the lack of resources available to her to run classes. As stated earlier, while conducting field research, the sample often builds over time, and though the initial access to the setting was dependent on my contact, gradually, the sample snowballed and gained definition and structure as I collected data in the field.

I accompanied Sodha to camps where the most recent refugees had arrived. I made observations as he interacted with them about shelter, food, jobs, and medical check-ups, among other topics. As a rule, I refuse food, water, or any gifts during field research. However, I was guided by Sodha to accept tea from refugees as it would indicate to them that they were treated with dignity and acceptance. It also helped to gain their trust by sitting on a floor with them. Many of them have faced the class- and caste-based discrimination, along with religious persecution and are marginalized based on multiple factors. Additional intensive interviews were conducted at Sodha's home, which doubles up as the UJAS's office. Respondents were comfortable in this setting and talked without hesitation; many noted that they felt safest in that space. Nonetheless, I ensured that the interviews were conducted one on one to avoid unwitting pressure from the organization that helps them in resettlement and advocacy. These interviews were conducted later in the afternoon. During summer, the temperature in Jodhpur could easily reach 90 to 100 degrees Fahrenheit; therefore, mornings were considered better for the field trips.

The language was largely not a problem except while interviewing those who had recently arrived in India. Those who had been living in India conversed in broken Hindi that was liberally punctuated with words of Sindhi, Punjabi, and Urdu. One of the volunteers working with UJAS accompanied me on most of the visits (not part of the interviews though), and, when needed, I could rely on him and other volunteers for translation.

As most interviews were semi-structured and built on conversations in the field, it was important to maintain eye contact. Instead of using paper and pen, the respondents were asked if they were comfortable in answering questions using a recorder. Most of them consented to it; however, when they wanted to share something off the record, the recorder was switched off for those portions of the interviews. The respondents were also comfortable with their video recordings[11] and photographs, though I constantly wondered if they understood the meaning of a photo essay or a research poster. When I tried to explain it to them, they expressed willingness to share their stories with "the world." Even after exiting the setting, I reached out to UJAS and shared the content of the photo essay and other material to ensure that there was nothing that could potentially be upsetting, factually incorrect, or put their cases or applications in jeopardy.

Ethical dilemmas: Talking about violence, displacement, trauma, and loss

The first and foremost concern was that of harm to subjects. Many respondents in the study had experienced and witnessed extreme abuse and violence. A few of them talked about young girls who had been kidnapped and raped for days. One respondent carried a photograph of his brother's dead body: that was the only picture he had of his brother. Also, even without violence, displacement causes much frustration and anxiety; the trauma of forced displacement is far deeper and difficult to grasp for an outsider. As the respondents talked about their experiences of leaving with nothing except clothes, little money, and their faith, many started to get emotional. They were further disillusioned by the treatment that was meted out to them in India. The lack of mobility due to visa restrictions, lack of adequate jobs, the fear of being displaced from the settlement (as it is government-owned land), not having access to basic amenities, and facing inexplicable delays in getting citizenship and caste and BPL certificates contributes to hopelessness. They feel extremely disenfranchised, helpless, and even "invisible." An elderly man in his eighties was in near tears while wondering what he needed to do in order to prove that he was an Indian.

Another respondent carried a newspaper cutting that contained a photograph of his wife and two children. They had suddenly disappeared, and after a week or so their photograph was published in a local newspaper reporting that the woman had married someone else and converted to Islam along with her children. As he narrated the threats that he received while trying to search for his family, lack of any legal assistance, and the decision to come to India that practically ended all hope of ever finding or reuniting with his family, his sense of helplessness was palpable. As a field researcher, it is a hard task to balance when to stop the interview to minimize causing emotional harm and when to continue the interview to capture raw emotions. Therefore, it is important to access and exit the setting with sensitivity. The subject vulnerability sometimes could also impact their expectations. For example, it was important for me to convey my limited role as a researcher. On the other hand, given the emotional nature of the content, I also had to maintain my own objectivity and composure throughout the data collection.

During field interviews, some people would walk up to me to voluntarily share their stories even if they were not the primary respondent that I had identified. As noted earlier, after the initial reluctance, more respondents were comfortable sharing their experiences. Many respondents would even call on women and young men to share their dilemmas. It was not always clear if the additional respondents felt compelled to talk due to the group dynamic. One of the limitations that I felt while collecting data was the limited voice of women respondents. The elderly women were more vocal than the younger women but did not go into the specific trauma and violence that many women had feared and/or faced. They would often change the topic to convey that what had happened had happened and that they wanted to only secure their and their children's future. During field research, one may not right away recognize all the gaps in data or be able to get information from every subject relevant to the study. However, multiple visits to the setting for data collection could provide better direction to the researcher.

Generalizability in qualitative research

One of the limitations of using qualitative methods is limited generalizability. It is pertinent to keep it in mind while presenting data in various forums, including conferences, books, newspapers, magazines, and journal articles. At times, unless the news is presented as a melodrama (Thrift, 2007), it does not garner enough interest. In other words, there has to be a face to every story for it to make an emotional connection and cause a reaction. The qualitative methods allow for presenting in-depth individual stories and, therefore, can establish an emotional connection. However, if the sample size is small and experiences are individualistic, it would affect generalizability. While presenting qualitative data, one has to be mindful of these limitations, and not get caught up in awe of one's own research.

As reasoned earlier, in many qualitative studies, a larger sample may be built by making multiple trips to the setting. It is especially helpful when time is limited and thus restricts getting information from a large sample in the field in one visit. In my work, the initial phase of data collection largely went as planned, but for the follow-up interviews, the meetings with UJAS were difficult to set up even in Delhi due to the unpredictability of the topic and respondents. For example, my meetings with the Director of the UJAS were canceled twice due to unforeseen events. In one instance, the Crime Investigation Department (Rajasthan, India) deported a family of refugees to Pakistan without any notice. Even during the holiday, the Jodhpur High Court (Rajasthan, India) held a bench meeting to hear this case, but by the time the stay order was issued, the train had crossed the international border to Pakistan. The family was deported for visa-related violations without any consideration for their safety. Though the UJAS contacted the social workers and activists in Pakistan to receive the family, no progress had been made in the matter by the time this chapter was being written.

Qualitative research often carries strong validity as the information is provided first-hand, but the experiences shared may be unique, personal, and subjective. Though certain patterns and commonalities can be identified as respondents share similar narratives about crime, abuse, escape, and resettlement, there is limited opportunity to verify information from another source. This is not a problem of validity in the methodological sense but presented as a need to keep in mind the limitations caused by a lack of replication. For example, to understand the push factors and nature of religious and economic persecution of Hindus in Pakistan, the secondary sources were accessed after the data collection in the field. During this process, I realized that many of the themes and concerns that the respondents in Kali Beri had shared were also reported in some of the news outlets in Pakistan and Rajasthan (though mainstream news media in India has largely ignored the topic) and in other forums, particularly social media, pre- and post-data collection, thus providing this study with a larger foundation and deeper understanding of the shared reality of loss and trauma.

The local customs, contacts, safety, and risk influence what aspects of the setting a researcher can observe and through what lens. There might be gaps in data, it may be tainted, or both. In many instances, it is not possible to conduct follow-up work, and therefore, the understanding may be shaped by one-time access (not to be confused with the problem of helicopter researchers that are not interested in understanding the larger context, gaining a deeper understanding, etc.). This limited information is often shared in multiple forums, where if not fully contextualized, it may result in creating facts by repetition, stereotypes, and misconceptions. As qualitative research methods gain more visibility and utility in studying topics of crime and justice, there is also concern about helicopter researchers and ethnocentrism not only when they travel abroad, but also when they study topics about diversity in their own backyard.

In summation, qualitative research provides immensely valuable opportunities to study phenomenon as it unfolds. One has to be prepared for unanticipated events and be willing to learn. Any researcher may become interested in a certain topic due to emotional, personal, academic, or policy interest, but it is imperative to control subjective views while collecting, analyzing, and presenting data: filtering information as per personal or audience biases defeats the purpose of conducting field research. Lastly, limited or no generalizability does not take away from the value of qualitative work but necessitates continuously building on these efforts to gain a broader and deeper understanding over time. It should not stop lawmakers responding to the individual or group's immediate needs but requires re-assessing situations and settings as they evolve. In fact, despite their individual struggles and trauma, most refugees in this study complained about similar problems and challenges and had similar demands that must be addressed irrespective of the individual journeys that brought them to India. There may be unique challenges for this group compared to other refugee populations, but there are commonalities within the group that have been brought to the surface by using qualitative research methods. When used properly, qualitative methods allow victims to tell their stories in their voices rather than imposing the researcher's own lens of what qualifies as pain, trauma, and victimization.

Notes

1 Some presentations in the West include using turbans, burqas, knives, and guns *without* any relevance or reason.

2 It was a Bill of Exchange and an integral part of the Indigenous banking system in India. Despite the difference in their origin and histories, in India, the terms Hundi and Hawala are often used interchangeably as for many people they serve the same purpose.

3 Many researchers and policymakers see it only as an Islamic banking system, but in India, many people who are using the Hawala system have nothing to do with any religion, including Islam; that is, non-Muslims also use it.

4 Infamy as reflective of the mindset that any publicity is good publicity.

5 H.S. Sodha, a migrant himself, runs an organization called Universal Just Action Society (UJAS) that organizes assistance for refugees including food, shelter, jobs, legal advice, medical help, and so on. It was formerly known as the Seemant Lok Sangthan and formally founded as UJAS in 1999. It carries out social and legal advocacy work on behalf of migrants and refugees.

6 Ghosh (2012) refers to a report in the *Los Angeles Times* about a 16-year-old girl named Rachna Kumari; she was abducted in a crowded marketplace by a police officer himself who "demanded that she convert to Islam and marry him" (para. 6).

7 For example, Roop Chand Bheel was tortured and set on fire for allegedly stealing cotton (Khan, 2010; Naveed, 2011). He received 80 percent burns and still managed to give a detailed account of what had happened to him. He died after struggling for four days ("Tortured cotton picker," 2010). Muno Bheel's case also stands out as he sought justice and escape for his family that had been held in a "private jail" by his landlord for 13 years and used as bonded laborers (Kassar, 2011).

8 Seventeen-year-old Anila Dhawan belonged to Hyderabad, Sindh. The court freed her as, despite threats to her life, she gave a statement in favor of her family.

June 7, 2017, another Meghwar, 16-year-old Ravita was abducted by men from the influential Syed community. She was converted and married off to one of her kidnappers.

Arti Kumari, a teacher, and 17-year-old Sikh girl Priya Kaur were kidnapped and married off after conversion to Islam.

January 2019, 16-year-old Anusha Kumari was kidnapped and forcefully converted.

Summer 2018, 14-year-old Jeevti Kohli was kidnapped while asleep. She was converted and married off to an aging landlord as his second wife.

"January 2019: 16-year-old Anusha Kumari abducted. Indian High Commission took up the matter but no action was taken.

June 2017: 16-year-old Ravita Meghwar abducted in Sindh.

April 29, 2017: 17-year-old Sikh girl Priya Kaur abducted in Buner district.

September 23, 2014: Joti Kumari, a student of Electrical Engineering, abducted from Larkana City, Sindh.

December 31, 2006: 17-year-old Deepa abducted from Tharparkar district in Sindh province.

August 2, 2006: 16-year-old Komal abducted from Hawks bay, Karachi.

July 23, 2006: 15-year-old Pooja abducted from Lyari Town, Karachi. A judge ruled in her favor and she was released by her tormentors, only to be abducted again and missing ever since.

March 3, 2005: 14-year-old Raji abducted from Aslam Town Jhuddo, Mirpurkhas.

December 22, 2005: 13-year-old Mashu kidnapped from Jhaluree village in Mirpur Khas.

January 4, 2005: 18-year-old Marvi and 16-year-old Hemi abducted from Kunri village in Umerkot district" (Inayat, 2019).

9 *Bhil* refers to the caste and *basti* is a local term for an unauthorized and unorganized colony.

10 After exiting the setting, I printed pictures and sent them to UJAS to give them to the kids and families.

11 The video recordings were lost due to the SD card getting corrupted on my last day in Jodhpur. I had made an amateur mistake of not backing up data after every field trip or day's work. However, none of the audio content was lost as I had also used a digital recorder for all interviews. That is, the respondents held the audio recorder and talked while the camera rolled.

References

Ackerman, Reuben. (2018). Forced Conversions & Forced Marriages in Sindh, Pakistan. CIFoRB, The University of Birmingham. Retrieved from https://www.birmingham.ac.uk/Documents/college-artslaw/ptr/ciforb/Forced-Conversions-and-Forced-Marriages-in-Sindh.pdf

Ambert, Anne-Marie, Adler, Patricia A., Adler, Peter Adler, and Detzner, Daniel F. (1995). Understanding and Evaluating Qualitative Research. *Journal of Marriage and Family*, Vol. 57, No. 4, pp. 879–893.

Armstrong, K. (2002). Ghosts of Our Past. AARP Modern Maturity, January/February 2002, pp. 44–47, 66. In: T. Badley (Ed.), *Annual Editions: Violence and Terrorism,* 08/09. Guilford, CT: McGraw Hill, pp. 2–5.

"BBC Cut Out International Rape Statistics from India's Daughter, Accuses Leslie Udwin." March 19, 2015. Firstpost. Retrieved from https://www.firstpost.com/india/bbc-cut-out-international-rape-statistics-from-indias-daughter-accuses-leslee-udwin-2162095.html

Berger, Peter L., and Luckmann, Thomas. (1966). *The Social Construction of Reality: A Treatise in the Sociology of Knowledge.* New York: Doubleday.

Blumer, Harold. (1969). *Symbolic Interaction: Perspective and Method*. Berkeley, CA: University of California Press.

Bogdan, R., and Biklen, S. K. (1992). *Qualitative research for education* (2nd ed.). Boston, MA: Allyn & Bacon.

Bradley, Jana. (1993). Methodological Issues and Practices in Qualitative Research. *The Library Quarterly: Information, Community, Policy*, Vol. 63, No. 4, *Symposium on Qualitative Research: Theory, Methods, and Applications* (October 1993), pp. 431–449.

Campbell, D. T. (1979). Degrees of freedom and the case study. In: T. D. Cook and C. R. Reichardt (Eds.), *Qualitative and Quantitative Methods in Evaluation Research* (pp. 49–67). Beverly Hills, CA: Sage.

Clarke, J. J. (1997). *Oriental Enlightenment. The Encounter between Asian and Western Thought*. London: Routledge.

Dillon, D. R. (1989). Showing Them That I Want Them to Learn and That I Care about Who They Are: A Microethnography of the Social Organization of a Secondary Low-Track English-Reading Classroom. *American Educational Research Journal*, Vol. 26, pp. 227–259.

Dutt, Barkha. (2017). The *New York Times* Tried to Explain Sari Fashion and Became the Laughing Stock of India. *Washington Post*, November 17, 2017. Retrieved from https://www.washingtonpost.com/news/global-opinions/wp/2017/11/17/the-new-york-times-tried-to-explain-sari-fashion-and-became-the-laughingstock-of-india/

Eisenhardt, K. M. (1989). Building Theories from Case Study Research. *Academy of Management Review*, Vol. 14, pp. 532–550.

Erchak, Gerald, M. (1992). *The Anthropology of Self and Behavior*. New Brunswick, NJ: Rutgers University Press.

"Forced Conversion of Minority Girls and Women in Pakistan." (2017). Unrepresented Nations and Peoples Organization, Avenue Louise 52, Bruxelles, Belgium. Retrieved from https://www.upr-info.org/sites/default/files/document/pakistan/session_28_-_november_2017/js9_upr28_pak_e_main.pdf

Fox, Maggie. (2018). Fake News: Lies Spread Faster on Social Media Than Truth Does. *NBC News*, March 8, 2018. https://www.nbcnews.com/health/health-news/fake-news-lies-spread-faster-social-media-truth-does-n854896

Ghosh, Palash. (2012). Pakistan to Issue ID Cards to Hindus, but Discrimination, Forced Conversions Continue. *International Business Times*. Retrieved from https://www.ibtimes.com/pakistan-issue-id-cards-hindus-discrimination-forced-conversions-continue-692826

Gishkori, Zahid. (2012). 'Hindu Girls Being Forcibly Kept in Sindh Madrassas.' *The Express Tribune Pakistan*. Retrieved from https://tribune.com.pk/story/350431/hindu-girls-being-forcibly-kept-in-sindh-madrassas/

Glaser, B. G., and Strauss, A. (1967). *The Discovery of Grounded Theory*. New York: Aldine.

Gray, Richard. (2017). Lies, Propaganda and Fake News: A Challenge for Our Age. March 1, 2017. Retrieved from https://www.bbc.com/future/article/20170301-lies-propaganda-and-fake-news-a-grand-challenge-of-our-age

Hadi, Abdul. (2015). Injustice and Persecution: Forced Migration of Sindhi Hindus in Pakistan. *Mediterranean Journal of Social Sciences*, Vol. 6(2)S5, pp. 11–14.

Haines, David, Rutherford, Dorothy, and Thomas, Patrick. (1981). The Case for Exploratory Fieldwork: Understanding the Adjustment of Vietnamese Refugees in the Washington Area. *Anthropological Quarterly*, Vol. 54, No. 2, Metropolitan Ethnography in the Nation's Capital, pp. 94–102.

Heyink, J.W., and Tymstra, T.J. (1993). The Function of Qualitative Research. *Social Indicators Research*, Vol. 29, No. 3, pp. 291–305.

Human Rights in Pakistan: Excerpts from Hindus in South Asia and the Diaspora, 2011. (2012)." Hindu American Foundation. Retrieved from https://www.hinduamerican.org/wp-content/uploads/2020/03/HAF-human-rights-report-2011.pdf

Inayat, Naila. (2019). Brides of Despair. *The New Indian Express*. March 31, 2019. Retrieved from http://www.newindianexpress.com/magazine/2019/mar/31/brides-of-despair-1956753.html

Jay, Alexis. (2014). Independent Inquiry into Child Sexual Exploitation in Rotherham 1997–2013. Retrieved from https://www.rotherham.gov.uk/downloads/file/279/independent-inquiry-into-child-sexual-exploitation-in-rotherham

Jones, S. (2004). Depth Interviewing. In: C. Swale (Ed.), *Social Research Methods: A Reader*. London: RoutledgeAldershot, pp. 257–260.

Karthikeyan, Suchitra. (2020). Complaint Filed Over its Reporting of Ankit Sharma's Murder; Here's What WSJ Reported. February 29, 2020. Retrieved from https://www.republicworld.com/india-news/general-news/complaint-filed-over-wsjs-misreporting-of-ankit-sharmas-murder.html

Kassar, Abbas. (2011). Hindu Peasant Family in Jail of Landlord for 13 Years. *Pakistan Christian Post*. Retrieved from http://www.pakistanchristianpost.com/head-line-news-details/2617

Khan, Fareed. (2009). Hindus and Sikhs Threatened by the Taliban and Sharia. *Asia News*. Retrieved from http://www.asianews.it/news-en/Hindus-and-Sikhs-threatened-by-the-Taliban-and-Sharia-15903.html

Khan, Faridullah. (2016). Pakistan's Hindus and Sikhs Forced to Bury Their Dead. Retrieved from https://www.dw.com/en/pakistans-hindus-and-sikhs-forced-to-bury-their-dead/a-19297607

Khan, Uzaira. (2010). Tortured Cotton Picker Identifies Tormentors. *Dawn*, November 16, 2010. Retrieved from https://www.dawn.com/news/582317

Kumar, Suneel. (2008). Linkages Between the Ethnic Diaspora and the Sikh Ethno-National Movement in India. *Faultlines*, Vol. 19, April 2008. Retrieved from https://www.satp.org/satporgtp/publication/faultlines/volume19/article4.htm

Martin, Gus. (2015). *Understanding Terrorism: Challenges, Perspectives, and Issues*. 5th edition. Beverly Hills, CA: Sage.

Merchant, Minhaz. (2020). Understanding the Bias of the Western Media in covering Delhi violence. March 6, 2020. *DailyO*. Retrieved from https://www.dailyo.in/politics/western-media-wall-street-journal-the-guardian-caa-nrc-protest-delhi-riots/story/1/32547.html

Merriam, S. B. (1988). *Case Study Research in Education: A Qualitative Approach*. San Francisco, CA: Jossey-Bass.

Miles, M. B. and Huberman, A. M. (1984). *Qualitative Data Analysis*. Beverly Hills, CA: Sage Publishing.

Naveed, Shayan. (2011). Minorities: 'Us and Them' – What Divides Pakistani Identity. Retrieved from https://tribune.com.pk/story/184740/minorities-identify-with-pakistan-despite-persecution-report/

OpIndia Staff. "When in 2012 NDTV Featured Prominently and Was Mocked in a Segment about 'Spreading Lies' on American Series 'The Newsroom.'" December 7, 2019. Retrieved from https://www.opindia.com/2019/12/ndtv-mocked-2012-american-tv-show-the-newsroom-for-fake-news/

OpIndia Staff. "The Wire Once Again Shields Islamist Mobs by Shamelessly Downplaying the Brutality of Dilbar Negi's Murder: Here's How." March 7, 2020 Retrieved from https://www.opindia.com/2020/03/the-wire-downplays-dilbar-negi-murder-details/

Osborne, Louise. (2015). German Professor Rebuked for Rejecting Intern Over 'India's Rape Problem.' March 9, 2015. Retrieved from https://www.theguardian.com/world/2015/mar/09/german-professor-rebuked-for-discrimination-over-indias-problem

Purewal, Shinder. (2011). Sikh Diaspora and the Movement for Khalistan. *The Indian Journal of Political Science*. Oct-Dec 2011, Vol.72, No. 4, pp.1131–1142.

Qadri, Asgar. (2017). In India, Fashion Has Become a Nationalist Cause. *The New York Times*. November 12, 2017. Retrieved from https://www.nytimes.com/2017/11/12/fashion/india-nationalism-sari.html

Reuters India. [@ReutersIndia]. (2020, May 6). Indian Troops Kill Maths Teacher-Turned-Rebel Commander in Kashmir. Retrieved from https://in.reuters.com/article/india-kashmir-idINKBN22I1JD [Tweet]. Retrieved from https://twitter.com/ReutersIndia/status/1258101753570041857

Rosen, Steven L. (2000). Japan as Other: Orientalism and Cultural Conflict. *Journal of Intercultural Communication*. No. 4, pp. 17–24. http://immi.se/intercultural/past-issues.html

Scruton, Roger. (2014). Why Did British Police Ignore Pakistani Gangs Abusing 1,400 Rotherham Children? *Political Correctness. Forbes*, August 30, 2014. Retrieved from https://www.forbes.com/sites/rogerscruton/2014/08/30/why-did-british-police-ignore-pakistani-gangs-raping-rotherham-children-political-correctness/#11acff40754a

Sehgal, Majeet. (2014). Hindus, Sikhs Compelled to Bury Dead in Pakistan as Cremation Grounds Vanish. January 6, 2014. Retrieved from https://www.indiatoday.in/india/north/story/hindus-sikhs-bury-dead-pakistan-cremation-grounds-lahore-161274-2014-01-06

Shakil, F.M. (2017). Forced Conversions Given Seal of Approval in Pakistan. *Asia Times*. Retrieved from https://www.asiatimes.com/2017/05/article/forced-conversions-given-seal-approval-pakistan/

Sharma, Divya. (2006). "Historical Traces of Hundi, Socio-cultural Understanding and Criminal Abuses of Hawala." *The International Criminal Justice Review*, Sage. Vol. 16, No. 2, pp. 99–121.

Sharma, Divya. (2008). "Research Ethics and Sensitive Behaviors: Underground Economy." In Donna M. Mertens and Pauline Ginsberg (Eds.), *Handbook of Social Research Ethics*. Thousand Oaks, USA: Sage, pp. 426–441.

Sharma, Divya. (2011). Growing Overlap Between Terrorism and Organized Crime in India: A Case Study. *Security Journal*, Macmillan Publishers Ltd., vol. 26, pp. 0955–1662.

Sharma, Divya. (2015). The People of Kali Beri Settlement: Pakistani Migrant Struggles in India. A Photo Essay. *Berkeley Journal of Sociology*, Vol. 59, pp. 92–101.

Sharma, Puneet Kumar. (2020). 51 Injuries Found on IB Staffer Ankit Sharma's Body, Postmortem Says He Was Attacked with Knives, Rods. March 14, 2020. Retrieved from https://www.indiatoday.in/india/story/postmortem-of-ib-official-ankit-sharma-shows-51-injuries-1655400-2020-03-14

Singh, Gurharpal, and Heewon Kim. (2018). The Limits of India's Ethno-Linguistic Federation: Understanding the Demise of Sikh Nationalism. *Regional & Federal Studies*, Vol. 28, No. 4, pp. 427–445.

Smith, L., and Geoffrey, W. (1968). *The Complexities of an Urban Classroom: An Analysis Toward a General Theory of Teaching*. New York: Holt, Rinehart & Winston.

Smith, Valerie J. (2009). Ethical and Effective Ethnographic Research Methods: A Case Study with Afghan Refugees in California. *Journal of Empirical Research on Human Research Ethics: An International Journal*, Vol. 4, No. 3, pp. 59–72.

Strauss, A., and Corbin, J. (1990). *Basics of Qualitative Research: Grounded Theory, Procedures, and Techniques*. Newbury Park, CA: Sage.

Struthers, R., Lauderdale, J., Nichols, L.A., Tom-Orme, L., and Strickland, C. (2005). Respecting Tribal Traditions in Research and Publications: Voices of Five Native American Nurse Scholars. *Journal of Transcultural Nursing*, Vol. 16, pp. 193–201.

"The Long Road to Cremation for Peshawar." Radio Free Europe. June 3, 2017. Retrieved from https://www.rferl.org/a/pakistan-hindu-cremation/28575449.html

Thompson, Edwina A. (2007). Misplaced Blame: Islam, Terrorism and the Origins of Hawala. In A. von Bogdandy and R. Wolfrum (Eds.), *Yearbook of United Nations Law*, Max Planck. Volume 11, 2007, pp. 279–305. Koninklijke Brill N.V., The Netherlands: Max Planck Yearbook of United Nations Law by Max Planck Institute, Martinus Nijhoff Publishers.

Thompson, Edwina A. (2008). An Introduction to the Concept and Origins of Hawala. *Journal of the History of International Law*. Vol. 10, No. 1, pp. 83–118.

TNM Staff at The News Minute. "Love for Sarees not Political: Indians Hit Back at New York Times." November 16, 2017. Retrieved from https://www.thenewsminute.com/article/love-sarees-not-political-indians-hit-back-new-york-times-71710

"Tortured Cotton Picker Dies." Dawn, November 17, 2010. Retrieved from https://www.dawn.com/news/889351

Thrift, Nigel. (2007). Immaculate Warfare? The Spatial Politics of Extreme Violence. In Derek Gregory, and Allan Pred (Eds.), *Violent Geographies, Fear, Terror, and Political Violence*. New York and London: Routledge, pp. 273–294.

"*Washington Post* Criticized, and Lampooned, Over Baghdadi Headline." October 28, 2019. *BBC News*. Retrieved from https://www.bbc.com/news/world-us-canada-50205592

Wehlage, G. (1981). The purpose of generalization in field-study research. In T. Popkewitz and R. Tabachnik (Eds.), *The study of schooling*, pp. 211–226. New York: Praeger

Yusuf, Huma, and Syed Shoaib Hasan. (2015). Conflict Dynamics in Sindh. United States Institute of Peace. Retrieved from https://www.usip.org/sites/default/files/PW104-Conflict-Dynamics-in-Sindh-Final.pdf

Yusufzai, Ashfaq. (2014). Minorities in Pakistan Fear 'Forced Conversion' to Islam. Inter Press Service. Retrieved from http://www.ipsnews.net/2014/05/minorities-pakistan-fear-forced-conversion-islam/

Chapter 2

(In)visibility of emotions and ethical concerns in (Indian) prison research

Reena Mary George

Introduction

The (in)visibility of emotions and ethical concerns in prison research is a contested topic. Drawing on empirical research in Indian prisons, this chapter focuses on ethical principles and its application in prison research; methodological limitations and the limitations one encounters as a researcher; the responsibilities as a (prison) researcher; the vast nature of criminological research leading to peculiarities of prison research; value conflicts and emotions of such research studies; and finally some ways to better equip oneself for prison research. My first encounter with ethics began during the research methods classes for my Master's in Social Work program. We did not, however, have an elaborate ethics course or an ethics committee through which the study passed. Students needed to be bound by the Code of Ethics for Social Workers. When I joined a research institute later, I had the opportunity to attend an ethics meeting led by Ruth Macklin in Mumbai in 2007. We were all excited about the meeting, and the opportunity to interact with the great Macklin, who wrote that *dignity is a useless concept* in (medical) ethics and "it means something over and above the respect for persons or for their autonomy." Nevertheless, Macklin makes a caveat for references to dignity in the many international human rights instruments, such as the Universal Declaration of Human Rights (Macklin, 2003, p. 1420).

This chapter is based on the four empirical prison studies that I conducted: (1) Rights-based assessment of children of recidivist women prisoners, 2005–2006 (qualitative – 28 participants,); (2) Health status of women prisoners in Maharashtra, 2007–2009 (quantitative – 900 participants); (3) Death penalty – A human rights perspective, 2008–2009 (qualitative – 13 participants); (4) Experiences and perceptions of prisoners surviving the death row in India, 2010–2014 (qualitative – 111 prisoners on death row and their families). Most of the studies had a strong qualitative aspect. Qualitative research is about a person's life, lived experiences, behaviors, emotions, and feelings, as well as organizational functioning, social movements, and cultural phenomena. The work is interpretive and "carried out for the purpose of discovering concepts and relationships in raw data and organizing these into a theoretical explanatory scheme" (Strauss & Corbin, 1998, p. 11). To understand the meanings of these experiences or perceptions in the prison context, any study needs to bear in mind that the interactive process takes place in a "total institution" (Goffman, 1957, pp. 43–84).

Prison is not a new phenomenon; it antedates its systematic use in the penal system, constituting itself outside the legal apparatus (Foucault, 1977, p. 231). Moreover, there have been "outsiders" going to prison with the aim of "reforming" it from the time prisons existed. Two of the most prominent of these reformers were Jeremy Bentham, and leading Quaker reformer, Elizabeth Fry (Cooper, 1981). As an outsider, I interacted with prisoners in various capacities – as a professional social worker, researcher, interpreter, lecturer, and counselor, thus visiting 22 prisons[1] in India and two prisons[2] in Austria. Over the years, I had the opportunity to interact with a vast number of people in diverse circumstances: among them women prisoners, children of women prisoners, under trials, convicted prisoners, prisoners on death row and their families, and families of victims of custodial death and torture. The chapter is divided into five sections. They are (i) ethical principles and their application; (ii) methodological concerns and limitations as a researcher; (iii) the labyrinth of actors in prison research; (iv) peculiarities of prison research and the (continuous) need to conduct it; and (v) value conflicts, emotions, and the label of "overidentification."

Ethical principles and their application

Interacting with prisoners and their families as a researcher has certainly allowed me to reflect upon the ethical concerns in research. Gilbert refers to ethics as a matter of principled sensitivity to the rights of others and suggests that being ethical limits the choice that we can make in the pursuit of truth. Researchers have to consider the effect of their actions on participants to preserve their rights and integrity as human beings (Gilbert, 2008). Lo points out that prisoners are vulnerable as research participants because their liberty is restricted in several ways. This is exacerbated as the voluntariness of consent, privacy, and confidentiality may be compromised in prisons. Also, because prisons are closed institutions, it is difficult to monitor adverse events in research. Prisoners may also have other characteristics such as poor education, mental health problems, and/or possible substance abuse issues which can make them more vulnerable (Lo, 2009). In this context, ethical principles are abstract, and it is not always obvious how they should be applied in given situations. Some of the most intractable ethical problems arise from conflicts among specific principles and the necessity of trading one against the other (House, 1993, p. 168).

The Belmont Report is a statement of basic ethical principles and guidelines intended to assist in resolving ethical problems associated with research involving human "subjects." It refers to the Nuremberg Code, noting that codes often provide rules intended to guide (research) investigators' appropriate conduct (NCPHSBBR, 1978). The three basic principles particularly relevant to the ethics of research involving human subjects are respect of persons, beneficence, and justice. The principle of respect for persons stipulates that individuals are to be treated as autonomous agents and that persons with diminished autonomy are entitled to protection. The principle of beneficence abides by the philosophy of "do no harm" not only by respecting the decisions of the research participants but also by making efforts to secure their well-being. The principle of justice ensures that reasonable, non-exploitative, and well-considered procedures are administered fairly and equally. The applications under each principle are as follows: informed consent and voluntary participation; anonymity (*respect*); risk minimization; confidentiality; data sharing (*beneficence*); non-exploitation and upholding dignity; relationship with participants and other actors; and promotion of integrity in research (*justice*). The section below discusses the application of ethical principles with examples from the prison setting.

Informed consent and voluntary participation

Informed consent provides that persons who are invited to participate in social research activities should be free to choose to take part or refuse, having been given the fullest information concerning the nature and purpose of the research, including any risks to which they would be exposed to, and implies appropriate arrangements for maintaining the confidentiality of the data, and so on (Gilbert, 2008). In the research studies that were conducted, participants were provided with a "Consent Note" which stated the purpose of the study, the questions that were going to be asked, official address, telephone number, that they had the right to withdraw their consent at any point, that participation would be voluntary, there would not be any payment associated with it, their identities would remain confidential, the report would not reveal names or identities of the participants, and that they were free to refuse to discuss anything that they did not want to discuss. These were explained to the participants in the language they understood, i.e., Hindi, Marathi, Malayalam, Kannada, Tamil, Assamese, Punjabi, Urdu, and English. Prisoners were reluctant to give written consent, i.e., they largely rejected signing any document as they have had the experience of signing confessional statements that were later used against them in court. The prisoners who participated in the interviews thus gave oral "informed consent."

Informed consent is taken because those who are being researched upon have the right to know what they are being researched about. However, informed consent is particularly dubious and tricky when it comes to a captive population, I call it "*the irony of informed consent.*" Most prisoners talk to an "outsider" such as a researcher because they are eager to see what the external person could "offer" them. They are also happy to "vent out" their stories to someone. However, informed consent is not always straight forward. For instance, an interview with a prisoner was set in the superintendent's office. The prisoner sat down, and I "informed" him about the study and sought his "consent." The prisoner "consented" for the interview. I observed that the prisoner was uncomfortable and had closed body language (i.e., closed arms, raised eyebrows). I stopped the interview and asked, "*What would you like to speak about?*" The prisoner said, "*What you are doing is bullshit. This is crap and this is not helping us in any way. And I don't want to be part of this.*" Had I continued with the interview without looking at the non-verbal signs, it would have been an ethical violation. So, getting an oral or written consent every time is not enough. One should be prepared to stop the interview in the middle as well.

In another instance, two prisoners refused to participate in the interview and returned to their cells. A few minutes later, a prison official brought one of the prisoners back to the room where the interviews were being conducted and asked me to interview him. I responded by saying that if the prisoner does not wish to be interviewed, I would not force him. The prisoner was happy that he did not have to talk to me and told, "*You cannot do anything regarding my case; hence I do not wish to talk to you.*" It was difficult to obtain trust in a short period and it was even more difficult to explain the study in a short time and obtain voluntary participation and informed consent from prisoners. The difficulty of the situation was exacerbated by the fact that prisoners have no liberty and are controlled, scrutinized, and held responsible by the system for everything they say. I never refused to talk to a prisoner, but some prisoners refused to talk to me, and I think this was a good sign. Prisoners were able to show agency in the restricted framework of the prison.

Consent from gatekeepers

The "gatekeepers" in prison researches are the highest officials from the Prison Department (generally the Inspector General of Prisons) and the Minister of Home Affairs from the Home Ministry of a particular state. Remembering the role they played in my research, I am tempted to refer to "Fluffy" from *Harry Potter and the Philosopher's Stone* (Rowling, 2014, pp. 153–174). Fluffy is a three-headed fierce dog who guarded the Philosopher's Stone – which if consumed, made the possessor immortal. Fluffy's heavy paws guarded the Stone. Fluffy evoked fear and intimidation in anyone who encountered him. From the interrogation I faced by the gatekeepers of India's prison system while conducting the study on the death penalty, I felt as if I was encountering "Fluffy" from time to time. I was asked, "*Why do you want to spoil India's name in the international arena by doing such a study?*"; "*This study is unconstitutional*"; "*Why do you want to talk to the garbage of the society?*"; "*You are from a "good" family; why do you want to talk to rapists and murderers?*" Another statement voiced in a different mode by most gatekeepers was, "*It is because of human rights activists like you that we lose power over them [prisoners] and people like you cause all problems.*" Or, "*It is people like you who spoil the society. You want to interview goons and dons who are a menace to the society, but you don't want to help out the poor on the streets.*" My entry into the prisons as an outsider was perceived as a threat and inconvenience, and it seemed to be irrelevant whether I was an academician or a human rights activist. While seeking permission in one of the states in India which was primarily a tribal belt, I was asked, "*So why are you so interested in this region? You will have to explain in the letter why you have chosen a region which has a high percentage of Naxalites.*[3] *What is your connection with them?*" I explained to the officer that it was not just that particular state which had been chosen, but all the other states in India as well. I was forced to send them copies of the permission letters issued to me by the authorities in other states, where the prisons did not house many "*Naxalites.*" Dealing with gatekeepers thus required flexible strategies.

Anonymity

Anonymization is a procedure to offer some protection of privacy and confidentiality for research partners, but it cannot guarantee that harm may not occur. People's reactions to research reports cannot be foreseen in advance. The context, unless massively disguised, often reveals clues for the identification of individuals, even when names and places are changed (Piper & Simons, 2005, pp. 56–63). In the studies which used a case-study method, the names of the prisoners were changed to pseudonyms to protect their identity and the study did not mention any details of their case. The suggestions for the pseudonyms came from prisoners themselves which further strengthened their participation in the research. However, certain aspects of prisoners' lives could not be camouflaged beyond a certain degree. If details were mentioned by prisoners who claimed to be on death row because of their religious or ethnic backgrounds, it could reveal their identities to mention the circumstances, even if their names were anonymized. There was also no scope to provide physical anonymity to certain participants because everyone knew death row prisoners in a particular prison. However, a prison in concern could also be identified based on the type of gallows (for the execution of prisoners) it had – a manual or automatic one.

Pre-publication access

Not all people in a research study can be anonymized and the number to whom this applies is often more than we frequently envisage. In such situations, a sound ethical principle is to seek clearance from the individuals concerned for the use of the data in a specific context or report. The principle of giving participants the opportunity to read research reports before it goes public, appears, at first sight, to adhere to the principle of respect for persons. However, much depends on the intent. If it is merely to warn participants of critical elements so that they will not be shocked when a report goes public, it offers more protection to the researcher than the participants. If sharing the report provides an opportunity for the participants to comment upon and possibly add to the draft report, this demonstrates greater respect for the potential difference of interpretation and the right to a fair voice (Gilbert, 2008). In smaller-scale studies, this is possible. In the study with 13 death row prisoners in Maharashtra in 2008–2009, during their pre-publication access, prisoners asked me to remove their religion and mother tongue from the personal profile section because that could have led to them being identified. They were also given access to the cross-case section on which some of them commented and provided me with inputs and ideas on how the concluding chapter could be framed.

Confidentiality

Confidentiality during the process of conducting the research and the anonymization of individuals in report writing is the general assumption of an ethical research study. As researchers, we tend to mix these concepts. Gilbert states that both these need separate consideration. Providing pseudonyms to the participants is not "anonymization." Confidentiality is a principle that not only allows people to talk in confidence but gives them the power to refuse the publication of any material which they think might harm them in any way (Gilbert, 2008). The interviews in all the studies that I conducted were supposed to happen in a place where no one could hear what the prisoners spoke. However, all the prison manuals state that a prison officer should be present while an interview is conducted. I negotiated with the guards evoking the *hearing–seeing-distance* principle, i.e., that a prison officer can be at a *seeing-distance* but not at a *hearing-distance.* Nevertheless, I must admit there were interviews where I could not negotiate this *hearing–seeing-distance* principle. These interviews took place in the superintendent's office, where the latter could hear the conversation between the prisoner and me. In these cases, I did not ask too many questions. It was interesting to observe how the prisoners spoke in these interviews – they provided mainly vague, general information about their lives. Every research participant seemed to know by instinct what they ought to filter. Such interviews lasted less than 15 minutes. Under such circumstances, the principle of anonymity and confidentiality is blown off the roof.

In terms of maintaining confidentiality, raw data needs to be protected as well. Prisoners have told me, "*We know, nothing goes out of the prison without the prison official looking at the data.*" Studies conducted as a team had to assure the prisoners that we indeed kept the data confidential. I was often pressurized by prison officials to share raw data with them, or endure questions like, "*What did this particular terrorist tell you?*" or "*Did the woman prisoner (name) tell you that she has AIDS? Did she share how many men she slept with?*" or "*I am the father of this prison, they (prisoners) are my children, I want to know what they said! Can the father not know what is going on in the house?*" As a young woman, it was often difficult to stand-up or voice my opinion in this male-dominated setting and tell these officials, "*I am not going to talk about this.*" Nevertheless, I never shared confidential information despite the immense pressure from prison officials and told them "*I am not going to talk about this.*" Of course, this also meant that the following day's data collection would be completely disorganized and that none of the prison staff would help us in reaching out to the prisoners. Moreover, the raw data had the identity of each individual and we had already stated in the letter of permission that the raw data of the research study would not be shared with anyone under any circumstances. One of the responsibilities of a researcher is to protect and promote the interests and rights of the participants. There was also a considerable amount of sensitive information such as experiences of being tortured, names of police officers who tortured, many cases of sexual exploitation of family members and prisoners themselves, and diaries and letters written by prisoners detailing torture in police custody.

Risk minimization

Discussing research interviewing in prisons, Newman stresses that face-to-face sources of data are vital to progress in any science of human behavior (Newman, 1958, p. 132). That said, all research conducted face-to-face in prison carries a certain risk for the participants, especially regarding aspects of confidentiality and anonymization. It is essential to take adequate precautions to protect the participants in order to minimize and mitigate risks. In the context of prisons, these risks might be existential. For instance, some prisoners maintained their innocence even after having been convicted of crimes and being awarded the death sentence. While on death row, six such prisoners were released in 2018 in Maharashtra after 16 years of being in prison (Doval, 2019). It is one's duty as a researcher not to share data that could jeopardize the case of the participants.

Non-exploitation and upholding of dignity

It was important that as a researcher I did not take unfair advantage of my relationship with the prisoners by asking them questions that could cause discomfort or violate their dignity in any manner. During the interviews, none of the prisoners was asked to describe their case or the crimes they were imprisoned for. Some of them shared details of their cases but I never explicitly (or implicitly) asked them to share the same. Documenting details about their cases was not the objective of any of the studies. Also, during the interviews, asking them questions about torture could have added to their mental stress. But most of them spoke about the torture they faced in police custody. Prisoners on death row often said that they felt good to have a visitor and talk about their lives in the prison as a person sentenced to death. I have tried my best to respect each prisoner and maintain dignity while listening and speaking about such sensitive topics. Such an approach reiterates principles of not unnecessarily consuming the time of participants or making them incur an undue loss of resources (NCESSRH, 2004).

Relationship with participants and other actors

Prisoners were indispensable partners in the research studies that I conducted. Most of them trusted me as a research partner. Many of them still write letters to my office address in India and inform or enquire with me about their cases and families. I am also in touch with some of the family members of prisoners as they seek information regarding their case status on the Supreme Court or High Court websites, request me to call their lawyers to enquire about the status of their cases, or to have more information on educational courses that they could do from within the prison. I have known these prisoners since 2007–2008. For the studies I conducted independently, I informed the prisoners about the status of the study via letters. For a researcher, it is an important ethical duty to inform the participants on the status of the study, as reposed trust in a stranger to whom they opened up their lives and homes.

Responsibilities of the researcher

One of the responsibilities of a researcher is the promotion and protection of integrity in research. This means that participants are only asked to share that information which corresponded with the scope of the study. As a researcher, it is also one's duty and responsibility to make all the necessary efforts to bring the research and its findings to the public domain in an appropriate manner. It is also one's duty to make all efforts to anticipate and to guard against possible misuse and undesirable or harmful consequences of research. In all the studies that I was part of, all the written documents and raw data have been preserved. Israel and Hay state that it is only by showing care and concern about ethics and by acting upon that concern that one promotes the integrity of research. They further say that since much of what we do occurs without anyone else "watching," there is ample scope to conduct ourselves in improper ways (Israel & Hay, 2006, pp. 112–128). Hence there is an even greater need to uphold our integrity in every aspect of the research.

Further, a researcher's responsibility also includes being accountable and transparent, bringing the findings to the public domain, and bearing the totality of the responsibility for the due observance of ethical principles (NCESSRH, 2004). I find it unethical to interview participants and not even have a ten-page report in the event of failure to complete your doctoral or master thesis or leave the research institute. One of the questions that prisoners asked was "*What are you going to do with all this information collected from us?*" As a researcher, I am accountable and ethically bound to take all steps to follow-up on the implementation of recommendations, which is generally a tool for advocacy.

I may have partly succeeded. The studies added to the body of knowledge in the criminal justice system. Bringing the study to the public domain meant large-scale dissemination. Prisoners suggested that I should send it to the President, the National Commission for Human Rights, and the courts. I disseminated this to the government as I was required to, and also to civil society and in academic circles. Further, the totality of responsibility for the due observance of all principles of ethics and guidelines devolves on all those directly or indirectly connected with the research. These include institution(s) where the research is conducted, researcher(s), sponsors/funders, and those who publish material generated from research. The responsibility of sharing and disseminating the results, however, lies with the researcher. In my case, the reports were duly submitted in various reporting formats to the institution and the funding partners. This, if done "correctly" would reflect the ethical principle of justice mentioned in the Belmont Report.

Methodological concerns and limitations as a researcher

The ethical principles and their application intersect with several methodological limitations and the limitations of the researcher in any empirical research. However, in a prison study, there are specific additional concerns and limitations than those listed below. Some of the limitations (both methodological and as a researcher) include time and financial resources; lack of prior research studies, especially in the Indian context (specifically on women prisoners, death row prisoners, families of prisoners, children of prisoners inside and outside the prison); data collection challenges and the habitat around them; issues related to the bias in self-reported data, including hearing information outside the scope of the research study; the challenges of using a translator; the binaries of conducting research with prisoners; and being a woman researcher in a male-dominated setting. The below section highlights these limitations.

Time and resources

I would start with the limitation most common to most empirical research: time and (financial) resources. All the interviews were conducted after receiving due permissions from the Inspector General of Prisons of the particular state in India or from the Home Ministry of the particular state under which the Prison Department fell. To obtain these permissions took me between six months to a year from the date of my application for the same. Traveling the length and breadth of a large country like India consumed a lot of resources. I was fortunate to have been funded for the bigger research studies, without which, these would not have been possible.

Lack of prior data

Another limitation that is common to several research studies is the lack of reliable prior research or data on the topic itself. Lack of reliable data will likely require one to limit the scope of the analysis, i.e., the sample size. It could also be a significant obstacle in finding a trend and a meaningful relationship. In prison research in India, one can hardly rely on the data on prisoners in particular states. This data is published by the Government of India through the National Crime Records Bureau (NCRB) gathered through the rigorous methodology. I do not wish to undermine the effort put in to gather this massive quantitative data, and I am sure that the whole research community which works in the criminal justice system appreciates the available data (NCRB, 2018). However, since prisoners are a floating population, these numbers change drastically even over a short time. For instance, a prison that officially recorded 16 prisoners on death row in a particular year had 60 prisoners on death row at the time I visited the prison.

In terms of the lack of reliable data on prison statistics, I underestimated the fact that it would also lead to a delay in gathering data. This was because the then-existing data on prisoners through "Prison Statistics India" did not match the actual number of prisoners (at the time of my study/prison visit); it was either higher or lower. When I realized that the numbers did not match, when taking the next appointment for the prison visit, via phone, I asked prison officials for the approximate number of (death row) prisoners so that I could plan my stay in that particular state. Some officers gave me this information because they understood the rationale behind this question, but most of them refused to give me this information citing "security" reasons.

As far as prior research studies on prisoners are concerned, there are several in the United States on death row prisoners, prisoners in general, children of prisoners, and women prisoners. However, when I conducted my death penalty study, there was no prior empirical research data on the death penalty in India. This made my study, an empirical one, the first study ever conducted in India on death row (George, 2009). The only legal research that existed was an analysis of death penalty cases from the Supreme Court Judgements in India (AI and PUCL, 2008). Again, regarding the death penalty, the large empirical data collection was first conducted in 2010–2014 for my doctoral dissertation in India. In the meantime, there is some research available that was produced based on affiliations with universities or civil societies on the death penalty in India. These studies corroborate with my findings that the most vulnerable and marginalized end up on death row in India (NLU, 2016; CES, 2018). There is scope for further research on experiences in courtrooms or with the media.

There are many studies in the area of criminology, such as on the dignity of prisoners (Dawes, 2002; Oyero 2004; Schlanger, 2010; Ploch, 2012; Spates & Mathis, 2014); on effects of imprisonment on families of prisoners (Schneller, 1976; Travis & Waul, 2003; Murray & Farrington, 2008; Codd,

2013; Liebling & Maruna, 2013; Condry & Smith, 2018); and on death row prisoners (Johnson, 1979; Abu-Jamal, 1996; Hood, 1996; Nowak, 2001; Schabas, 2002; George, 2015; Hood & Hoyle 2015; Johnson, 2017; Cooper, 2017; Bar-Hillel & Lavee, 2019; Liu, 2019). These studies may show that there is enough data about prison research. The similarities in results about prisoners on death row in the United States in the 1980s and George's study in 2014 in India (Jackson & Christian, 1980; George, 2015) are astonishing. They reveal how prisoners are similar beings all over the world. However, when one looks at methodological and ethical reflections in prison research, there is only a handful (Liebling, 1999; Scheper-Hughes, 1995; Huggins & Glebbeek, 2003).

Data collection habitat

The habitat surrounding data collection is tricky. A rule of thumb is "*Good time to gather data is 'now'; tomorrow won't be better.*" One of the lessons learned during data collection in prison was – gather data when you have the opportunity as there will not be a better time "*tomorrow*" to gather data. If you have a chance to talk to a prisoner, do it then and there. The elaborate two-phased and three-phased interviews often go topsy-turvy in an actual field situation. If I could do something differently, I would give the prisoners the closed-ended questions as a questionnaire and ask them to fill it out and return it to me the next day. Even though most of the prisoners could not read or write, the ones who could always helped the ones who could not. One must also not underestimate the risk of the *bad mood* of the prison officials or an emergency like a custodial death, an escape from the prison, and illness or hunger strikes by prisoners during the collection of data. Prison as a research setting can be quite intimidating. A prison official once told me, "*When a person comes to the prison, his/her smartness reduces by half.*"[4] This substantiates with all the claims that prison can be cruel and painful (Sykes, 1958; Liebling, 1999).

Similarly, denying permission to gather data is a huge limitation in prison research. Empirical studies with prisoners depend on whether one has access to the prisoners themselves. Additionally, the more "dangerous" the category of a prisoner is, the less likely is one to get permission or access to such a prisoner. In my experience, permissions have been denied citing political, security, and "sociological" reasons. The last one is rather funny. In a particular prison, the prison official "decided" that since mine was a "sociological" study – only prisoners who have murdered their own families should be interviewed. In this particular prison where there were 22 prisoners on death row, I could only interview three prisoners who were convicted of killing their family members.

While conducting interviews during data collection, a researcher in India is not allowed to use an electronic recording device. Hence, one needs to be prepared with adequate writing pads, pens, pencils, and folders to store one's papers while making sure that none of them is lost, as one has to respect and protect the confidentiality of the participants. At the same time, not using a recorder is a blessing in disguise. Imagine the resources that would be required to transcribe these data, including translating interviews. Furthermore, prisoners would not be very happy to have their voices recorded as they already feel vulnerable in such situations and recording their experiences about being tortured by particular police officers or treated badly by a certain judge could land them in trouble, should the data be stolen or misplaced.

Self-reported data

In prison studies, where the participants are prisoners, the data is often self-reported. This kind of data is limited by the fact that it can rarely be independently verified while conducting a research study, especially while gathering the data on one's own. Therefore, self-reported data contains several potential sources of bias that act as methodological limitations. These include selective memory, telescoping, attribution, and exaggeration (Harris & Brown, 2010, pp. 1–19). For instance, prisoners often spoke about being tortured in custody while they forgot or did not recall whether they had been produced in court within 24 hours of their arrest. Also, interestingly, most prisoners spoke about life on the outside and how they had enjoyed life before going to prison. Some prisoners would share a multitude of information outside the scope of the study. One is never prepared to hear these stories about "seeing ghosts" at night, lesbianism, rape, sex among prisoners, sexual abuse by prison officials, torture, and sometimes even death by neglect.

The question that researchers are often asked is: "*How can you know if there is any truth to what the prisoners say?*" I rely on Jackson to answer this. Jackson conducted a study with death row prisoners in Texas in the 1980s. To this question of "truth," Jackson says that the statement (which a prisoner makes) is a fact, a social fact, one as valid as any other. The *whys* of these facts are other matters entirely, but none of them is simple to be determined. He further says that one may never know why the prisoners present themselves the way they do, but neither may one ever know. Jackson argues that whether we *believe* the prisoner or not is not important, what is important is that they feel the need to organize their verbal presentations of themselves so that they are rational, and second, they know how to do it. The truth of the statement has only partly to do with the truth or accuracy of the facts in the statement. He further goes on to ask, "*What does 'true' mean in such a context?*" and that the stories most people give of themselves and the explanations they have for themselves are always narrative and always after the fact; life is never narrative and the moment in which things happen is never after the fact. He adds that all reconstructive discourse – a statement by a murderer waiting in a tiny cell in Texas, the autobiography of Henry Kissinger, the letter of a lover to a lover who is presently angry – is *craft* (Jackson, 1987).

"Tryst" with translators

The most significant part of using translators is the risk of biased responses resulting from the use of local translators or research assistants, thus transgressing political, social, or economic fault lines of which the researcher may not be aware (Jacobsen & Landau, 2003). Even though Jacobsen and Landau mention bias only by respondents/research participants, in reality, the bias could be from either side (both translators and research participants). I had my own "tryst with translators" during the data collection phase. For instance, one translator refused to ask sensitive questions related to torture and sexual assault, despite rehearsing the questions. Some of the translators dealt with their own values and biases. For instance, one of the translators was shocked to hear that a certain male prisoner's mother was an alcoholic. This translator asked the prisoner with big wide eyes, "*Your mother drinks alcohol?!*" while turning to me immediately and telling me, "*His MOTHER drinks alcohol!*"

In another case, the translator had heard about a certain death row prisoner who was convicted of killing a *large number* of innocent people. The details will reveal the identity of the prisoner, and hence I refrain from reproducing those here. This local translator grew up reading about this case and was always angry with the people who were convicted for this particular crime. However, this translator had not expected to encounter the same prisoner he had grown up reading about. The translator was visibly angry during the whole interview. In another case, the translator carried out his conversation with the prisoner for over ten minutes and translated one word to me. In another instance, a male translator wanted to translate the woman prisoner's interview in the women's prison, and when I refused, he asked me, "*Are you objecting to my translating the woman prisoner's interview on your own, or are these the prison rules?*" I responded by telling him, "*Indian prison rules do not allow men in a woman's prison but even if they make an exception in our case, I would prefer a woman translator to respect the dignity of the woman prisoner who we are going to interview. I am not sure if she will be comfortable with two strangers, especially when one of them is a man.*"

Risk of being incarcerated is high

One of the limitations as a prison researcher is the risk of being "incarcerated" while conducting an empirical prison study. When I went to a certain prison, I was asked to write on a sheet of paper that I would keep the data secure, and that no personal information about the prisoners would be made public. All the personal information has been kept secured, and the raw data is still preserved. However, in one of the prisons, I was asked to sign a document already prepared by the prison official which stated that if I "violated" any rules (the document did not specify the rules), the state could take legal actions against me – very much implying that I could be arrested and imprisoned. I refused to sign such an undertaking and instead wrote a letter stating that as a researcher I was bound by research ethics and duties to protect the research participants and bring no harm to them. The officer was annoyed with me for not signing the document that he had already prepared. Often, academics who are considered left-leaning are synonymized with being Naxal-sympathizers. If one wants to conduct interviews in a particular prison with a large number of alleged "Naxalites," one is questioned on why by the gatekeepers. This could be seen as a potential risk of being incarcerated.

The binary of conducting research with prisoners

Prisoners can be intimidating or very respectful to your presence and your time. This is rather binary. Prisoners either care for the study (and therefore extend this care to the researcher), or they do not. I have hardly observed a middle ground. There were two situations where I felt threatened and intimidated. One was when I was placed in a small office used by the Welfare Officer in the prison with just the prisoner and the Welfare Officer. The prisoner sat opposite the table, and the door was behind him. The Welfare Officer sat on the left of the table, reading or writing something. There was a wooden ruler which the Welfare Officer was using before the interview. This prisoner tapped the ruler on the desk whenever he answered any question. I stopped the interviewing quoting "*confidentiality*" was violated. The Welfare Officer and I went to the Superintendent's office where I informed him that the principle of confidentiality was violated when the Officer sat right next to me. The Superintendent informed me that the Welfare Officer was there to "protect me." I responded by saying, "*If the prisoner hits me, this kind Officer will not be able to help me until I actually receive a few blows. Therefore, please put me in an open space or a bigger room, so that if there is an attack, I can at least run or try to escape.*" The negotiation helped me, and I was placed in an open space. In the open space, the Welfare Officer was not present. In another instance, one prisoner I was to interview was reported to be mentally disturbed. I insisted on at least seeing him. The officer took me outside the prisoner's locked cell and additionally informed me that on the previous day, this particular prisoner had hit a prison guard from inside his cell. This prisoner laughed uncontrollably on seeing me, which considerably intimidated me. The interview was not conducted because this prisoner was not mentally fit for one. In either case, I was not physically harmed. Also, I have never been verbally threatened or physically harmed by a prisoner on any of my visits.

Some of my research supervisors were not prescriptive and instructed me as follows, "*You are a professional and will know how to respond when you are in a particular situation.*" However, for several research studies, there were prescriptive tones for "behaving" in prison. As a student social worker, I had worked in the prison on the issue of the rehabilitation of recidivist women prisoners, yet when I went back to the prison as a researcher, I could not acknowledge the women I knew from before because I was not permitted to interact outside the scope of the study – a condition imposed by both the gatekeepers and by the research ethics committee.

Prisoners have always treated me with much affection and respect. When I stayed in prison from morning until evening, the prisoners often offered me biscuits, juice, or sometimes even their food. Prisoners have recited poems and sung songs penned by them about getting justice, presented me with the Holy Koran, cried, laughed, shared their deepest thoughts, vulnerabilities, shame, regret, and on occasion have confessed the crimes for which they were convicted. I have seen remorse up-close and witnessed what it is to feel burdened after conviction of a crime. The first time I heard about an incident of torture, I was shocked. Each successive narration of torture shocked me even further. I heard accounts of petrol being poured in the private parts of prisoners to "teach them a lesson" for raping and murdering, and heard accounts of prisoners being forced to sign a confessional statement they had never made because of extreme torture and police brutality or being threatened to be shot while trying to "escape." Some prisoners showed marks of torture, such as scars, and had visibly impaired speech. The binary of caring or not caring, and/or of being intimidating or respectful, contributes to the data that is being gathered and maybe even lead to some unexpected findings.

"Being a woman researcher" in a male-dominated setting

In a male-dominated setting like a prison which houses male prisoners, one is constantly reminded of the fact that one is not a man, and of "*not having a man*" by one's side. During my fieldwork, I was on occasion refused accommodation in hotels on the specious ground that it was "dangerous" to allot rooms to "single" women. I was asked by almost all prison officials why I was not yet married. There were instances where prison officials who had access to my cellphone number strictly for professional reasons (as I had to write it down at the security desk in the prison), misused the same, and sent me "frandship" (friendship) messages late in the night. In another instance, the prison guard shouted at the translator and me for getting up from our seats to stretch our legs after a long interview. At that point, I felt that this would not have happened had I been a man.

All accounts are not negative. For instance, since I used to be in the prisons from morning until evening gathering data, and, of course, I had to use the bathroom in between. The prison official accompanied me to the women's section, which was at quite a distance from death row. This was at the cost of leaving hundreds of prisoners whom this officer was is in-charge of in that yard. This officer would hand over his charge to the deputy or sometimes even a "warder."[5] Naturally, the official was not very happy with his "additional" duty of accompanying me to a bathroom! Nevertheless, prison officials made sure that I could use the bathroom whenever I wanted to. There were also prison officials in-charge of my "security" inside the death row yard, who treated me to lunch from their homes.

One of my supervisors Dr. Manfred Nowak, ex-United Nations Rapporteur on Torture advised me that I should always sit in a place from where I can escape in case of an attack. This advice was based on his experience of having talked to thousands of detainees all over the world. But I am sure Dr. Nowak would have (perhaps) given the same advice (in terms of protecting oneself) to all researchers irrespective of their gender. Being a woman researcher may not have always been disadvantageous. My interpretation of the high turnover of participants in the study with male prisoners was that they thought of me as "non-threatening." Being short, for once, worked in my favor, at the same time, being short is also a risk as studies have shown that "short people" are prone to be attacked or targeted more than taller people. Again, I was perhaps perceived as a gender that did not "torture" them and perhaps could be trusted more than men, or perhaps the prisoners just wanted to talk to someone to distract themselves from the boring prison routine. Whatever was the case, it worked in my favor.

Further, as part of these research studies and work in prisons, I have interacted and worked with several women researchers or women working in prisons in India and South Africa. However, none of our names appears in any major research reports; neither are our experiences recorded systematically nor even acknowledged. There is a wealth of information from all these women in this field that is still buried somewhere in the corners of our minds or shelves. The only names that appear in prison research in India and around the world are male authors, male social workers, and male lawyers. My lawyer friend (a woman) says that clients would "bargain" regarding the fees with women lawyers but would not open their mouths when a male lawyer quoted a high fee. I do not want to sound disgruntled; nevertheless, this is an attempt to highlight some of the structural inequalities that lie in the field of criminology. Several women have researched in this field, and they are acknowledged, yet not everyone has shared the emotional and/or ethical aspects of criminological research. In this context, it is refreshing to read accounts from Chenwi (Chenwi, 2007), Scheper-Hughes, Liebling, Huggings, and now George.

The labyrinth of actors in prison research

The above section discussed methodological limitations and limitations as a (prison) researcher. This section discusses the labyrinth of actors involved in prison research. While this is not an all-inclusive list of actors, some of them are victims, fellow researchers, prison officials, lawyers, media, mental health professionals including prison doctors, social workers, magistrates, prisoners, and researchers themselves. Although each of these actors is equally significant in prison research, this chapter does not have the scope to discuss them all. Also, one would notice that it is difficult to isolate each of these actors as all of them intersect when one deals with prison and/or prisoners. This section highlights three of these actors – victims, prisoners, and fellow researchers.

Victims

As a social worker and a researcher in the prison system, working for the rehabilitation of prisoners, I never reflected on the victims who were on the "other side" of the criminal justice system. It changed over the years after experiencing the loss of friends and family members to death. Going through the process of grief enabled me to reflect on the fact that many lost their dear ones and made me reflect on their process of coming (or never coming) to terms with the loss of their loved ones. I do not know how the father of the Bhotmange family (Khairlanji Rape Case) lived with the loss of his daughter and wife. This mother and daughter were found in a stream, brutally raped by a whole village with wooden logs inserted in their private parts ("Khairlanji: The Crime and Punishment," 2010). I often wonder how the parents of "Nirbhaya" (the fearless one) live each day. Nirbhaya was gang-raped in 2012 in a bus in Delhi, and following the injuries, she passed away a few days later. The rapists were hanged on March 20, 2020, and it brought a sense of justice to the family, but the process of grief is long. Perhaps it is only after this "sense of justice" that the family will be able to even grieve "properly." I have been troubled by the thoughts of all those parents who lost babies to gruesome crimes or the families that dealt with the loss of loved ones in terror attacks. The question of whether one can conduct unbiased research with participants who have gone to the extent of raping little children, cutting and bagging them in gunny sacks, and leaving them in front of a police station, remains open.

As an older researcher, I would say that the so-called "progressive individuals" or what the prison officials would call "useless human rights people" (titles I am perhaps guilty of) could be more sensitive and acknowledge not only the lives of prisoners (perpetrator) but also the victims. I must admit that none of my studies did. Individuals who work with perpetrators, fight tooth and nail for their dignity, yet, sometimes, we forget that acknowledging the lives of victims would restore dignity for the friends and families of these victims. My interpretation of researchers not going down this road is because of our very human nature – if we keep thinking or engaging with victims, it would make it very difficult to speak to the prisoners who are charged with these crimes. This is akin to who take up clients who may or may not have committed the crime they are charged with. The "job" is to defend the client. As researchers, the "job" is to gather data based on the objectives of the prison research study than entangling ourselves with the details of the crime or the (convicted/under trial) prisoner themselves.

As researchers, we engage deeply with prisoners, and so it would not be completely out of place to bring in reconciliation teams to work with prisoners and families of the victims. But this again stems from me being a social worker and a researcher. In the pure sense of research, this might seem to be a case of "over engaging" with participants. But anthropologists like Scheper-Hughes might understand my side. There is a certain obstinacy to include anything about victims in research conducted with prisoners. A research report may not be the ideal place, but one must acknowledge that the families of the victims deserve closure, and perhaps an apology from prisoners who wish to apologize to the families. Nevertheless, the victim's families should not be forced to offer their forgiveness, nor should the prisoners be forced to ask for forgiveness. This "compulsion" to forgive is dubious in more than one way. Desmond Tutu's reconciliation projects are not without criticism – be it Tutu advocating forgiving the people who committed genocide in Rwanda or the ones in Nazi Germany and other parts of Europe ("Tutu Criticized; Told Jews to Forgive Nazis," 2020). Also, more recently, there was an article that suggested that Nirbhaya's parents should forgive the rapists/murderers. It is the same kind of violation of the dignity of victims or survivors of crimes when we "human rights activists" (in this case, Advocate Indira Jaising) request for such "forgiveness" (Gupta, 2020).

(Prison) researchers

Another actor in this labyrinth is the researcher. I have come across many researchers in India who would "brag" about the "category or type" of research participants that one engages with. For instance, interviewing prisoners on death row or custodial torture survivors occupied the "top-tier." Women prisoners or children of prisoners occupied a "lower-rung" in the hierarchy. I have also come across researchers who brag about having eaten "prison food" during their visits to the prisons. I chose to work in the criminal justice system, mainly prisons, because of the "exotic" nature and the "thrill" it would carry. I only realized much later that the people we engage with, are very much like us – just plain individuals. This is not an attempt to diminish the crimes that prisoners are charged with or convicted for. These are despicable, gruesome crimes where precious lives are lost.

Again, as a researcher – experience, knowledge, political understanding, and maturity play a big role. To cite my example, when I started researching in the prison, I sometimes did not understand the gravity of what was reported by prisoners. For instance, we were interviewing women prisoners about their health status. Prior to our study, there was a study on HIV/AIDS where the women were asked about their sexual activity. I must confess that a younger me was not sensitive enough to understand how these questions might affect the dignity of women, especially in a society where matters regarding sexuality and sexual activity are still taboo. One of the women I attempted to interview about her health status thought that we were going to ask her the same questions posed during the HIV/AIDS study, and asked me, "*What do you want to know? How many times do I sleep with my husband? I slept five times with him. Three times willingly and twice by force.*"[6] What I did not realize at that point was she was referring to marital rape. This particular woman refused to give an interview, understandably so.

Despite having several actors (non-inclusive list: prison doctors, social workers, magistrates, prisoners, and researchers) in this labyrinth of prison research, I have mentioned only two – victims and researchers. There is scope to reflect on other actors and the roles they "play" in this system.

Peculiarities of prison research and the (continuous) need to conduct it

The labyrinth of actors in a prison research setting opens doors to certain peculiarities of prison research which affect the very nature of the research. To me, these peculiarities are prisoners, prison, and punishment itself.

Prisoners

Prisoners, some of them, speak about the crime (even when you do not ask) and regret deeply what they did. Some mention that they are wrongfully convicted; others do not speak about it at all. Rich prisoners will try and convince you about what a great life they had on the outside. Poor prisoners, on the other hand, would tell you that at least they get regular meals in the prison. Studies show that most prisoners who end up on death row are individuals from marginalized backgrounds. Most of them are *threatened, tortured*, and *tutored* to narrate a particular story that would go on to become the "rarest of the rare" narrative – criteria to be given the death penalty in India (George, 2015, pp. 65–74). Some of the prisoners are (in)famous for the crimes they are convicted for, and I had seen their photographs before entering the prison. Possibly, I could have been biased after "knowing" that a certain prisoner was convicted for raping a mentally challenged child or burning down his/her family. Although it pained me, I did realize (even though I may not have articulated it) that the exclusion of any prisoner while conducting a study to understand the "experiences and perceptions of prisoners within the criminal justice system" would pose not only serious methodological challenges but also ethical ones. Thus, this peculiarity of "prisoners" is far more complex than one would like it to be.

Prison

A prison is a place for rehabilitation and reintegration. This institution is supposed to better the lives of the ones who are confined in them. But research has suggested that prison is a cruel and harmful institution (Sykes, 1958). Wacquant states that ghettos and prisons both belong to the same class of organizations, namely, *institutions of forced confinement*: the ghetto is a manner of "social prison" while the prison functions as a "judicial ghetto." He mentions that both ghettos and prisons are entrusted with enclosing a stigmatized population so as to neutralize the material and/or the symbolic threat that it poses for the broader society from which it has been extruded. The prison is thus formed of fundamental constituents of stigma, coercion, physical enclosure, and organizational parallelism and insulation that make up a ghetto. Much as the ghetto protects the city's residents from the pollution of intercourse with the tainted but necessary bodies of an outcast group in the manner of an "urban condom," the prison cleanses the social body from the temporary blemish of those of its members who have committed crimes. Wacquant follows Durkheim and states that individuals who have violated the socio-moral integrity of the collectivity by infringing on "definite and strong states of the collective conscience." Thus, prison acts as an "urban condom" which keeps the "disease" (prisoners) away from the "healthy" ones (Wacquant, 2000).

Punishment

In the "judicial ghetto" (prison), prisoners undergo various forms of punishment such as simple or rigorous life imprisonment, simple imprisonment, and sometimes the death penalty. This would, however, exclude undertrials and detainees, as they are not "punished" in the real sense. Either way, the barrier "urban condom," i.e., the prison, keeps the "diseased?" (people) away till they receive their "punishment" or are acquitted. Garland describes punishment as a "complex set of interlinked processes and institutions rather than a uniform object or event." He draws from Foucault and Durkheim's position that punishment is the key to developing moral standards and that locking up offenders condemns the offense and reinforces society's values. He further considers punishment as fundamental to society which encapsulates and reinforces its values (Garland, 1990). Garland also argues that punishment (imprisonment) is not only an exercise of power but also an expression of the moral community and collective sensibilities, in which penal sanctions are authorized responses to shared values individually violated (Garland, 1991).

Need for (continuous) engagement in prison research

The above mentioned three peculiarities – prisoners, prison, and punishment – are the very factors that make it compelling for academicians and researchers to continue gathering evidence for an informed decision on the lives of people who are marginalized, who are supposedly "judicially ghettoized" to serve the moral community and collective sensibilities of the society. As criminologists, one reflects on the reasons for visiting this "judicial ghetto" and the need to engage with prisoners, prisons, and punishment. One of the reasons that we are able to engage and conduct research with the three peculiarities, under various labels (sociologists, criminologists, anthropologists) is because we know that we'd be out by the end of the day. Our liberty is not at stake. Prison does break a person. The question often raised by various actors (prison officials, media, family members, families of victims) is this: "*Is engaging with these peculiarities not pervert in some way?*" The arguments of the actors are strengthened because we (prison researchers) talk to a population that is arrested, charged, under trial, and/or convicted for rape, murder, theft, dacoity, vagrancy, sexual assault, breaking and entering, terrorism, Naxal links, sedition, terrorism-related offenses, or something even worse.

One can, therefore, argue that prison research *may* border around *perversion* when one looks at it from a certain perspective. However, the reasons for this "*supposed perversion*" is precisely the fact that we live in a society that is governed by the Rule of Law, that we live in a democracy, and we have a system that allows every individual to go through due processes, where one has the right to a fair and just judicial process. It is relevant to provide evidence that the lives of people who are on the "conflictive" side of the law. It is also crucial to provide evidence on the criminal justice system (police, prison, and court) and to have informed policy decisions in place. Therefore, the need to engage in these peculiarities is not just out of the "curiosity" of the researcher but also for the benefit of the state. The three peculiarities – prison, prisoners, and punishment – however, conglomerate to create an exigency of (in)visible ethical concerns.

Value conflicts, emotions, and the label of "overidentification"

This exigency of (in)visible ethical concern also leads to the (in)visible function of emotions in empirical prison research. Some would say our job as a researcher should be unbiased, unaffected by emotions. Some would highly rely on the principle of "non-engagement," both with data and the participants. I was very happy to read Liebling and Scheper-Hughes in this context. An education that drills into your head, "*Don't start crying with your clients*" is not necessarily correct. In a sense, it would be disastrous to be too involved with any research participant. No parent would ever admit to having a (secret) favorite child, (un)knowingly, we researchers do have our "favorite research participant." This is not to be construed for a parent-child relationship between a researcher and a participant and the power that it carries. Nevertheless, research studies do lay the groundwork for a life-long relationship with participants, and I am not shy to admit that some of my research participants and their families are still in touch with me.

Feminist critics have maintained that feelings, beliefs, and values shape our research, and are a natural part of an inquiry. However, in positivist sociological research, when subjective emotions get mixed with reflexivity, the data is perceived as unscientific. This premise did not remain uncriticized by feminist methodologists. Emotions influence our research, and our research can affect us emotionally. Consequently, feminist researchers have explored their own research experience, including feelings and emotions, rather than dismissing them as unscientific and irrelevant (Huggins & Glebbeek, 2003).

Similarly, Devereux argues that any investigation of other human beings is necessarily a self-investigation as well because the beliefs and behavior of one's subjects arise in the researcher's own unconscious (and usually infantile) fears, wishes, and fantasies. This countertransference phenomenon, a term borrowed from psychoanalytic therapy, evokes much anxiety and is extremely painful. The selective recruitment of anthropologists (and criminologists), and the nature of our data, countertransference, and its attendant anxieties, remains a characteristic of anthropology or criminology research (Devereux, 1967). I call this characteristic, "*bilateral damage*" caused through research with human participants. The ethical conundrums make me rely on Gilbert when he states that there are no cut-and-dried answers to the many ethical issues one faces as a social researcher. He further says that very often, the issues involved are multi-faceted and there are contradictory considerations at play. There is not necessarily one right and one wrong answer, but this indeterminacy does not mean that ethical issues can be ignored. He suggests that the best counsel for the social researcher is to be constantly ethically aware (Gilbert, 2008).

Despite being ethically aware, the constant "bilateral damage" (countertransference and its attendant anxieties) does get to us. During my prison research, there was adequate support in terms of emergency backup, infrastructural facilities, and monetary compensation. However, one thing I did not foresee as a consequence of dealing with prisons, prisoners, and punishment was the sheer magnitude of emotional stress that one would go through. While dealing with the data during analysis, I have had nightmares, bloody dreams, and heard the voices of prisoners when I closed my eyes. I was especially disturbed to hear accounts such as a certain prisoner's wife being electrocuted when she was five months pregnant and later dying in a hospital, or the execution of two death row convicts in November 2012 and February 2013, or the death of a prisoner who was part of the study in 2013. The distress I faced during the writing process was immense. I have until today not watched a single movie related to the death penalty. It took me a long time to watch a prison series such as *Orange Is the New Black*, and certainly not without emotional triggers. I do not read articles from the United States that talk about "*What is the last meal that you wish to eat?*" (Rayner, 2020). I do not engage in discussions on social media or with friends and family about the execution of death penalty prisoners, including the four prisoners convicted of rape and murder of Nirbhaya in 2012, which apparently shook the "collective conscience" of Indian society (Mashi & Slater, 2020).

In this context, I would propose some *Do's and Don'ts,* recommendations for prison researchers: (i) do not underestimate the emotional stress, take care of oneself during the entire process; (ii) be prepared to get information outside the scope of the study, the rule of thumb is to reflect on the objectives of the study; (iii) do not overtly or covertly try to dig up details of the crime from prisoners, as we are not investigating crime, we get access to the prison and prisoners to gather data to (mostly) improve the conditions of the criminal justice system and contribute to evidence-based laws and policies and the body of knowledge; (iv) be prepared to speak to men and women who have brutalized and killed other human beings in the most horrific and undignified manner; (v) be prepared to hear confessions of crime, stories of torture, sexual abuse, rape, scams, and ghosts and perhaps everything under the sun; (vi) be prepared and rehearse all possible situations with translators before actually conducting the interviews; (vii) acknowledge the victims in the research reports; bearing in mind that lives were lost; (viii) make appointments with a professional counselor right at the beginning to talk about the emotional stress and make provisions in the research budget for such a situation; (ix) acknowledge and be mentally prepared that the risk of physical harm is real and for this always demand open spaces to conduct interviews; (x) gather data while you can, there will not be a better opportunity later, prison conditions and situations keeps changing; (xi) (it is given) do not share information that might harm the prisoners in any manner and keep data confidential; and (xii) prepare a list of (un)forseen research projects.

The *Do's and Don'ts* or recommendations may or may not be helpful, and they may or may not assist prison researchers. If methods are applied properly and there is a system that allows for evidence in policymaking, prison research will continue to happen. A study in prison opens up a plethora of issues that one deals with. This may be related to our interactions with the *labyrinth of actors*, the *peculiarities of prison research,* the methodological concerns or limitations, or ethical principles. Liebling hits the bull's-eye by asking, "*Why is this emotional function of prison so invisible in most empirical research?*" (Liebling, 1999, p. 165). My interpretation of this invisible emotional function in empirical research is the fear of being labeled as "overidentifying" with the research participants. Staying in prison for the whole day and working at night to transcribe the data can exhaust and distress a researcher. As a researcher, it is constantly drilled in our heads to "maintain distance" or "non-engagement." Liebling deliberates that any methodological approach which asks for separation between being a criminologist (work) and human being (life) is deeply flawed. She says that many behave, read, and write as though the criminological lives and human lives are separate. Liebling further states that research in any human environment without subjective feeling is almost impossible – particularly in a prison and goes on to state that the pains of imprisonment are tragically underestimated by conventional methodological approaches to prison life. She says prison is all about pain – the pain of separation and loss, the wrench of restricted contact in the context of often fragile relationships, and of human failings and struggles (Liebling, 1999, pp. 165–166).

Overidentifying or romanticizing or demonizing the participants or the (prison) environment is frowned upon, but one has to cease being human to have these robotic responses of not "*feeling*" something. I would also not call these emotional feelings "overidentification." This is because I constantly remind myself and my participants of my boundaries as a human being and as a researcher.

Setting boundaries may help us in not "overidentifying." Interestingly, Scheper-Hughes proposes a combination of an academician and *companheira*. She was in the field to observe, to document, to understand, and later to write about the lives and their pain as fully, truthfully, and sensitively as she could. She says that we are privy to community secrets that are generally hidden from the view of outsiders or historical scrutiny until much later. She asks academicians what exempts us from the human responsibility of taking an ethical and even a political stand when working out of historical events as we are privileged to have witnessed them. Scheper-Hughes says that she was drawn back to the people and places not because of the exoticism and their "otherness," but in the pursuit of those small spaces of convergence, recognition, and empathy that she and her participants shared, realizing that they were not so radically "*other*" to each other. Scheper-Hughes further says that seeing, listening, touching, and recording can be, if done with care and sensitivity, acts of solidarity, and the work of recognition. Not doing any of those can be hostile acts, acts of indifference and of turning away. (Scheper-Hughes, 1995, pp. 410–419).

In any case, if I could change one aspect from my prison research experience, that would be acknowledging the women prisoners whom I knew from my internship (2004–2005) in the prison, with whom I have shared a meal, who taught me to cook the famous Maharashtrian peanut egg-plant roast in a women's prison. I take Scheper-Hughes position that witnessing is in the active voice, and it positions the anthropologist inside human events as a responsive and morally committed being, one who will "take sides" and make judgments. She says that "taking sides" certainly flies in the face of anthropological non-engagement with either ethics or politics. The following is what I agree with the most and perhaps follow. *Non-involvement was, in itself, an "ethical" and moral position.* I also take Scheper-Hughes' position that we can make ourselves available not just as friends or as "patrons" in the old colonialist sense but as *comrades* (with all the demands and responsibilities that this word implies) to the people who are the subjects of our writings, whose lives and miseries provides us with a livelihood (Scheper-Hughes, 1995, p. 410–419).

Creation of visibility of emotions and ethical concerns

The chapter deals with ethical principles and its applications with several examples from (Indian) prison research studies; explicates methodological concerns and limitations as a researcher; attempts to analyze the labyrinth of the (few) actors in prison research; crystalizes the peculiarities of prison research and the (continuous) need to conduct it; and finally situates the value conflicts and emotions and the label of "overidentification." There is perhaps nothing new that was said regarding research ethics or methodology, as the arguments, principles, and applications essentially remain the same. When it comes to prison research, it would be encouraged to share the emotional aspect of conducting these empirical studies. To destabilize the invisibility of the emotional aspect and ethical concerns of prison research, we must record, keep logs of our debriefing, and publish these emotions. Sykes, way back in the late 1950s, in his subtle way conveyed this message that "*the study of crime, in spite of the inherent interest of the subject matter, is in danger of becoming a dull parade of unattached facts*" (Sykes, 1958, pp. 115–116). It should be a concerted and coherent effort from all actors engaging with prisoners, prisons, and punishment to make the emotions and ethical concerns visible.

Notes

1 Akola District Prison; Amravati Central Prison; Amritsar Central Prison; Bangalore Central Prison; Belgaum Central Prison; Cuddalore Central Prison; Guwahati Central Prison; Jalgaon District Prison; Jorhat Central Prison; Kalyan District Prison; Kannur Central Prison; Madhurai Central Prison; Mumbai District Prison; Nagpur Central Prison; Nashik Road Central Prison; North-Lakhimpur District Prison; Patiala Central Prison; Poojapuram Central Prison; Puzhal Central Prison; Trichy Central Prison; Vellore Central Prison; Yerwada Central Prison.

2 Vienna-Josefstadt Prison (Justizanstalt Wien Josefstadt) and Vienna-Simmering Correctional Institution for Adult Male Prisoners (Justizanstalt Wien-Simmering).

3 Naxalites are a group of far-left radical communists, supportive of Maoist political sentiment and ideology. The term Naxalites comes from Naxalbari, a small village in West Bengal.

4 Quote translated from Marathi to English – original quote – "*Jhevha tho aath madhe yeyetho, tho ardha shahana bantho.*"

5 Warder is a trusted convicted prisoner.

6 Quote translated from Hindi to English – original quote – *"Tu kya janana chahathi hai? Mein kitne baar sothi hoon mere aadmi ke saath? Paanch baar soyi thi. Theen baar apne marzi se aur do baar jabardasti se."*

References

Abu-Jamal, M. (1996). Live from Death Row. *Journal of Criminal Justice and Popular Culture*, 4(2), 42–47.

Amnesty International India and People's Union for Civil Liberties (AI and PUCL). (2008). *Lethal Lottery: The Death Penalty in India – A Study of Supreme Court Judgement in Death Penalty Cases 1950–2006*. TN, India: Amnesty International India. Retrieved March 10, 2020 from https://www.amnesty.org/download/Documents/52000/asa200072008eng.pdf

Bar-Hillel, M., & Lavee, J. (2019). Lay Attitudes toward Involuntary Organ Procurement from Death-Row Prisoners: No, but. *Behavioural Public Policy*, 1–17. http://doi.org/10.1017/bpp.2019.16

Chenwi, L. (2007). *Towards the Abolition of the Death Penalty in Africa: A Human Rights Perspective*. Cape Town, SA: Pretoria University Law Press.

Codd, H. (2013). *In the Shadow of Prison: Families, Imprisonment and Criminal Justice*. New York: Routledge.

Condry, R., & Smith, P. S. (Eds.). (2018). *Prisons, Punishment, and the Family: Towards a New Sociology of Punishment?* Oxford: Oxford University Press.

Cooper, D. T. (2017). Death Row. *The Encyclopedia of Corrections*, 1, 1–5.

Cooper, R. A. (1981). Jeremy Bentham, Elizabeth Fry, and English Prison Reform. *Journal of the History of Ideas*, 42(4), 675–690.

Dawes, J. (2002). Dying with Dignity: Prisoners and Terminal Illness. *Illness, Crisis & Loss*, 10(3), 188–203.

Devereux, G. (1967). *From Anxiety to Method in the Behavioural Sciences*. The Hague/Paris: Mouton & Company.

Doval, N. (2019, May 12). Life in the Hangman's Shadow. *First Post*. Retrieved March 20, 2020 from https://www.firstpost.com/india/life-in-the-hangmans-shadow-6608051.html

Foucault, M. (1977). *Discipline and Punish*, translated by Alan Sheridan. New York: Pantheon.

Garland, D. (1990). *Punishment and Modern Society: A Study in Social Theory*. Chicago, IL: University of Chicago Press.

Garland, D. (1991). Sociological Perspectives on Punishment. *Crime and Justice*, 14, 115–165.

George, R. M. (2009). *Death Penalty: A Human Rights Perspective*. (unpublished Master thesis, Mumbai, India: University of Mumbai).

George, R. M. (2015). *Prisoner Voices from Death Row: Indian Experiences*. London: Routledge.

Gilbert, N. (Ed.). (2008). *Researching Social Life*. Thousand Oaks, CA: SAGE.

Goffman, E. (1957). On the Characteristics of Total Institutions. In *Walter Reed Army Institute of Research: Symposium on Preventive and Social Psychiatry*. Washington, DC: National Academies Press. https://doi.org/10.17226/20228.

Gupta, P. (2020, January 18). Nirbhaya's Mother on Why She Won't Consider Request to Pardon the Rapists. *shethepeople – The Women's Channel*. Retrieved March 11, 2020 from https://www.shethepeople.tv/news/asha-devi-no-merit-indira-jaisings-request.

Harris, L. R., & Brown, G. T. (2010). Mixing Interview and Questionnaire Methods: Practical Problems in Aligning Data. *Practical Assessment, Research and Evaluation*, 15(1), 1–19. Retrieved March 10, 2020 from https://scholarworks.umass.edu/pare/vol15/iss1/1

Hood, R. (1996). *The Death Penalty: USA in World-Wide Perspective*. New York: Oxford University Press.

Hood, R., & Hoyle, C. (2015). *The Death Penalty: A Worldwide Perspective*. Oxford: Oxford University Press.

House, E. R. (1993). *Professional Evaluation: Social Impact and Political Consequences*. Newbury Park, CA: SAGE.

Huggins, M. K., & Glebbeek, M. L. (2003). Women Studying Violent Male Institutions: Cross-gendered Dynamics in Police Research on Secrecy and Danger. *Theoretical Criminology*, 7(3), 363–387.

Israel, M., & Hay, I. (2006). *Research Ethics for Social Scientists: Between Ethical conduct and Regulatory Compliance*. London: SAGE.

Jackson, B. (1987). *Fieldwork*. Urbana, IL: University of Illinois Press.

Jackson, B., & Christian, D. (1980). *Death Row*. New Brunswick, NJ: Transaction Publishing.

Jacobsen, K., & Landau, L. B. (2003). The Dual Imperative in Refugee Research: Some Methodological and Ethical Considerations in Social Science Research on Forced Migration. *Disasters*, 27(3), 185–206.

Johnson, R. (1979). Under Sentence of Death: The Psychology of Death Row Confinement. *Law and Psychology Review*, 5, 141–192.

Johnson, R. (2017). Living and Working on Death Row. In Bohm, Robert M., & Lee, G. (Eds.), *Routledge Handbook on Capital Punishment* (pp. 589–594). New York: Routledge.

Reader's Editor (opinion piece), The Hindu. Khairlanji: The Crime and Punishment (2010, August 23), *The Hindu*. Retrieved March 11, 2020 from https://www.thehindu.com/opinion/Readers-Editor/Khairlanji-the-crime-and-punishment/article16149798.ece

Liebling, A. (1999). Doing Research in Prison: Breaking the Silence? *Theoretical Criminology*, 3(2), 147–173.

Liebling, A., & Maruna, S. (Eds.). (2013). *The Effects of Imprisonment*. London: Routledge.

Liu, S. (2019). Female Offenders on Death Row. *The Encyclopedia of Women and Crime*, 1, 1–4.

Lo, B. (2009). *Resolving Ethical Dilemmas: A Guide for Clinicians*. Philadelphia, PA: Lippincott Williams & Wilkins.

Macklin, R. (2003). Dignity is a Useless Concept. *British Medical Journal (Clinical Research Edition)*, 327(7429), 1419–1420. https://doi.org/10.1136/bmj.327.7429.1419

Mashi, N., & Slater. J. (2020, March 20). India Executes Four Men Convicted in 2012 Delhi Rape and Murder Case. *Washington Post*. Retrieved March 20, 2020 from https://www.washingtonpost.com/world/asia_pacific/india-2012-delhi-gang-rape-executions/2020/03/19/65d223f6-468a-11ea-8949-a9ca94a90b4c_story.html

Murray, J., & Farrington, D. P. (2008). The Effects of Parental Imprisonment on Children. *Crime and Justice*, 37(1), 133–206.

National Commission for the Protection of Human Subjects of Biomedical and Behavioral Research (NCPHSBBR). (1978). *The Belmont Report: Ethical Principles and Guidelines for the Protection of Human Subjects of Research*. Bethesda, MD: The Commission. Retrieved March 10, 2020 from https://www.hhs.gov/ohrp/regulations-and-policy/belmont-report/read-the-belmont-report/index.html

National Committee for Ethics in Social Science Research in Health (NCESSRH). (2004). *Ethical Guidelines for Social Science Research in Health*. Mumbai: Satam Udyog. Retrieved March 10, 2020 from http://www.cehat.org/go/uploads/EthicalGuidelines/ethicalguidelines.pdf

National Crime Records Bureau (NCRB). (2018). *Prison Statistics India, 2018*. Delhi: Ministry of Home Affairs. Government of India. Retrieved March 20, 2020 from http://ncrb.gov.in/prison-statistics-india

National Law University (NLU). (2016). *The Death Penalty India Report*. Delhi: National Law University.

Newman, D. J. (1958). Research Interviewing in Prison. *Journal of Criminal Law, Criminology, and Police Science*, 49(2), 127–132.

Nowak, M. (2001). *The Death Penalty: An Inhuman Punishment?* in Orlin, T. S., Rosas, A., & Scheinin, M. (2001). The Jurisprudence of Human Rights Law: A Comparative Interpretative Approach. *Refugee Survey Quarterly*, 20(3), 42–43.

Oyero, R. O. (2004). An Appraisal of the Right to Dignity of Prisoners and Detainees with Disabilities: A Case Study of Ghana and Nigeria. (Doctoral dissertation, University of Pretoria, Pretoria, South Africa). Retrieved March 20, 2020 from http://hdl.handle.net/2263/1099

Piper, H., & Simons, H. (2005). Ethical Responsibility in Social Research. In Somekh, B., & Lewin, C. (Eds.), *Research Methods in the Social Sciences* (pp. 56–64). London: SAGE.

Ploch, A. (2012). Why Dignity Matters: Dignity and the Right (or not) to Rehabilitation from International and National Perspectives. *New York University Journal of International Law and Politics*, 44(3), 887–949.

Rayner, J. (2020, March 10). Last Meals on Death Row, a Peculiar American Fascination. *New York Times*. Retrieved March 11, 2020 from https://www.nytimes.com/2020/03/10/dining/death-row-last-meals-jay-rayner.html

Rowling, J. K. (2014). *Harry Potter and the Philosopher's Stone* (Vol. 1). London: Bloomsbury Publishing.

Schabas, W. A. (2002). *The Abolition of the Death Penalty in International Law*. Cambridge, UK: Cambridge University Press.

Scheper-Hughes, N. (1995). The Primacy of the Ethical: Propositions for a Militant Anthropology. *Current Anthropology*, 36(3), 409–440.

Schlanger, M. (2010). Regulating Segregation: The Contribution of the ABA Criminal Justice Standards on the Treatment of Prisoners. *American Criminal Law Review*, 47(4), 1421–1440.

Schneller, D. P. (1976). *The Prisoner's Family: A Study of the Effects of Imprisonment on the Families of Prisoners*. San Francisco, CA: R and E Research Associates.

Spates, K., & Mathis, C. (2014). Preserving Dignity: Rethinking Voting Rights for US Prisoners: Lessons from South Africa. *Journal of Pan African Studies*, 7(6), 84–105.

Strauss, A., & Corbin, J. (1998). *Basics of Qualitative Research Techniques*. Thousand Oaks, CA: SAGE Publications.

Sykes, G. M. (1958). *The Society of Captives: A Study of a Maximum Security Prison*. Princeton, NJ: Princeton University Press.

The Centre for Equity Studies (CES). (2018). *India Exclusion Report 2017-18*. Delhi: Yoda Press.

Travis, J., & Waul, M. (Eds.). (2003). *Prisoners Once Removed: The Impact of Incarceration and Reentry on Children, Families, and Communities*. Washington, DC: Urban Institute Press.

Tutu Criticized; Told Jews to Forgive Nazis (1989, December 29), *Los Angeles Times*. [Los Angeles Times has reprinted it]. Retrieved March 11, 2020 from https://www.latimes.com/archives/la-xpm-1989-12-29-mn-1127-story.html

Wacquant, L. (2000). The New 'Peculiar Institution': On the Prison as Surrogate Ghetto. *Theoretical Criminology*, 4(3), 377–389. https://doi.org/10.1177/1362480600004003007

Chapter 3

Social science research in Canada

Ethical and methodological issues

Shahid Alvi

Introduction

This chapter provides a discussion of selected methodological and ethical issues associated with conducting social science research in Canada. The chapter is based on the premise that research methods and questions about ethics should take account of the social context in which research is conducted. Therefore, a good deal of attention is directed toward the description of the Canadian social environment and some of the social problems associated with it, particularly for underserved populations often viewed as undeserving. It is, of course, impossible to cover the myriad underserved and under-researched populations in Canada, and omitting them from the discussion in no way diminishes their importance or relevance. To accommodate space limitations, the chapter focuses on a handful of issues and populations, although readers should note that many of the arguments presented have relevance for the study of other groups elsewhere.

Canada is the second-largest country in the world by area with a population of 37 million people. As such, it is a sparsely populated nation in comparison with countries like the United States and India. Canadians are often characterized as polite, discreet, and rational people living peacefully under the rule of law within a parliamentary democracy – the embodiment in its constitution of the principles of peace, order, and good government. With its neighbor, the United States, Canada shares the longest unguarded border in the world and is its number one trade partner. Not surprisingly, the size and cultural power of the United States has meant ready diffusion of its popular culture into Canada, making Canada very similar to the United States in certain ways. However, in terms of social problems, on a per capita basis, Canada has lower crime, poverty, and ill-health rates compared with the United States.

Like many other industrialized nations, Canada's population is aging. Population scenarios derived by Statistics Canada suggest that between 15 and 28 percent of Canadians will be over the age of 65 by the year 2063 (Bohnert, Chagnon, Coulombe, Dion, & Martel, 2015). Canada is a "nation of immigrants," widely considered to be one of the most multicultural societies in the world. By 2036, nearly 40 percent of the working population of Canada is projected to be visible minorities, nearly one-third will be immigrants, and nearly one in five people will observe a non-Christian religion (Morency, Malenfant, & MacIsaac, 2017). People of color in Canada represent about one-fifth of all poor people compared with 12 percent of non-racialized individuals (Government of Canada, 2016). In terms of the United Nations Human Development Indices measuring longevity, health, education, and standard of living, Canada ranks 12th out of 189 countries (United Nations Development Programme, 2018).

The country is also well known for its relative economic and political stability, and its putative embrace of cultural and ethnic diversity. The country has historically taken a path differing from nations such as the United States with respect to immigration and integration of newcomers, eschewing a "melting pot" approach in favor of a "tossed salad" strategy. This metaphor conveys the idea that Canada has historically rebuffed the notion that one should be "Canadian first" with culture or heritage acting in a complementary way. Rather, the country has tried to integrate immigrants while simultaneously encouraging the elevation, preservation, and indeed, celebration of "non-traditional" cultural, religious, and political belief systems. Thus, the image of Canada around the world is often that it is a peaceful, stable, benevolent, peacekeeping middle power.

On the other hand, as Henderson and Wakeham (2009, p. 1) report, former Canadian Prime Minister Brian Mulroney once erroneously stated that:

> There are very few countries that can say for nearly 150 years they've had the same political system without any social breakdown, political upheaval or invasion. We are unique in that regard. We also have no history of colonialism.

In fact, although Canada is a prosperous and peaceful country relative to many others, it is also one that experiences its fair share of social problems, including a history of colonialism, warranting methodologically sound and rigorous research unpacking unwarranted assumptions and thus driving sound policy decisions. Taking the homicide rate as an example, while it is true that Canada has a lower rate of such crimes compared with the United States, there are still about 50 countries with rates lower than Canada (Braithwaite, 2014). All countries experience social problems such as poverty, violent crime, poor health, and environmental degradation, and many of the issues discussed in this chapter are as common in social science research as they would be anywhere in the world. Nonetheless, all countries are also unique in terms of their socio-political contexts, the extent and potency to which certain social problems are experienced, and the resources directed to ameliorate them. Accordingly, the realities of context shape both the methods and research questions social scientists engage with. The issues discussed in this chapter are set against the backdrop of the Canadian social, political, and cultural landscape. The critical approach I utilize is a position that rejects the idea that science can or should be value-neutral. My basic contention is that all social science is political.

The issues discussed here are therefore organized within the contemporary context in which researchers are working in Canada and employ a critical perspective on some key methodological and ethical issues confronting social scientists. Specifically, I place methodological and ethical issues regarding the purpose of research within the context of neoliberalism, the alarming escalation of "othering," the experiences of Indigenous peoples, and the increasing importance of digital technologies in Canada. I begin with a necessarily brief discussion of dilemmas facing social science, paying particular attention to the question of the purpose of social science research. The section that follows that discussion provides some basic background on well-known ethical challenges in social science. The remainder of the chapter examines some of these ethical and methodological questions with respect to particular issues in contemporary Canada.

What is social science for?

Social science faces challenges to its authenticity from within and outside its disciplines. For many decades, much of the social sciences have operated within a framework positing that knowledge of the social world can only be gained by testing hypotheses and quantifying results, the central tenets of positivist epistemology. As a set of epistemological assumptions, and in its most basic form, positivism assumes that there is a distinct correspondence between the methods of the social and natural sciences (Bierne, 1996). The implications of this perspective on knowledge are that deviations from the norm, as one might see observed differences between criminals and non-criminals for example, exist because such groups possess certain characteristics that have their roots in either individual or social pathologies. Moreover, it is posited that these differences can be understood via quantitative methods, with the goal of establishing cause-effect understandings of social phenomena. For instance, criminology and the social science enterprise to which it belongs are considered to be a system of science, distinct from and sometimes dismissive of beliefs, hunches, or feelings. Criminology, remarks Brodeur (1999, p. 131), "aims to produce knowledge… intended to change the social environment through its application," but it is knowledge as distinct from "research" because the former implies validity, while the latter can imply anything. Reiss (1993) points out that some social scientists working within positivist epistemological frameworks often claim to be "value-free," "impartial," or "reporting not promoting" an "antiseptic" view of science. Young (2004), a criminologist, argued that social scientists must be careful to appreciate the limitations of statistical "voodoo," but mindful of its utility where appropriate. For many social scientists, the limitations of positivism have fostered a post-positivist stance on the nature of knowledge, one that recognizes the importance of the assumptions and values scientists bring to the design, method, and interpretation of social phenomena. As such, post-positivism challenges positivist assumptions that empirical data should be interpreted in terms of the logic of cause and effect, that research is conducted to support a preconceived theory, and that researchers should maintain distance and objectivity in relation to the research problem and its subjects.

Positivism contends that there is one "real" world that is truly unknowable, and that alternative accounts of that world must be grounded in a particular scientific method. As such, these approaches have been questioned as positions of supposed "detached neutrality and objectivity" (Burgess-Proctor, 2015, p. 124), one example of which is evident in the alternative approaches (discussed later in this chapter), suggested by scholars pursuing research about, for, and with First Nations peoples.

Further, positivism is a perspective on science that assumes that one can have an objective and certain knowledge of the world around, which for Braithwaite (2014) has resulted in a "dysfunctional disciplinary structure." He contends that this condition stems from over-reliance on the study of categorical objects and behaviors rather than theoretical inquiry driven by a thirst for discovery. For instance, he argues that disciplines such as criminology and sociology are more inclined to study criminal justice institutions such as prisons, police, and organizational behavior, rather than prisoner experiences, police corruption, and corporate fraud. He wants to draw attention to what matters in social life; to decide whose side we are on in light of the realization that all research brings with it the biases and preconceptions of the researcher (Becker, 1966).

Qualitative researchers will be familiar with questions of what constitutes knowledge when knowledge is defined through a positivist lens. In the past and to some extent still, qualitative research has been accused of not being "real science" because it does not necessarily test hypotheses based on representative samples drawn from sample frames and is therefore not generalizable to populations. But this characterization of qualitative research completely misses the point of doing such work and relies upon a narrow definition of epistemology. While it is certainly true that a great deal of qualitative work tends to focus on micro relations rather than links to the macro level of analysis, it is also true that qualitative research can provide us with in-depth understandings of the social world, of experiences, and the construction of meaning that is just not possible with quantitative techniques. As public health researcher Irving Selikoff once opined, statistics are people with the tears wiped away.

Some social scientists have successfully used mixed methods designs integrating quantitative and qualitative techniques (see, for example, Wilson, 1990), but a more cogent objection to the idea that qualitative research is not scientific is that such research is often used to generate theory or hypotheses, and is therefore unconcerned with generalizability issues. In his analysis of this generalizability problem, Small (2009) points out via his discussion of Burawoy's extended case method that qualitative research can be seen as a way of revealing the relationship between broader structural forces and the case or cases the researcher is studying – we study the deviant or unique case to generalize about theory or society. Generalizability is not the goal of qualitative research and should not be reported to suggest that such research is representative of larger populations. It offers logical not statistical inference (Small, 2009).

The question of why we do the research we do is germane to the types of methods we employ and has complex ethical implications. For example, in medicine, research on drugs for treating terminal cancer may yield health benefits outweighing the ethical obligations of doing the research but may never see the light of day because the intervention is not profitable. Here, there are two ethical dilemmas – should the research be done even though it violates ethical principles but potentially results in cancer remission, and should corporate interests be allowed to dictate what potentially beneficial drugs go to market based on profit margins? In research on homelessness, we may find that the gravity of issues confronting the homeless, coupled with their unmet needs may create a situation calling for research that may be seen as intrusive or, in the case of work offering monetary incentives to participate in research, as coercive by some research ethics boards. We could argue that corporate interests are outside the purview of science, and we could simply ignore the homeless. Contrary to this position, however, is the idea that we must consider the extent to which the impetus to do empirical research to inform theory and policy entails more than simply describing social reality, but also engaging with questions around what kind of world is desirable (Keucheyan, 2013).

In part, reflecting on the purposes of social science is also tied to debate over our identity as social scientists, public intellectuals, or both. In the context of debates over the purpose of research as "agitation for justice" or to make our work accessible to the general public (Burawoy, 2005; Lupton, 2014), there is growing unease among the general public as to the utility and "truth" of science. These perceptions derive from numerous sources. The business models of mass media demand that they promulgate information that sells advertising. In turn, this objective drives truth claims that are often titillating or emotionally tinged, and often misleading or wrong. Moreover, the proliferation of social media platforms, which by their nature are designed to disseminate "information" often without reference to sources, credibility, truth, or verifiability, has created an environment of distrust and skepticism of science. There are numerous examples of this situation ranging from the dangerous to the bizarre, including climate change denial, amplification of the alleged dangers posed by "foreign" others, disavowal of electoral fraud, alien abduction, and flat-earth theories. Sound, reliable information is at a premium nowadays and challenges to the truth of a claim are often made more on the basis of political confirmation bias and emotional reaction than they are on careful evaluation of scientific findings.

In short, social science research is political either inherently or by design, and even to claim that research can be value-free is in itself a political statement (Luker, 2008). It is not surprising therefore that the relationship between policy decisions and sound research is also political. One cogent example of this is evident in the recent history of the Canadian Census. For decades, Canada has conducted a census of its population involving the mandatory completion of a survey conducted by Statistics Canada every four years. In 2010, the Conservative federal government decided to make the long-form census voluntary, repackaging it as the National Household Survey. The Director of Statistics Canada, Munir Shaikh, resigned his post arguing, with support from statisticians, academics, and some 370 organizations that a voluntary survey would not provide information of the same quality as a mandatory one (people are less likely to fill out voluntary surveys) and that scientists were being "muzzled" by a government that did not care for data contradicting its political agenda (Savoie, 2015). The long-form census was reintroduced in 2016, a move that economists, social scientists, and bureaucrats have hailed as a return to a nominal commitment that "intelligent policy development is not possible without good data," but which has left a gap in data (Sheikh as cited in Gorbet & Sharpe, 2011, p. 333).

Ethics in research: Contemporary issues

In planning and executing their investigations, researchers must consider, at minimum, issues of confidentiality, anonymity, liberty to withdraw from the research, informed consent versus coercion of research subjects, and the minimization of harm to researchers, participants, and institutions. Such rules sometimes present researchers with challenges related to the design and execution of their work, and there are times in all research where unanticipated problems arise (thus requiring contingency plans).

In Canada, research ethics are governed by research ethics boards, which in universities must comply with rules as set out in the second version of the Tri-Council Policy Statement (TCPS-2). This document, the result of a collaboration between bodies governing social sciences, humanities, the natural sciences and engineering, and medicine, covers a range of ethical issues, including research with vulnerable populations, inclusive research, privacy and confidentiality, conflict of interest, and minimizing risk. The guidelines are rooted in lessons learned from well-known accounts of ethical problems in research, such as the Nuremberg doctors' trials, the Tuskegee experiments, Humphrey's study of homosexual men, and the Stanford Prison experiments. It is a comprehensive benchmark relying on international norms and standards, and any research funded by government agencies must adhere to criteria delineated in the document, although compliance is administered and monitored by affiliated institutions (such as universities). It is important to remember that the TCPS2 (and policies like it) are guidelines, which means that the design and intent of research studies need to be considered on a case-by-case basis in light of the ethical principles outlined in the document and with a measure of common sense.

These guidelines are understandably robust and critically important because they are reflections of human social and community values. However, one of the most significant challenges faced by Canadian (and other) social science researchers, particularly those engaging in qualitative research pertains to the increasing use of a biomedical model to evaluate social science methodology and even the appropriateness of the kinds of research questions social scientists ask. The preemptive nature of biomedical research (again understandably) tends to lean toward strict standards because there are often clear implications of such research for the health and well-being of living organisms. Yet similar standards cannot always be adopted for social science research, leading some scholars to argue that sometimes, ethics boards (which are most often composed of evaluators with different backgrounds) simply do not understand social science research, employ inappropriate definitions of harm which constitute obstacles to advancing knowledge, and engage in "ethics creep" as a risk avoidance strategy which in turn is part of the "audit culture" of neoliberal societies (Haggerty, 2004; Dingwall, 2008; Allen, 2009; Doyle & Buckley, 2017). The reality of digital technology is also raising important questions (considered later in this chapter) for social science because these technologies are forcing us to re-evaluate very fundamental questions about harm, privacy, democracy, and even free will.

Social science research in the neoliberal era

As noted earlier, research is conducted in a social and political context, and it would be naive to believe that such contexts do not play a role in the kinds of research that are funded by external agencies such as governments and foundations. Since the 1970s, that context has been given many names, including post-industrialism, late modernity, post-modernity, and fourth-wave capitalism. The term employed in this chapter is neoliberalism, which Harvey (2007) defines as an "institutional framework characterized by private property rights, individual liberty, unencumbered markets, and free trade [in which…] The role of the state is to create and preserve an institutional framework appropriate to such practices" (Harvey, 2016, p. 22). Thus, neoliberalism prioritizes research on economic investment and profit over social policies (such as living wages, job security, healthcare, pensions, and racial and gender equality) designed to mitigate or transcend the numerous negative consequences of a deregulated free-market economic system. Neoliberalism is therefore implicated as a catalyst and accelerant of many social ills, compounding living conditions and social difficulties for many people in Canada, and in particular those who are already vulnerable. In addition, since the bulk of funding for social science research in Canada is provided by the state, the research funding domain is also shaped by neoliberal ideology in numerous ways.

At a macro level, neoliberal economic, political, and social policies have meant that research funding for social science studies is increasingly tied to augmenting the prosperity and economic well-being of Canada and Canadians. At face value, this seems like a worthwhile goal. No one would deny the importance of economic prosperity and well-being for all citizens. However, this kind of emphasis has gone hand-in-hand with the transformation of public sector organizations, including universities, in which the dominant narrative is one of the markets, competitiveness, and patents, increasingly at the expense of research that is critical of the vagaries and harmful consequences of neoliberal policies (Giroux, 2014; Kenny, 2017). Between 2005 and 2015, the federal government of Canada spent on average ten times more per year on research in the natural sciences and engineering than it did on the social sciences and humanities (Statistics Canada, 2015). In effect, research aiming to unpack the contradictions and negative social outcomes of economic, environmental, and cultural trends or to enhance education, decrease poverty, gender inequality, and racism pale in comparison with research and development advancing the aims of capital.

The results of neoliberalism have been to widen social inequality, diminish human rights, and instill a culture of fearful acceptance of the social system as a taken for granted and insurmountable reality (Stanford, 2015). In her study of the views of elder faculty (those who have been academics for 20 years or more) in Canada, Kawalilak (2012) shows that such faculty call attention to the devaluation of fields of study seen to be unrelated to acquiring job skills, an emphasis on pedagogy favoring corporate and commercial discourse, and the devaluation and cheapening of professional academic work as evidenced by increased reliance on contingent faculty (see Dobbie & Robinson, 2008; Giroux, 2014). At the same time, there has been great emphasis on the centrality of science, technology, engineering, and mathematics (STEM) fields as those worthy of research funding, especially if they advance industry objectives. This emphasis is not in itself problematic as such areas of inquiry are important to human development and well-being. However, it is important to remember that STEM fields should proceed with a clear understanding of the moral, ethical, and social consequences of research conducted in those fields as well as the outcomes of that research. Self-driving cars, genetic engineering, and the use of algorithms to determine sentencing outcomes or the legality of online hate speech must be guided by insights from the social sciences, particularly with regard to issues around meaning, context, nuance, reliability, and validity.

Such developments mean that for some social scientists, the environment in which research is conducted in Canada now prioritizes research often uncritical of status quo social and political configurations. Others make the stronger argument that more emphasis for research funding is being placed on efforts that promise to create profits, improve efficiencies, enhance productivity, and reduce costs within extant social arrangements (Metcalfe, 2010). Although the raison d'être of research should be to advance the human condition by unpacking inequalities and the unreasonable exercise of power, much research reproduces the current state of affairs under the cloak of neutrality and objectivity (Jeppesen & Nazar, 2012). Regardless of one's point of view, it is clear that neoliberalism now sets limits upon, and conditions the impetus to critically reflect upon and transform social relations in ways that might remake the status quo (Polster, 2004).

Social scientists study variation in human societies. To study difference is to engage not only with statistical variation from averages but to try and understand theoretically why such distinctions exist and how differences are experienced. As noted earlier, we should not study the difference with indifference. Such approaches to understanding variation evince little or no commitment to a healthier, more just world, often ignoring issues of morality, ethics, and politics and buttressed by the claim that such concerns are outside the purpose of social science.

As also described earlier, Canada is a very heterogeneous country, and this diversity has meant increasing attention to issues around assimilation, adjustment, acceptance, and prejudice on a wide range of differences, including but not limited to age, gender, sexuality, ethnicity, and religion. In a limited space, it is impossible to comprehensively cover the research challenges that would apply in studying all these issues, let alone the complex ways in which they interact. Therefore, the remainder of this chapter focuses attention on some methodological and ethical challenges associated with what I consider to be two important trends in Canadian society. The first set of issues pertains to the lives of "the other," or people who are objectified as less worthy of respect and are thus often the victims of unequal treatment in different streams of life. Here the focus is on issues around multiculturalism, racialized women, and First Nations people. The second considers another important development common to the majority of richer countries – the increasing importance of the internet and the digitalization of social life.

Researching the "other" in multicultural Canada

Neoliberal policies have changed employment and work relations and have fostered an increase in precarious employment, the disappearance of many industrial manufacturing jobs, the rise of automation in the service sector, volatility in primary sector markets (e.g., oil, gas, and agricultural products important to the Canadian economy), and the outsourcing of work. These economic problems have been accompanied by social anxiety and political and cultural polarization. Manifestations of these crises can be seen in increased racism, the backlash against progressive groups and ideas, xenophobia, and calls for a return to an imaginary past of ostensible stability, harmony, and productive well-paying jobs. In effect, there has been a palpable and well-documented rise in fear and sometimes hatred of "the other," a closing of minds and political polarization in Canada. This "ontological insecurity" as Young (1999) refers to it requires research attention to clarify social phenomena, debunk myths, and help forge rational policy. Firmly entwined in the mesh of neoliberal ideological and political practices, "others" in Canada have received increased, often negative attention because it is easy to blame the troubles that come with significant change on people possessing discernable physical and cultural characteristics. In what follows, I outline some methodological and ethical issues that should be considered in studying social issues in this context.

Minority populations are a substantial, growing, and increasingly important component of Canada's population. Canada aspires to be a multicultural nation whose inhabitants live harmoniously, and where the difference is both acknowledged and celebrated. In 1971, Canadians formalized their commitment to multiculturalism in reaction to the recommendations of the Royal Commission on Bilingualism and Biculturalism, which had been appointed in 1963 and proposed that Canada acknowledge and develop as a country on the basis of its "two founding races." Prime Minister Pierre Elliott Trudeau responded by stating that biculturalism and indeed no one culture defined Canada and that the country would recognize that diverse ethnic and cultural communities made up "essential elements" of the nation. This commitment granted all Canadians the right to preserve, develop, and grow their own cultures, to participate in mainstream life with equal rights and obligations, and to promote cultural exchange. Li (1999) points out that this policy was largely symbolic, lacking the force of law and seen by many as rhetoric more than reality (Wayland, 1997). Today, as in many other nations, multiculturalism, diversity, and difference are at the center of political and social debate, thus creating some urgency for systematic investigation. For example, hate crimes against visible and religious minorities, LGBTQ communities, and people defined as the "other" have risen in the past decade. In 2015, police-reported incidents of hate-motivated crimes in Canada increased by 5 percent, half of which were motivated by hatred of a "race" or ethnicity. Hate-motivated crimes against Muslims increased by 61 percent. Of all hate crimes, nearly one-third involved violence (Leber, 2017). Many of the communities to which these victims belong are experiencing "in terrorem" harms in that they live in shock, anger, and the fear that they too could be victimized (Perry & Alvi, 2012).

The concomitant increased visibility and presence of extreme right-wing groups on and offline has only served to make such fears worse and has contributed to the amplification of fear and distrust among the general population. Often, discussion of complex issues is replaced by simplistic narratives, the tendency to responsibilize individuals or groups for their alleged deficits, accusations of "fake" news, and an upsurge in nationalistic myths. In this kind of environment, the role of social scientists is surely to unpack the complexity of such views, understand their roots, and offer all stakeholders potential solutions to social problems, as well as clear, accessible information to help dispel fictions. Moreover, such projects rely on scientific systematic inquiry, rather than conjecture for their utility and credibility. Indeed, the current environment has done much social science research with, about, and for marginalized groups imperative, as they are increasingly targeted for ridicule and blamed for much that has gone wrong in recent times. Thus, while researchers know what subjects and issues require investigation, they must also be aware of the interests and perspectives of those with whom they are conducting the research.

Researchers need to be aware of cultural norms and values as potential obstacles to conducting their research, but also how such elements of social life intersect with one another and other social identities. For instance, in research involving immigrant women conducted by the author and colleagues, it was clear that topics like sexuality were not to be discussed. The author has also faced difficulties accessing survivors of woman abuse from certain deeply religious cultures because they do not consider violence against women and girls to be a "problem" in their community. Similarly, Acquisti and colleagues (2015) have noted that Americans tend to be more open about sexual issues compared with Chinese, who in turn are more likely to be open about financial matters. These researchers also suggest that there are differences in perceptions of the importance of privacy both within and between cultures.

It may be difficult to approach cultures with a strong in-group/out-group orientation or those that see themselves as isolated from mainstream, secular-pluralist Canada. Some groups also feel that any research being conducted on their behalf will not amount to much in the way of changing their situation. This is not a surprising sentiment, as the voices of many such groups, such as Indigenous peoples, immigrants, or the poor, have been ignored in the past. Other collectives may display misgivings about talking to anyone who appears to be in a position of authority as they may have immigrated from war-torn countries or one where it is dangerous to speak about political and social issues.

In addition to creating problems in terms of what can be discussed and who can be accessed, it may be difficult to build rapport and trust with vulnerable populations because of language barriers, cultural biases, or misunderstandings from all parties. Thus, research with such groups entails a careful assessment of the culture being scrutinized, including value orientations toward sensitive or taboo subjects and standpoints on mainstream society considering attitudes toward the separation between public and private domains, language, and religious beliefs, to name a few. The point here is not to establish a checklist of items to complete, but to make the best attempt to understand the culture in appreciation of *emic* strategies; that is, from the point of view of a culture's inhabitants using their definitions of reality, prior to, and throughout the research process. One difficulty emerging from this approach is that researchers will often have to reconcile their own cultural and scientific biases with those of the minority group they are studying (Fontes, 1998).

For example, in addition to speaking either or both English and French, Canadians speak over 200 languages as a mother tongue. As more people immigrate to Canada, the proportion of people who do not speak English or French as a first language increases, although fluency in English and French becomes the norm for these groups over the span of one or two more generations (Chui, 2013; Morency, Malenfant, & MacIsaac, 2017). Newcomers are a small but increasing portion of the population and are more likely to experience the kinds of social problems of concern to social scientists. To be sure, many standard research methodologies can be employed with such populations in either majority language, but in other cases, one difficulty stems from the idea that while a person may be able to speak English, for example, they may "think" in terms of their mother tongue. Thus, there may be English words, expressions, and idioms that are not interpreted the same way in a person's native language or may not exist at all.

A good example of the challenges posed by this situation can be seen in research on violence against women where language barriers make it difficult for English speaking qualitative researchers to fully appreciate what is being said by non-English speaking research participants. In addition, researchers choosing quantitative survey methods may be presented with the challenge of wording questions appropriately to accurately capture data, operationalize concepts, and interpret results. Similarly, questions should be properly worded in the native language of the respondent, so that such questions take into account cultural and linguistic customs and idioms, or linguistic relativity (see the discussion of the Sapir-Whorf hypothesis in Kay & Kempton, 1984). In some cultures, for instance, there is no word that easily corresponds to the terms "strongly agree" or "strongly disagree," two standards of Likert scale construction. Instead, some of these cultures only see the world in terms of the binary construct of "agree or do not agree," thus necessitating the reconstruction of scales and caution in statistical analysis and interpretation. As another example, healthcare researchers studying the Hmong, an ethnic group originating in the south and east Asia, have encountered such difficulties in that the Hmong have no words for "mental health," including words like depression, anxiety, or schizophrenia (Cha, 2003). Chen et al. (1995), and colleagues found that Japanese and Chinese students were more likely than North American students to choose the midpoint on Likert scales. Similar work by Hui and Triandis (Hui & Triandis, 1989) found that Hispanics were more likely to choose extreme responses on five or ten-point scales. Similarly, Tohe (2000) relates that in the Diné native language, there is no word for feminism because the Diné is a matrilineal culture in which women are valued, honored, and respected as leaders of families and the tribe. Thus, language concerns should be considered both in terms of methodological conventions of back translation and the involvement of native language speakers in the design and implementation of research projects and the operationalization of concepts. In addition, care should be taken to understand the role of linguistic and cultural differences in the interpretation of data (van Nes, Abma, Jonsson, & Deeg, 2010).

Similar issues are at play in studies of victimization and abuse of racialized women. Those working in this field are familiar with practical issues (such as safety and recruitment) as well as theoretical and methodological issues around the definition and measurement of abuse. They are also aware of the role of cultural variation in perceptions of what constitutes violence and abuse. Moreover, while survivors of woman abuse are hard to sample because many women do not report their victimization or are unwilling to participate in research studies, racialized and immigrant women are even more difficult to find since they often live in isolated communities.

In one Canadian study of Tamil women, interpersonal violence was defined broadly and showed little variation from definitions used widely in the field, although forms of psychological abuse had specific meanings for this community (Mason et al., 2008). Notably, the study utilized representatives from local organizations to gain an understanding of Tamil culture, question construction, and translation, thus illustrating the value of collaborative, inclusive research. Without taking such an approach it would be easy to misinterpret the lack of a word in some cultures for domestic violence as an indication that it does not happen in those communities (Krauss, 2006). Indeed, in other cultures, belief in patriarchy and obedience in marriage is acceptable and behaviors such as neglect, isolation, or threats of deportation do not fit neatly within Western categories of abuse and victimization (Raj & Silverman, 2002; Alvi, Clow, & DeKeseredy, 2005; Morash, Bui, Yan, & Holtfreter, 2007; Bui, 2016). These cultural differences coupled with the isolation immigrant women often experience, mean that gaining access for research purposes may prove difficult. What this means methodologically is that researchers should strive to understand the characteristics of their subjects, ideally involving members of that community to facilitate research, while also weighing creative ways to find participants and build rapport.

On another level, and as a general rule, the utmost care should be taken to ensure the safety of women (or other vulnerable groups) when conducting research of this nature. Conducting a phone interview, or an online survey, for instance, may endanger a woman because the abuser may have access to those conversations or interactions. Similarly, women reporting abuse should be made aware of the existence of support services because it is the responsibility of researchers to ensure that no harm is done, but also that they have some commitment to the well-being of their subjects. Researchers should not engage in "drive-by" research or helicopter research, where the subjects of inquiry are seen as data points rather than human beings. There is always a distinct possibility of harm coming to these research participants because they are being asked about sensitive matters that also carry with them the potential of stigmatization within the community to which the person belongs (Bender, 2017). One issue that has received some attention from research ethics boards is the concern around trauma recall – the possibility that opening up about one's experiences may recall vivid and harmful memories and feelings. While there is no good evidence to suggest that it is a common occurrence (Burgess-Proctor, 2015), researchers should always pay attention to the possibility of secondary trauma.

Violence against women is multi-faceted, and therefore it is critical that researchers embrace multi-disciplinary perspectives on the problem, as well as multiple methodologies to study it and instigate change. Research designs must examine not only the lived experiences of immigrant women and women of color but also the interplay between the cultural contexts from which they emerged, and the ones they live in now. This type of research, then, must employ a culturally competent, intersectional analysis of economic insecurity, xenophobia, and racism, as well as patriarchy and the psychology of violence. This type of research thus requires a willingness to engage in the deep study of the culture one is studying, and a reflexive understanding of one's own cultural beliefs, attitudes, and values in relation to those being studied (Nandan, 2007).

First Nations peoples

First Nations, Inuit, and Metis peoples (here I will use the terms Indigenous or First Nations interchangeably) occupy a unique position in Canadian society. Scholars of the Indigenous experience in Canada generally agree that their status has been conditioned and shaped by colonialism, prejudice, and ongoing neglect. In short, it has been the experience of cultural genocide. Colonial practices included the destruction and prohibition of native cultures, languages and spiritual practices, the deliberate introduction of disease, family disruption including separation of children from their parents, the imposition of residential schools, imposed assimilation, the appropriation of land and termination of treaties, and forced impoverishment. Many of these injuries continue to this day (Jull, Morton-Ninomiya, Compton, & Picard, 2018). Recognition of the harm these practices have caused to First Nations peoples has taken centuries, culminating in the 2015 Truth and Reconciliation Commission Report which has called for reconciliation efforts in law, access to education and pedagogy, and healthcare (Truth and Reconciliation Commission of Canada, 2015).

The legacy and persistence of these policies and practices have politically marginalized Indigenous peoples and left them with numerous economic, social, and health problems. Despite a lack of up-to-date data owing to shifts in census data collection policy discussed earlier in this chapter, we do know that Indigenous peoples are overrepresented among the homeless, experience higher rates of HIV, tuberculosis, type II diabetes, suicide, have a lower life expectancy, and lower perceived mental health than their non-Indigenous counterparts (National Collaborating Centre for Aboriginal Health, 2013; Public Health Agency of Canada, 2016).

These communities are over-policed, disproportionately incarcerated, and under-housed (Cesaroni, Grol, & Fredericks, 2019). Aboriginal adults in some provinces represent 70 percent of the incarcerated population, and despite being just 3 percent of the total adult population, they make up 27 percent of provincial/territorial prisoners and 28 percent of federal ones (Cunneen & Tauri, 2019). Indigenous women are nearly four times likely than other women to have experienced sexual assault and there are currently at least 1000 missing Indigenous women and girls in Canada (Bailey & Shayan, 2016). As of 2016, nearly one-third of Indigenous people reported that that they were the victim of a crime, and the overall rate of violent victimization regardless of type was double that of their non-Indigenous counterparts. As criminologists know, crime is a multi-causal phenomenon, and in the case of Indigenous people, factors such as poverty, drug addiction, homelessness, and poor mental health all play a role in crime perpetration and victimization (Boyce, 2016).

This necessarily brief and incomplete overview of the significant situations faced by Indigenous people in Canada points to the centrality of analyzing colonialism when engaging in research into the lived realities of Indigenous peoples (Cunneen & Tauri, 2019). It is also important to abandon the attitude that First Nations people are another group in the pantheon of vulnerable populations that we do research "on" instead of "with." As pointed out earlier in this chapter, it is important to reflect not only on why we do research and for whom, but on one's own position as a researcher relative to those we study. With respect to Indigenous peoples, taking these guidelines seriously means reflecting on and resisting the temptation to represent knowledge as "truth," and the presentation of the studied as "others" to the non-Indigenous world (Deckert, 2016; Cesaroni et al., 2019, p. 115). In turn, this recognition calls for research establishing Indigenous voices, ways of knowing and interpretations of their own experiences as central to research methodology, while acknowledging and integrating the legacy of (neo)-colonialism into the method, theory, and analysis. As Battiste and colleagues make clear (2008, p. 504), there is no "one" Indigenous form of knowledge standing in opposition to Eurocentric knowledge. Rather, there are numerous kinds of Indigenous knowledge, each existing in webs of relation to specific contexts containing:

> linguistic categories, rules, and relationships unique to each knowledge system; has localized content and meaning; has customs with respect to acquiring and sharing knowledge; and implies responsibilities for possessing various kinds of knowledge. No uniform or universal Indigenous perspective on Indigenous knowledge exists – many do.

One difficulty is that sometimes researchers are caught up in the task of discovering problems in populations, rather than trying to understand how such communities have attempted to deal with adversity. This point is well illustrated in the research reported by Ball and Janyst (2008, p. 37), in which one respondent states:

> We are tired of researchers coming in and documenting all the things wrong with our communities: youth suicide, child neglect, alcohol abuse, family violence, poor nutrition, embezzlement. You would think people would want to figure out how we survived white people for so many hundreds of years. How we kept our children alive, kept our stories, kept our knowledge about how to live on the land, kept our ceremonies, kept our fires burning with hope for generations yet to come. How about some research on what's right with us? About what makes us resilient?

To ignore these guidelines is to revert to research where the non-Indigenous researcher "interprets" what they find "for" the research subject, rather than also engaging with the subject to help to interpret the findings. Further, research with Aboriginal peoples demands that we consider our relationship to those we are researching in all phases of the research enterprise. For example, the Opaskwayak Cree researcher Wilson (2001, p. 177) recounts that "My father was saying how a couch or sofa in Cree translated literally means 'someplace where you sit.' Rather than calling it a sofa, rather than calling it an object, you name it through your relationship to it." Concepts and ideas, from this perspective, are not as important as one's relationship to concepts and ideas. Moreover, such accountability means that researchers do not stop at questions of operationalization, validity, and reliability, but also consider how their research meets obligations to the researched (Wilson, 2001). Different conceptions of knowledge between non-Indigenous researchers and Indigenous peoples may also pose challenges because, for the latter, knowledge is rooted in collective identity. Much of that communal character has traditionally been expressed in oral traditions which require researchers to consider new (relative to standard research protocols) ways of collecting data, such as photovoice, storytelling, and through participation in circles, which are similar to focus groups but integrate and acknowledge the cultural significance of circles as representations of the life cycle, nature, and their purpose as ways of promoting healing and transmitting knowledge (Wright, Wahoush, Ballantyne, Gabel, & Jack, 2016). The authenticity of these methods rests on non-Indigenous researchers acknowledging that Eurocentric ways of knowing do not necessarily correspond to Indigenous conceptions of knowledge. They also entail undertaking the work of finding a compromise between conventional methodological canons of Western science and traditional points of view making up the tapestry of Indigenous communities.

Accountability to community values also poses challenges for obtaining informed consent since agreeing to release certain kinds of information may violate moral obligations to family and community, whereas from a Western point of view, providing consent is a choice made by individuals (Ermine,

Sinclair, & Jeffery, 2004). In the same vein, privacy laws in Canada protect individuals but do not do the same with respect to communities, which as we have seen, is a core element of Indigenous culture (Bruhn & Stratéjuste, 2014).

These kinds of considerations have been acknowledged in the Tri-Council Policy Statement (TCPS2) which emphasizes the unique history and culture of First Nations peoples, their valuation of reciprocity in relationships, and the importance of reflecting their world views respecting research. The guidelines also point out that since such norms have been ignored or violated in the past, it is understandable that these communities often approach research and researchers with apprehension or mistrust. As Denzin and Lincoln (2008) observe, when non-Indigenous researchers impose ethnocentric standards of "truth" and authenticity on what they are observing, they will inevitably, but erroneously conclude that the social relations they are studying are backward compared with their own standards.

Another important issue to consider is that knowledge generated in First Nations communities, sometimes centuries old, has a value not just to these communities, but in the market and that great care should be taken to ensure that the financial benefits that accrue as a result of this wisdom be shared with those who generated the knowledge. For instance, Battiste (2008, p. 504) has pointed out that the pharmaceutical industry has bypassed trials on plants by appropriating Indigenous expertise and knowledge on the ways in which such plants are used and then patenting and selling the resulting products without proper consideration of intellectual and cultural property rights. This kind of flagrant, unfair treatment is another reminder of the importance of considering what research is for and for whom.

Challenges of research in the digital age

Like other wealthy countries, Canada is an increasingly digital society whose people are trying to come to terms with important and rapid shifts in social relations that come with digitization. As it is both new and unstable, the study of potential problems associated with using digital technologies to form research questions, gather data, and analyze and interpret results is in its infancy. In this section, some of the pros and cons of digital research are examined.

When Tim Berners-Lee "invented" the World Wide Web in 1989, he probably did not realize how the technology would revolutionize so many aspects of social, political, and cultural life. A mere three decades after its conception, digital technology has transformed the way we interact with one another, the ways we do politics, and everything else from consumption to culture. Research methods in the social sciences are no exception, although it would be overstating the case to suggest that all subdisciplines have taken advantage of digital methods at the same rate or with the same degree of optimism. Criminology, for instance, has been relatively slow to adopt the methodological tools now available, while those scientists working in fields related to the business world, such as marketing and organizational behavior, have been at the forefront of adoption and development.

The internet both constitutes and represents the modern social world. Our social institutions and the relationships we enter into are reflected, to a great extent, in online interactions. What we say and do "in real life" in our consumer product preferences, our political or religious views and our desires, demographic characteristics, and social identities are at once reflected in the digital world and made by it. At the same time, the emerging digital world is forcing us to reconsider age-old questions. Consider for a moment the problems of cyberbullying, or trolling. One of the key research questions to emerge in tandem with the ubiquity of online interaction is the question of the extent to which people actually believe "in real life" what they are saying online. In the literature on cyberbullying of teens, for instance, scholars have pointed to the fact that the internet affords anonymity that permits people to make statements they would never make to people in a face-to-face situation (Barlett & Gentile, 2012; Barlett et al., 2013). A related question is why many people believe information posted online despite its falsity, and even in light of the capacity of that information to create harm. Explanations for this question are being debated, with some pointing to individual responsibility, thus prioritizing human actions and desires, and others indicting the characteristics of internet technology itself. Thus, scholars are trying to answer the question: "is it the net or the netizen?" (Omotoyinbo, 2014). This is an important question because it touches on matters of what can be done to curb the increasing presence of "e-bile" (Jane, 2014), incitements to violence, and the dissemination of falsehoods. Research suggests that people tend to consume online news that aligns with their interests and views (Schmidt et al., 2017), thereby suggesting that people are not passive recipients of information that makes them do things. In turn, this suggests that polarization or disagreement between people in the real world can be reproduced in internet forums but may also be intensified due to repeated exposure to particular messages and self-assurances of anonymity. In relation to the question of what social science research is for, then, and given that internet research subjects are not easily anonymized and that online incivility seems to be growing, researchers might ask new questions about the duty of care owed to participants in, and consumers of research, as well as the obligations that the researchers may have to make the findings accessible to authorities.

An important staple of ethical research involves the promise to keep the identifying information of research participants anonymous. Yet the internet makes it much easier to identify people than traditional pen and pencil survey methods. For someone possessing the right skills, it is relatively easy to ascertain a research participant's Internet Protocol (IP) address, which in turn can provide all sorts of information that a person does not wish to disclose. Similarly, the search and networking capabilities characterizing modern cyberspace make it easier to identify locations (such as schools or hospitals, or villages) or individuals based on the descriptive (but supposedly anonymized) information routinely presented in research papers, particularly ethnographies (Walford, 2018). It is also important to consider the power of states to access information a researcher has promised to keep anonymous. For example, currently, the US government has the right to examine the content of data sets stored on servers in the United States, including any identifiers that normally would only be known to the researchers, based on national security concerns under the terms of the Patriot Act II. One service used by many researchers is Survey Monkey, which as of this writing has stated that "any government" (including the Canadian government) can obtain access to such information with a special warrant, that the US government's attempt to acquire such data is "just not a likely scenario," and that "the risk imposed by the US Patriot Act is greatly overstated." Given the highly sensitive nature of some of the data social scientists collect and current political uncertainties, researchers must determine how comfortable they are storing such data on servers in other countries (Loh, 2019).

Another useful perspective on this question is advanced by Alfano et al. (2018) and his colleagues who assert that we should not dismiss the nature of internet technologies themselves in creating such problems despite the fact that our initial premise might be to blame people for online malfeasance. Their research points out that the algorithms in search engines like Google point information seekers to links that the system "thinks" are most suitable for the searcher because Google collects information on user's likes, search histories, and demographic background. Once the user clicks on a potentially useful link, other algorithms take over, leading the user down a series of connections and pathways that often reproduce and strengthen the messages content creators wish to disseminate. In short, the web can easily lead people down rabbit holes of information that may or may not be true. In itself, this phenomenon is fascinating because of its implications for information literacy, public perception, responsible decision making, and the fact that it offers the opportunity to observe meaning-making in real time (Mills, 2017). It should be kept in mind, however, that the social scientific study of these phenomena poses numerous questions around the ethics of conducting "netnography," including the capacity of the researcher to influence research subjects, invasiveness, informed consent, the extent to which social media is a "public space," deception, and other issues (Kozinets, 2015).

The methodological challenges of trying to understand online behavior are at once immediate, but there are also technical issues. Social scientists are trained in social science, but not necessarily programming, the nuances and complexity of algorithms, IP addresses, or web hosting. We are not, as a rule, trained computer scientists. Yet the world we study has gone online, which confronts us with the problem of dealing with a relatively unknown terrain of society, a new representation of the very entity we try to understand. Further, this technological landscape changes quickly, such that new ethical and methodological challenges will undoubtedly emerge to challenge prevailing orthodoxies. This fluidity, in turn, means that researchers will have to be vigilant in ensuring that their research remains ethically and methodologically sound by ensuring they have a sound grasp of the essential parameters of responsible research coupled with reflexivity and awareness of the unique qualities of the digital world (Roberts, 2015).

One could argue that the advent of "big data" has enabled the collection of vast quantities of normally private information on variables such as demographic background, voting patterns, religiosity, and perspectives on child-rearing and punishment in society, thereby greatly expanding the scope of opportunities for research and analysis (Mayer-Schönberger & Cukier, 2013; Hesse, Glenna, Hinrichs, Chiles, & Sachs, 2018). Such information can now be collected very quickly, sometimes at low cost and with the advantage of generating huge sample sizes – one estimate of data generation from websites, social media, sensors, smartphones, cars, and other sources is 2.5 exabytes per day (an exabyte is equal to 1 million terabytes), and that was in 2016 (Bello-Orgaz, Jung, & Camacho, 2016). In light of the expansive nature of digital data collection, it is not surprising that some social scientists are predicting the demise of traditional survey methodologies (Couper, 2017; Savage & Burrows, 2017).

There are some issues with big data that will continue to present challenges to the field. Although much big data is readily available, some data could be prohibitively expensive for academic researchers. In addition, these data are "ready-made" in the sense that they already exist – usually for some other purpose. Thus, it may often be difficult to determine the quality of the information in big data sets, particularly in terms of potential sampling biases and errors, operationalization difficulties, self-selection bias, and the reality that such data sets are often not designed with social science questions in mind (Kitchin & McArdle, 2016).

There are also unresolved and alarming ethical consequences to consider surrounding digital anonymity with respect to big data. Keeping online data private and confidential should be a central tenet of ethical research. Yet as we have seen in various very public and potentially consequential data breaches affecting companies like Facebook and Equifax, as well as the Democratic National Committee, FEMA, and various banks, hospitals, and universities, maintaining confidentiality poses potential difficulties (Jamieson & Salinas, 2018). These challenges are related to data breaches, the capacity of pernicious actors to determine the identity of online research participants, lack of researcher knowledge about data security (e.g., encryption technologies or misplaced USB drives), or the failure of digital technologies themselves (e.g., storage drives or server failure). In terms of anonymity, it is quite easy to determine the identity of individuals from large data sets that often include location codes, credit card transactions, browsing behavior, medical histories, and personal identifying information such as social security or driver license numbers.

Indeed, some studies have estimated that between 63 and 87 percent of people can be identified on the basis of three pieces of information alone; ZIP code, birth date, and sex (Sweeney, 2000; Ohm, 2009).

In addition, how would we know if the information we are gathering on a particular social group discussing suicide or depression or victimization includes minors? What are our obligations to people we are studying online if they are claiming they wish to harm themselves? What are our legal obligations if we uncover palpable or implied threats to persons or national security? How do we distinguish between statements that are unmistakable, implied, and "just talk?" None of these questions offers straightforward answers but will definitely be questions researchers in the social sciences will have to contend with now and in the future.

Another issue is accessibility. Again, the extent to which people deviate from the norm and explanations for the spectrum of human behavior constitute core elements of the research enterprise. Although digital technologies offer new opportunities to gather data, not everyone has access to the internet. In Western societies, the internet is used by approximately 85 percent of Europeans and North Americans, but only one-third of Africans and half of those living in Asian countries enjoy reliable access to the internet (Internet World Statistics, 2019). Thus, the problem of accessing vulnerable, disenfranchised, or poor populations, those most likely to be ignored or underrepresented in policy decisions, may continue to be a problem for researchers claiming representativeness. As noted earlier, Canada is a vast country, and in northern Canada, there are communities without clean running water and adequate housing, let alone access to broadband internet. Thus, while the (mostly Indigenous) people living there are among the most impoverished in the country, they are far less likely to have access to digital technology, and consequently, less likely to be heard.

In addition to the broad ethical guidelines mentioned earlier, there are well known and pervasive difficulties often associated with the rigor researchers aspire to in social science. For instance, while generating and accessing representative samples of persons within a population of interest often requires a degree of ingenuity, older ways of generating such samples are increasingly becoming obsolete because there are fewer ways of accessing sampling frames. There are several reasons for this problem. Technological advances have made cheap and accessible phone lists obsolete (there are no phone books anymore), and more people are foregoing phone landlines for unlisted numbers on cell phones, thereby precluding random digit dialing. To make things worse, while master lists of potential survey research participants do exist, they are prohibitively expensive for most researchers. Internet technologies have also fostered legitimate privacy concerns among the general public, which are particularly salient in light of security issues mentioned earlier. Many people are reluctant to conduct a "short" phone survey with a person claiming to be a researcher. Relatedly, marketing and polling companies have flooded the public with requests to participate in self-administered research studies, resulting in respondent fatigue, associated refusal to participate, and resulting problems managing non-response bias and generalizability.

One promising solution to the problem of accessing "hidden" populations for whom there are no sampling frames is through the use of respondent-driven sampling (RDS). Respondent-driven sampling has been used successfully to study numerous difficult to reach populations such as the homeless, drug addicts, sex workers, and illegal immigrants. Essentially, the technique is a form of chain referral sampling (such as snowball sampling), where close ties between people are used to gather samples based on the association of the members in a network of people. The difficulty with standard snowball techniques is that they cannot be generalized to the larger population. RDS selects research subjects on the basis of friendships between known members of a group one wishes to study, called seeds. The seeds are used to recruit other participants within their social networks rather than from a sampling frame that might consist of "all those present at a homeless shelter in one night," or "all those present at lunchtime at the food bank." Those participants, in turn, are paid to recruit still more participants but must recruit on average at least one such person. Further, recruiters are given financial incentives to meet quotas of other potential participants, essentially a finder's fee. After successive waves of sampling this way, it is possible to reach an adequate sample size that is asymptotically unbiased. Moreover, because research subjects themselves recruit other subjects, RDS avoids problems arising when participants are reluctant to provide information to researchers on other people they know (for details see Salganik & Heckathorn, 2004; Abdul-Quader, Heckathorn, Sabin, & Saidel, 2006). Given that the internet is essentially a massive network of people, it will be interesting to see how methods like RDS can be employed to reach representative samples in the digital world.

Although such methodological advances are exciting, particularly for those studying the most vulnerable in society, all methods demand that great care be taken to ensure that ethical standards are not violated. Scott (2008) for instance, provides a "cautionary tale" of research using RDS conducted with injection drug users which resulted in respondents exploiting each other, deepening inequalities, and creating interpersonal conflict, violence, and coercion among other negative outcomes. In addition, recruiters working with an RDS methodology may intentionally or unintentionally misrepresent the risks and benefits of the research to potential participants. Informed consent may not be obtained (because elements in the network chain are not trained researchers), and new networks posing risks to individuals may be formed. This research should remind researchers that once again, those we study are more than research subjects – they are often people who will do what they need to survive and if that means gaming the system or taking advantage of other people, they may do so.

Conclusion

This chapter has focused on a necessarily small subset of ethical and methodological challenges for social science researchers conducting research in Canada, although it must be noted that none of these issues is unique to the Canadian context. Due to space limitations, the chapter does not cover a number of important issues, including insights from the long history of social science in the province of Quebec, debates in the Canadian political economy tradition, or the influence of both US and European sociology in molding a Canadian "perspective" in the social sciences.

Rather, the emphasis on this chapter has been on the importance of coming to terms with the fundamental question of what social science is for, a matter that is especially relevant in today's turbulent and often troubling social context. A position favoring praxis is taken in this chapter, that is, research conducted to create improvement in the lives of people. The chapter also covers some aspects of the relationships between research methods and ethical questions to some features of Canadian society currently receiving much national attention. Against the backdrop of its traditional commitment to multiculturalism, Canada is now confronting challenges from nationalist and sometimes hate-motivated groups that are not only alarming but also raise questions around integration, acceptance, and harmony among social groups. Major economic transformations, rooted in the logic of neoliberalism are creating palpable social restlessness, and for many, real economic hardships. While these changes are happening around the world, the Canadian experience has so far been less dramatic than we are seeing in countries like the UK and the US. Still, the general social malaise warrants careful examination and presents at the same time the opportunity for social scientists to truly examine the role of difference in shaping people's lives, to reconceptualize and better understand how cosmetic differences between people can have major consequences, and to prioritize an analysis of the broader politico-economic context that generates social problems.

Within this framework, the chapter points out some important ethical and methodological challenges posed in studying vulnerable groups that are increasingly seen as the "other." It also examines the role of colonialism and its aftermaths in the lives of Indigenous peoples, and how their histories and ways of knowing should be integrated into research methodology and the importance of avoiding the presumption of non-Indigenous "expertise" with respect to Indigenous lives. More fundamentally, it points to the importance of reconsidering social science research as an interaction between those who "know" and the research subject to be known. Rather, research efficacy can benefit greatly from a methodological framework recognizing the authenticity and value that comes with appreciating the idea of two knowing subjects.

The chapter also considers contemporary uncertainty around the meaning and direction of an increasingly digital society, highlighting questions and issues requiring ongoing scrutiny, including issues around the indefinite lines between public and private spheres, privacy, and the welfare of research subjects. It is incumbent upon researchers that we anticipate digital harms and develop methodologies and ethical frameworks to mitigate and perhaps prevent such harm from occurring. In turn, the goal of embracing digital technologies with a critical eye will demand that social scientists learn more about the technical dimensions of digital technologies so they may incorporate them into their methodologies and ethical protocols.

Finally, the chapter challenges conventional positivist stances on research, arguing that such approaches tend to erroneously assume that the only phenomena that count are those that can be counted, and emphasizing the importance of acknowledging the power and privilege accorded to researchers in the research enterprise.

References

Abdul-Quader, A. S., Heckathorn, D. D., Sabin, K., & Saidel, T. (2006). Implementation and analysis of respondent driven sampling: lessons learned from the field. *Journal of Urban Health, 83*(6 Suppl), i1–5.

Acquisti, A., Brandimarte, L., & Loewenstein, G. (2015). Privacy and human behavior in the age of information. *Science, 347*(6221), 509–514.

Alfano, M., Carter, J. A., & Cheong, M. (2018). Technological seduction and self-radicalization. *Journal of the American Philosophical Association*, pp. 298–322.

Allen, L. (2009). 'Caught in the act': ethics committee review and researching the sexual culture of schools. *Qualitative Research, 9*(4), 395–410.

Alvi, S., Clow, K. A., & DeKeseredy, W. (2005). Women abuse and resilience in a sample of minority low-income women. *Women's Health & Urban Life, 8*(2), 51–67.

Bailey, J., & Shayan, S. (2016). Missing and murdered indigenous women crisis: technological dimensions. *Canadian Journal of Women and the Law, 28*(2), 321–341.

Ball, J., & Janyst, P. (2008). Enacting research ethics in partnerships with indigenous communities in Canada: "do it in a good way." *Journal of Empirical Research on Human Research Ethics, 3*(2), 33–51.

Barlett, C. P., & Gentile, D. A. (2012). Attacking others online: the formation of cyberbullying in late adolescence. *Psychology of Popular Media Culture, 1*(2), 123–135.

Barlett, C. P., Gentile, D. A., Anderson, C. A., Suzuki, K., Sakamoto, A., Yamaoka, A. et al. (2013). Cross-cultural differences in cyberbullying behavior: a short-term longitudinal study. *Journal of Cross-Cultural Psychology, 45*(2), 300–313.

Battiste, M. (2008). Research ethics for protecting indigenous knowledge and heritage: institutional and researcher responsibilities. In: N. Denzin, Y. Lincoln, & L. Smith (Eds.), *Handbook of Critical and Indigenous Methodologies* (pp. 497–510). Thousand Oaks, CA: SAGE Publications, Inc.

Becker, H. S. (1966). Whose side are we on. *Social Problems, 14*(3), 239–247.

Bello-Orgaz, G., Jung, J. J., & Camacho, D. (2016). Social big data: recent achievements and new challenges. *Information Fusion, 28*, 45–59.

Bender, A. K. (2017). Ethics, methods, and measures in intimate partner violence research: the current state of the field. *Violence Against Women, 23*(11), 1382–1413.

Bierne, P. (1996). The invention of positivist criminology: An Introduction to Quetelet's "Social mechanics of crime." In: B. D. MacLean (Ed.), *Crime and Society* (pp. 25–50). Toronto, ON: Copp Clark Ltd.

Bohnert, N., Chagnon, J., Coulombe, S., Dion, P., & Martel, L. (2015). *Population Projections for Canada (2013 to 2063), Provinces and Territories (2013 to 2038).* Ottawa: Statistics Canada-Statistique Canada.

Boyce, J. (2016). *Victimization of Aboriginal people in Canada, 2014.* Ottawa: Statistics Canada.

Braithwaite, J. (2014). Hybridity in the Canadian craft of criminology. *Canadian Journal of Criminology and Criminal Justice, 56*(4), 399–416.

Brodeur, J.-P. (1999). Disenchanted criminology. *Canadian Journal of Criminology, 41,* 131.

Bruhn, J., & Stratéjuste, C. (2014). Identifying useful approaches to the governance of indigenous data. *International Indigenous Policy Journal, 5*(2).

Bui, H. N. (2016). Help-seeking behavior among abused immigrant women: a case of Vietnamese American women. *Violence Against Women, 9*(2), 207–239.

Burawoy, M. (2005). 2004 American Sociological Association presidential address: for public sociology. *British Journal of Sociology, 56*(2), 259–294.

Burgess-Proctor, A. (2015). Methodological and ethical issues in feminist research with abused women: reflections on participants' vulnerability and empowerment. *Women's Studies International Forum, 48,* 124–134.

Cesaroni, C., Grol, C., & Fredericks, K. (2019). Overrepresentation of indigenous youth in Canada's Criminal Justice System: perspectives of indigenous young people. *Australian & New Zealand Journal of Criminology, 52*(1), 111–128.

Cha, D. (2003). *Hmong American Concepts of Health.* New York: Routledge.

Chen, C., Lee, S.-y., & Stevenson, H. W. (1995). Response style and cross-cultural comparisons of rating scales among East Asian and North American students. *Psychological Science, 6*(3), 170–175.

Chui, T. (2013). Immigration and ethnocultural diversity in Canada, Ottawa: Social and Aboriginal Statistics Division and John Flanders of Communications Division, Statistics Canada, pp. 1–23.

Couper, M. P. (2017). New developments in survey data collection. *Annual Review of Sociology, 43,* 121–145.

Cunneen, C., & Tauri, J. M. (2019). Indigenous peoples, criminology, and criminal justice. *Annual Review of Criminology, 2,* 359–381.

Deckert, A. (2016). Criminologists, duct tape, and Indigenous peoples: quantifying the use of silencing research methods. *International Journal of Comparative and Applied Criminal Justice, 40*(1), 43–62.

Denzin, N., & Lincoln, Y. (2008). Introduction: critical methodologies and indigenous inquiry. In N. Denzin, Y. Lincoln, & L. Smith (Eds.), *Handbook of Critical and Indigenous Methodologies* (pp. 1–20). Thousand Oaks, CA: SAGE Publications, Inc.

Dingwall, R. (2008). The ethical case against ethical regulation in humanities and social science research. *Twenty-First Century Society, 3*(1), 1–12.

Dobbie, D., & Robinson, I. (2008). Reorganizing higher education in the United States and Canada: the erosion of tenure and the unionization of contingent faculty. *Labor Studies Journal, 33*(2), 117–140.

Doyle, E., & Buckley, P. (2017). Embracing qualitative research: a visual model for nuanced research ethics oversight. *Qualitative Research, 17*(1), 95–117.

Ermine, W., Sinclair, R., & Jeffery, B. (2004). *The Ethics of Research Involving Indigenous Peoples.* Indigenous Peoples' Health Research Centre Saskatoon, Saskatchewan.

Fontes, L. A. (1998). Ethics in family violence research: cross-cultural issues. *Family Relations, 47*(1), 53–61.

Giroux, H. A. (2014). *Neoliberalism's War on Higher Education*. Chicago: Haymarket Books.

Gorbet, F. W., & Sharpe, A. (2011). *New Directions for Intelligent Government in Canada: Papers in Honour of Ian Stewart*. Ottawa: Centre for the Study of Living Standards.

Government of Canada. (2016). *Backgrounder on Poverty in Canada*. Government of Canada.

Haggerty, K. D. (2004). Ethics creep: governing social science research in the name of ethics. *Qualitative Sociology, 27*(4), 391–414.

Harvey, D. (2007). *A Brief History of Neoliberalism*. Oxford: Oxford University Press.

Harvey, D. (2016). Neoliberalism as creative destruction. *The ANNALS of the American Academy of Political and Social Science, 610*(1), 21–44.

Henderson, J., & Wakeham, P. (2009). Colonial reckoning, national reconciliation?: Aboriginal peoples and the culture of redress in Canada. *ESC: English Studies in Canada, 35*(1), 1–26.

Hesse, A., Glenna, L., Hinrichs, C., Chiles, R., & Sachs, C. (2018). Qualitative research ethics in the big data era. *American Behavioral Scientist, 63*, (5), 560–583.

Hui, C. H., & Triandis, H. C. (1989). Effects of culture and response format on extreme response style. *Journal of Cross-Cultural Psychology, 20*(3), 296–309.

Internet World Statistics. (2019). *Internet Usage Statistics*. Retrieved April 11, 2019, https://www.internetworldstats.com/stats.htm.

Jamieson, T., & Salinas, G. (2018). Protecting human subjects in the digital age: issues and best practices of data protection. *Survey Practice, 11*, (2).

Jane, E. A. (2014). Your a ugly, whorish, slut. *Feminist Media Studies, 14*(4), 531–546.

Jeppesen, S., & Nazar, H. (2012). Beyond academic freedom: Canadian neoliberal universities in the global context. *Topia – Canadian Journal of Cultural Studies, 28*, 87–113.

Jull, J., Morton-Ninomiya, M., Compton, I., & Picard, A. (2018). Fostering the conduct of ethical and equitable research practices: the imperative for integrated knowledge translation in research conducted by and with indigenous community members. *Research Involvement and Engagement, 4*, 45.

Kawalilak, C. (2012). Navigating the neoliberal terrain: elder faculty speak out. *Workplace: A Journal for Academic Labor, 21*, 2–12.

Kay, P., & Kempton, W. (1984). What is the Sapir-Whorf hypothesis. *American Anthropologist, 86*(1), 65–79.

Kenny, J. (2017). Re-empowering academics in a corporate culture: An exploration of workload and performativity in a university. *Higher Education, 46*(7), 1–16.

Keucheyan, R. (2013). *Left Hemisphere: Mapping Contemporary Theory* (G. Elliott, Trans.). New York: Verso Books.

Kitchin, R., & McArdle, G. (2016). What makes Big Data, Big Data? Exploring the ontological characteristics of 26 datasets. *Big Data & Society, 3*(1), 205395171663113.

Kozinets, R. V. (2015). *Netnography: Redefined* (2nd ed.). Los Angeles, CA: Sage.

Krauss, H. H. (2006). Perspectives on violence. *Annals of the New York Academy of Sciences, 1087*, 4–21.

Leber, B. (2017). *Police-Reported Hate Crime in Canada, 2015*. Ottawa: Statistics Canada.

Li, P. S. (1999). *Race and Ethnic Relations in Canada*. Oxford: Oxford University Press.

Loh, S. (2019). How worried should Canadians be about the US Patriot Act. Retrieved April 4, 2019, from https://www.surveymonkey.com/curiosity/patriot-act/.

Luker, K. (2008). *Salsa Dancing into the Social Sciences*. Boston, MA: Harvard University Press.

Lupton, D. (2014). *Digital Sociology*. London and New York: Routledge.
Mason, R., Hyman, I., Berman, H., Guruge, S., Kanagaratnam, P., & Manuel, L. (2008). "Violence is an international language": Tamil women's perceptions of intimate partner violence. *Violence Against Women, 14*(12), 1397–1412.
Mayer-Schönberger, V., & Cukier, K. (2013). *Big Data: A Revolution that Will Transform How We Live, Work, and Think*. Boston: Houghton Mifflin Harcourt.
Metcalfe, A. S. (2010). Revisiting academic capitalism in Canada: No longer the exception. *The Journal of Higher Education, 81*(4), 489–514.
Mills, K. A. (2017). What are the threats and potentials of big data for qualitative research. *Qualitative Research, 18*, (6), 591–603.
Morash, M., Bui, H., Yan, Z., & Holtfreter, K. (2007). Risk factors for abusive relationships: a study of Vietnamese American immigrant women. *Violence Against Women, 13*(7), 653–675.
Morency, J.-D., Malenfant, E. C., & MacIsaac, S. (2017). *Immigration and Diversity: Population Projections for Canada and Its Regions, 2011 to 2036*. Ottawa: Statistics Canada-Statistique Canada.
Nandan, M. (2007). Waves of Asian Indian elderly immigrants: what can practitioners learn. *Journal of Cross-Cultural Gerontology, 22*(4), 389–404.
National Collaborating Centre for Aboriginal Health. (2013). *An Overview of Aboriginal Health in Canada*. Prince George: University of Northern British Columbia.
Ohm, P. (2009). Broken promises of privacy: responding to the surprising failure of anonymization. *UCLA Law Review, 57*, 1701.
Omotoyinbo, F. R. (2014). Online radicalisation: the net or the netizen. *Social Technologies, 4*(1), 51–61.
Perry, B., & Alvi, S. (2012). 'We are all vulnerable' The in terrorem effects of hate crimes. *International Review of Victimology, 18*(1), 57–71.
Polster, C. (2004). Canadian university research policy at the turn of the century: continuity and change in the social relations of academic research. *Studies in Political Economy, 71*(1), 177–199.
Public Health Agency of Canada. (2016). *Health Status of Canadians 2016*. Ottawa, ON: Public Health Agency of Canada.
Raj, A., & Silverman, J. (2002). Violence against immigrant women: the roles of culture, context, and legal immigrant status on intimate partner violence. *Violence Against Women, 8*(3), 367–398.
Reiss, I. L. (1993). The future of sex research and the meaning of science. *The Journal of Sex Research, 30*(1), 3–11.
Roberts, L. D. (2015). Ethical issues in conducting qualitative research in online communities. *Qualitative Research in Psychology, 12*(3), 314–325.
Salganik, M. J., & Heckathorn, D. D. (2004). Sampling and estimation in hidden populations using respondent-driven sampling. *Sociological Methodology, 34*(1), 193–240.
Savage, M., & Burrows, R. (2017). The coming crisis of empirical sociology. *Sociology, 41*(5), 885–899.
Savoie, D. J. (2015). The Canadian public service: in search of a new equilibrium. In A. Massey & K. Johnston (Eds.), *The International Handbook of Public Administration and Governance* (pp. 182–198). Cheltenham, UK: Elgar Publishing.
Schmidt, A. L., Zollo, F., Del Vicario, M., Bessi, A., Scala, A., Caldarelli, G., et al. (2017). Anatomy of news consumption on Facebook. *Proceedings of the National Academy of Sciences of the United States of America, 114*(12), 3035–3039.

Scott, G. (2008). They got their program, and I got mine: a cautionary tale concerning the ethical implications of using respondent-driven sampling to study injection drug users. *International Journal of Drug Policy*, *19*(1), 42–51.

Small, M. L. (2009). 'How many cases do I need?': On science and the logic of case selection in field-based research. *Ethnography*, *10*(1), 5–38.

Stanford, J. (2015). *Economics for Everyone: A Short Guide to the Economics of Capitalism* (2nd ed.). Nova Scotia: Fernwood Publishing.

Statistics Canada. (2015). *Gross Domestic Expenditures on Research and Development in Canada (GERD), the Provinces and Territories*. Statistics Canada – Catalogue no. 88–221-X.

Sweeney, L. (2000). Simple demographics often identify people uniquely (Data Privacy Working Paper 3). Pittsburgh, PA: Carnegie Mellon University. http://dataprivacylab.org/projects/identifiability/paper1. pdf, *671*, 1–34.

Tohe, L. (2000). There is no word for feminism in my language. *Wicazo Sa Review*, *15*(2, Native American Literature on the Edge of a New Century), 103–110.

Truth and Reconciliation Commission of Canada. (2015). *Honouring the Truth, Reconciling for the Future: Summary of the Final Report of the Truth and Reconciliation Commission of Canada*. Winnipeg: Truth and Reconciliation Commission of Canada.

United Nations Development Programme. (2018). *Human Development Indices and Indicators: 2018 Statistical Update*. New York: United Nations Development Programme.

van Nes, F., Abma, T., Jonsson, H., & Deeg, D. (2010). Language differences in qualitative research: is meaning lost in translation. *European Journal of Ageing*, 7(4), 313–316.

Walford, G. (2018). The impossibility of anonymity in ethnographic research. *Qualitative Research*, *18*(5), 516–525.

Wayland, S. V. (1997). Immigration, multiculturalism and national identity in Canada. *International Journal on Minority and Group Rights*, *5*(1), 33–58.

Wilson, S. (2001). What is an indigenous research methodology. *Canadian Journal of Native Education*, *25*(2), 175–179.

Wilson, W. J. (1990). *When Work Disappears: The World of the New Urban Poor*. New York: Alfred A. Knopf.

Wright, A. L., Wahoush, O., Ballantyne, M., Gabel, C., & Jack, S. M. (2016). Qualitative health research involving indigenous peoples: culturally appropriate data collection methods. *The Qualitative Report*, *21*(12), 2230–2245.

Young, J. (1999). *The Exclusive Society: Social Exclusion, Crime and Difference in Late Modernity*. London: Sage.

Young, J. (2004). Voodoo criminology and the numbers game. In J. Ferrell, K. Hayward, & M. Presdee (Eds.), *Cultural Criminology Unleashed* (pp. 13–27). London: Glasshouse Press.

Chapter 4

When research violates local Indigenous communities

Mogomme Alpheus Masoga, Allucia Lulu Shokane, and Lisa V. Blitz

Introduction

To voice the dreams, aspirations, interests, and freedom of its people in this age of globalization and globalism, Africans must stand up and insist on being studied on their own Indigenous terms (Chilisa, 2012; Chukwuokoko, 2010). There are 54 countries in Africa recognized by the United Nations with over a billion people speaking up to 2000 languages across almost 12 million square miles. Although there are some similarities in culture and values, it is crucial to honor and understand the many diverse cultures and communities throughout this vast continent. Most African countries went through some period of European colonization and apartheid, meaning that geopolitical boundaries were defined by others for economic and political reasons, not respecting culture. Prior to colonization, African communities endured the Maafa (African Holocaust or human trafficking for slavery; Eno et al., 2012), leading to global diaspora. Our research has been in two of these countries: Malawi and South Africa.

The unique historical, social, and economic circumstances and cultural heritage of African people must be heard and understood to appreciate and elevate the people who live on the African continent and those of the global diaspora. These concerns and challenges remain critical, especially in Africa where local communities are violated and alienated from the research processes introduced to them. Drawing upon our experiences engaging in participatory research with communities in South Africa and Malawi and offering a critical examination of Western epistemology, Afro-sensed frameworks, and Indigenous knowledge systems, this chapter explores: (1) the ways in which academic and research institutions are not addressing local needs and concerns; (2) how participatory research responds to differences in language and communication styles; (3) orality as a human-centered way of communication; (4) questions of ownership and control of knowledge; (5) ethical and methodological dilemmas we have encountered; and finally, (6) conclusions and recommendations to promote Indigenous approaches and participatory research methods.

Research and knowledge production can no longer be conducted with Indigenous communities as if their views do not count or their lives and personal experiences, including their experiences of the research process, are of no significance. Nor can their experiences be interpreted and voices heard filtered through Western scientific epistemology alone. In the absence or marginalization of the African voice, Western epistemology, including its methods, paradigms, and production and dissemination of knowledge, amounts to imperialism in the guise of modern scientific knowledge (Asante, 2003; Mogorosi & Thabede, 2017). The starting point for the production, recording, and dissemination of knowledge should be the community involved in the process, along with the researcher (Masoga & Kaya, 2013).

Much of existing knowledge production on Indigenous peoples is tainted by Eurocentric perceptions, assumptions, and prejudices (Masoga, 2018; Mkabela, 2005). Eurocentrism is the practice, conscious or otherwise, of placing emphasis on Western (and, generally, European) concerns, culture, and values at the expense of those of other cultures (Pop, n.d.). These may be unconsciously embedded in research methods and the data analysis processes or consciously defended as valid and rigorous. Institutional review of research protocols offers ethics protections, but review committees seldom include representation of the Indigenous community being researched and cannot shield a community from missteps in a cultural or linguistic interpretation of data. Major challenges of representation, accountability, and responsiveness in research are core ethical concerns.

It is the responsibility of any researcher conducting research with local Indigenous communities to adhere to essential ethical research principles and practices. These obligations include increased protection of confidentiality, privacy, and human rights that should be followed in any research. In Indigenous research, these obligations are particularly sensitive and essential for ensuring that scientific work and practices do not lead to harm, either by commission or by omission (Emmanuel, Wendler, Killen, & Grady, 2004; Mogorosi, 2018). Careful culturally attuned adherence to these principles is necessary to ensure that the rights and dignity of local Indigenous communities are protected.

This chapter discusses areas where research violates local communities using examples from our work in South Africa and Malawi to illustrate concerns and point to corrective action. We look intently at the contributions of Indigenous knowledge research to social science research today. We draw upon our experiences engaging in participatory research with communities in South Africa and Malawi and offer a critical examination of Western epistemology, Afro-sensed knowledge, Indigenous knowledge systems, and asset-based community development as frameworks for research with communities.

Discussions in this chapter present lessons learned and reflections on our research practice. Many scholars conducting participatory research emphasize the crucial role of reflexivity (Berger, 2015) and examinations of unequal power relations (Muhammad et al., 2015) when engaging with the community for research. We emphasize the importance of these processes as well. Beyond this, however, we engage in *researching back*, a term coined by Masoga (28 June 2018) to capture the collective and community participatory mandate to deeply understand the work together as equal partners to ensure the research process is meaningful to the community and honors Indigenous knowledge systems.

When Masoga was conducting research with the community of Majaneng in Hammanskraal, about 25 miles from Pretoria, South Africa, in 2004, he had an experience that moved his thinking into areas similar to but different from reflexivity and reflection. In this project, research participants challenged him and questioned the already completed research work. The research participants wanted space and time for "us" – themselves as part of the research team – to go through the entire research process. Questions from all arose such as: How did I perform ("I" being Masoga and participants questioning themselves)? Can we clarify my role? Does anyone have any misgivings, regrets, and/or positive feedback? It was clear that the process proposed by this community looked deeper into validity and reliability matters of the research, not only findings and action steps. Masoga recalls feeling like he was "undressed" and "re-dressed" by the research community, and he understood the profound value of this process to the research.

To communicate the nuanced experience, Masoga uses the term researching back and integrates it into all participatory research projects. Researching back refers to the research team's (including community participants) discussions on our process, often centering on feedback or reactions from community members who are also part of the research team. These discussions are a regular part of debriefings as we gather data, integral to data analysis and interpretation, and fundamental to ensuring that we have open and honest communication with our community partners.

Referring to the process as researching back has become an important term as it reminds us that this is a fundamental aspect of the research, not an added or optional component. Further, consistent with what we have learned from our engagement with African Indigenous communities, processes often cannot move forward until they have been revisited in a circling back fashion. For us, it is important to learn from what we are doing as we are doing it and to expand our reflections over time and across projects. Conducting research in communities provides us with a chance to learn and to unlearn. We grow and become better scholars when we enter into spaces of research with open minds and hearts when engaging with local communities. Researchers cannot be seen as people with answers and solutions, although answers and solutions are often what are sought. Local communities offer spaces where more authentic solutions and Indigenous knowledge can be blended with new knowledge (Nel, 2008).

Indigenous approaches and research methods

Indigenous knowledge systems (IKS) are grounded in local culture and contain the ways in which people who have lived in the same place over generations have learned, developed knowledge, and communicated their accumulated wisdom to teach the next generation and develop their community (Boven & Morohashi, 2002; Makhubele, 2008). While the focus on IKS brings a great depth of knowledge on specific areas or communities, it also has limitations on the transferability and confirmability (Guba, 1981) of information as applied to other communities. Care must be taken to not overgeneralize.

One interesting IKS definition offered by South African poet and writer Mongane Wally Serote (Masoga, M.A., personal communication, 6 June 2004) is that IKS emanates "from the human spirit are life experiences organized and ordered into accumulated knowledge with the objective to utilize it to the quality of life and to create a liveable environment for both human and other forms of life." The IKS are located in the context of utilitarian and creative forces to ensure comprehensive well-being for both humans and other forms of life. Indigenous knowledge is held by IKS practitioners such as farmers, traditional healers, herbalists, midwives, and rainmakers (Boven & Morohashi, 2002; Moreno Sandoval et al., 2016). The knowledge is stored in various forms which include traditional customs, folk stories, folk songs, folk dramas, legends, proverbs, myths, and more.

We acknowledge that Indigenous knowledge (IK) has been defined in different ways. The systems aspect of IKS emphasizes the process of developing and communicating knowledge and is often contrasted with scientific epistemology that is associated with Western European and North American cultures (Breidlid, 2009). Scientific epistemology is commonly taught as the highest standard for research. Imposing a foreign epistemology on culture in the attempt to learn about it, however, poses ethical dilemmas and contaminates the validity and reliability of the data (Dikko, 2016; Kapborg & Berterö, 2002). Using Afro-sensed frameworks and philosophies to analyze the problems of African people can be effective as an intervention tool in addition to generating knowledge more broadly (Shokane & Masoga, 2018).

It is essential for researchers to balance their sensitivity to local Indigenous culture by applying ethical participatory research principles and methodologies, thus avoiding causing harm that can violate people's rights and dignity (Owusu-Ansah & Mji, 2013). Protecting the dignity and rights of people requires the use of non-oppressive research methods that promote a culture of respect for the local Indigenous community's distinctive values, culture, and social practices. In the aftermath of colonialism, apartheid, and other forms of racial and economic oppression, IKS is often ignored and local Indigenous knowledge carries its own burden of stigma or discriminatory exclusion. Respect for cultural beliefs and traditions (such as language, ancestry, and impact of urbanization) should always be adhered to. Cultural norms, such as a desire to please, may be specific to some cultures and interact with perceived power imbalances among community members and researchers.

Participatory research methods offer researchers and local Indigenous communities ways to improve their understanding of insider/local knowledge and seek to find a balance that pushes back against the potential dominance of outsider/Western scientific knowledge (Kanji & Greenwood, 2001). Participatory research methods include collaborative research partnerships between researchers and local Indigenous communities and are used to avoid exploitation or further dominance by Western knowledge. The partnership could be developed by involving local Indigenous communities as research partners through sharing responsibilities for conducting research and focusing on aspects such as planning the project, conducting, and overseeing research (Emmanuel et al., 2004).

Through participatory methods, research design and interpretation of data can become Afro-sensed (Shokane & Masoga, 2018). The process of Afro-sensing in research does not exclude scientific epistemology but seeks to blend ways of knowing and disseminating knowledge (Ndlovu-Gatsheni, 2018; Owusu-Ansah & Mji, 2013). Afro-sensing is not an event that happens once for all at a given time and place, but an ongoing process of seeing others and ourselves clearly. A YouTube video (United States Institute of Peace, 14 March 2019, Youth-Led Peacebuilding: Participatory Action Research https://youtu.be/pvsNeKlbbss) provides an example of youth-led participatory research in Kenya. While the video depicts a process specific to violence and radicalization in a Kenyon city, it also illustrates the use of an Afro-sensed approach to engaging the community in addressing its own problems and has applications to other African community contexts. As demonstrated in this video, identity and self-determination in diverse and complex contextualities require that scholars and participants have clear self-understanding, respect, and trust among researchers and community, and make use of Indigenous knowledge and culture.

African culture and Indigenous knowledge should be incorporated into the training and practice of education from primary school through university (le Grange, 2016; Masoga, 2002). The education process should resemble the values and principles of those who are impacted and the communities that develop through the education process. Research and knowledge production are not innocent or distant academic exercises, they are activities that occur in a particular context of ideological, political, and social frameworks. Despite the catastrophic history of slavery, colonization, apartheid, globalization, and the disarticulation of knowledge production in Africa, the African intellectual and spiritual heritage survives. In the absence or marginalization of the African voice, however, Western epistemology amounts to imperialism in the guise of modern scientific knowledge. The wealth of knowledge among the elders in African communities is an important source of intellectualism to which researchers should turn, guided by Afro-sensed epistemology and IKS.

Our standpoint is that Afro-sensed epistemology and IKS expand other ways of knowing and center the African intellect and spirit as the core through which knowledge is developed and disseminated. Researchers in local Indigenous knowledge should disseminate research results to research stakeholders, including participants and communities, in a timely and competent manner so they can build upon what was discovered. Afro-sensed epistemology works from the base of an African worldview as the foundation for understanding African people. African beliefs, values, and traditions should be observed when conducting research with local Indigenous communities. This will be essential to avoid further violation and exploitation of the local knowledge of Indigenous communities by Western narratives and knowledge. To this end, we explore five areas of concern: (1) academic and research institutions not addressing local needs and concerns; (2) differences in language and communication styles among community members and researchers; (3) orality as a human-centered way of communication; (4) questions of ownership and control of knowledge; and (5) ethical and methodological dilemmas

Academic and research institutions are not addressing local needs and concerns

The field of Indigenous knowledge research and higher education throughout Africa is complex. The origins of the research in Africa are rooted in its colonial and apartheid past and, across the continent, higher education has been hesitant to embrace IKS or to regard Indigenous science as legitimate (Grenier, 1998; Owusu-Ansah & Mji, 2013). To seek to understand the truth of the people, higher education institutions and Indigenous communities should be empowered to generate knowledge and build power together through research (Nyong, 2007).

Participatory and community-engaged methods also offer ways to use the research process and skills as empowerment tools with Indigenous communities and the schools that serve children and families. Thus, participatory and community-engaged methods can inform education globally, beginning in primary school. Indigenous knowledge practitioners can be brought into primary and secondary classrooms to endorse an African social capital among students, school personnel, community members, and families (Masoga & Kaya, 2011; Shizha, 2007). Using participatory and community-engaged methods to guide research with the communities supports the Indigenous understanding that can be blended with scientific epistemology if the participating community-based research team deems appropriate.

Ethical and methodological dilemmas arise when researchers and scholars are expected to master Western epistemology, thus reducing investment in and removing research and theory from the Indigenous conceptual sphere (Mkabela, 2005). When this happens, academic and research institutions are not addressing local needs and concerns, but remain as floating islands without roots, ideologically and intellectually separate from the people and concerns they hope to understand.

Biases are found in African universities and research institutions as well as those in the Global North (Mamdani, 2018). African universities and research institutions, however, have a unique responsibility to act as guiding lights to the continent, to the societies within which they are located, and to the global community that seeks to repair the damage of history. The process of decolonization of higher education in Africa should commence in the classroom. Curriculum review must be done to promote the multicultural and Indigenous knowledge when training scholars in research suitable for African people and culture.

From our work, we have seen this dilemma in research undertaken by Shokane (2017), where she experienced an ethical dilemma of conducting participatory research with communities affected by natural disasters. The institutional ethics review committee had endorsed the project management plan to emphasize the community as co-researchers of the participatory action research design. However, some of the review panels expressed a concern that for a researcher with limited experience, producing academic articles and presenting conference papers within the period of the study was too ambitious. These questions directly impacted the feasibility and expected success of the study and had to be addressed. Shokane could not move at her pace as she had to deal with both her own issues of wanting to complete a PhD. thesis and to honor the participatory nature of the study. She needed to allow the process to unfold by itself. It was challenging not to be in the driver's seat when the community needed to drive the research project. Shokane had to adhere to the principles of community and participatory research in producing practical designs for solving a community problem by involving the community members throughout the research process. The process made the study labor-intensive, time-consuming, and exhaustive, as Shokane had prolonged and extensive engagement in the field for more than 12 months.

Differences in language and communication styles

Differences in language and communication styles between researchers and community members are also important considerations as they can result in misinterpretation and missed opportunities (Kapborg & Berterö, 2002; Larkin, Dierckx de Casterlé, & Schotsmans, 2007). Afro-sensing, approaching understanding through African ways of knowing, relating, and communicating, is liberating (wa Thiong'o, 1986) as it promotes the use of one's home language to engage in discourse and brings one closer to the individual and community truth. When research is translated from participants' home language to a different language for publication or other forms of dissemination, participatory and community-engaged methods provide opportunities for dialogue to agree upon word or image choice to best communicate Indigenous meaning (Larkin et al., 2007).

Opportunities should be provided for local Indigenous communities to communicate their research language and should also include the ability to hear and to speak the language or otherwise signal or express the participant's perspective. This should involve the capacity to decide and the ability to communicate that decision. Research with Indigenous local communities should be conducted in plain language and appropriate to the participant's level of understanding. It has been observed that most African scholarship activity is conducted in languages foreign to the participants, typically English (Nel, 2005). African scholars are expected to master English, removing research and theory out of the Indigenous conceptual space and reducing investment in developing Afro-sensed research approaches. The differences in language and communication styles can pose a challenge in working with a research team in which most of the participants do not read and write fluently in either their language or that of the researcher. In research conducted by Shokane (2017), this challenge compelled her to be involved in becoming more fluent in Sepedi, a language that was not her home language so that she could better communicate verbally what was not easily communicated in other ways. This challenge also motivated Shokane to work together with the community members who are familiar with the language and to learn from them. It was significant for the researcher not only to collect data but to engage the community in this way throughout the process of the research study.

Another example comes from our research in Malawi, where attention to language is crucial, as none of the researchers speaks Chichewa, the local language. We rely on community partners who are bilingual in English and Chichewa and native to Malawi to translate both words and cultural meaning. Blitz leads the Malawi research, and the overarching research questions typically come from researchers who are coming to the community to pursue their research agenda. Before work begins, however, elders and *mafumuwa* (traditional leaders) are consulted to ensure that the broader research questions are interesting to them and could generate knowledge or inform practices that build upon Indigenous knowledge.

Blitz, who lives in the U.S. and travels to Malawi annually, works very closely with multiple community partners. She keeps in touch through social media and will regularly seek guidance on cultural and translation issues between in-person visits. Questions asked of research participants are developed in English with the community partners, translated into Chichewa, and stated in ways that the community partners believe would be best understood by community members. The questions and responses often become lively conversations in multiple languages as Blitz, community partners, and respondents discuss the best English words to capture the meaning, feeling, and intent of the respondents (Blitz, Yull, Kufiyani, & Wapinski-Mooridian, 2018). The process is long and the notes copious and sometimes difficult to decipher, requiring careful member checking to ensure accuracy and confirmability (Lincoln & Guba, 1985).

Orality as a human-centered way of communication

Use of orality in research is a human-centered way of communication (Prah, 2017), utilizing words and gestures holistically to make use of channels through which the accumulated knowledge of a society can be expressed or transmitted. As Capra (1988) explains, orality includes informal body language such as gestures, twinkling the eye, and so on. One could look at some examples in orality and recording. An example comes from Masoga's research (2017), when he had the privilege of meeting and engaging with Mma (an honorific for mother) Maake of Makgane in the Limpopo province of South Africa. Masoga was engaged in research on Indigenous knowledge and medicine. Mma Maake was the community midwife. When Masoga met with her, she was busy attending to a mother-to-be who had a complicated pregnancy. Masoga was impressed by the level of recording that Mma Maake maintained. There were no papers on her table to recall the progress already done in this case, but she was able to provide dates and actions taken to remedy the problem experienced by the mother-to-be.

Mma Maake did not have a formal education. When Mma Maake was asked how she could recall and record all cases she was attending to, she led Masoga into her practice and on the floor, she had 85 strings tied differently. The 85 tied strings represented numerous cases that she has so far attended over her career. Each string told a story about the birth case: age, sex, date, and whether it was a complex or simple case. It was interesting how Mma Maake classified her cases, using nodes of strings as codes to unlock the confidentialities. Mma Maake made a point that all records about her clients were kept safe and managed accordingly. Unfortunately, one challenge with this type of special knowledge or expertise is that some knowledge is kept secretly and sacredly and not easily shared, making the Indigenous knowledge difficult to pass down to others. The unique communication and recording methods are serious challenges in preserving and protecting Indigenous knowledge. Research with Indigenous communities offers opportunities to formally record what might otherwise be lost.

Questions of ownership and control of knowledge

Research and knowledge production are activities that occur in a particular set of ideological, political, and social frameworks. Much of the existing knowledge production on Indigenous peoples is contaminated by Western/Eurocentric prejudices. Researchers in local Indigenous communities should engage with communities to define research priorities. Research in communities should be conducted focusing on Indigenous approaches and theories and include partnerships with the people who live in the communities. Community-engaged research that demonstrates respect for cultural differences can protect against outsider/Western contamination.

There are always questions of ownership and control of knowledge generated and documented in a community, including mechanisms and structures to ensure that the producers of knowledge have access to and control of their own knowledge for their sustainable development. It is our view that there must be mechanisms and structures in place to ensure that the local communities as producers of this knowledge have access to, and control of, their knowledge that enables them to create their sustainable livelihoods (Dondolo, 2005). Participatory research methods offer ways to identify and promote Indigenous approaches and methods that bridge gaps between African people and African scholars from outside the local community and those who come to Africa from other parts of the world to conduct research (Chilisa, 2012; Mkabela, 2005).

The question of ownership and control of knowledge has come up as a repeated concern in the work in Malawi. As an example, stemming from the process of participating in a research project assessing assets and community strengths, a group of women decided to form a collaborative business making and selling soap. A small local non-governmental organization (NGO) that works with children and families in the area offered to help the women launch their business (Blitz et al., 2018).

The women welcomed the help, but the project soon stalled as the ambitions of the NGO moved toward making a product suitable for sale to commercial businesses and tourists. A tension in values and priorities emerged. The women wanted to make a product they could sell to others in their community at the local marketplace. Their priority was getting a needed product to their neighbors at less cost than what was currently at the market. Consistent with their Indigenous culture, they valued relationships and supporting the community and noted coming together to love one another as the most important aspect of the project. Unfortunately, they could not make a profit, and without profit, they could not afford to continue to purchase supplies to make more soap. They needed the help of the NGO.

Tension grew between the women's desire for a small self-run business and the NGO's need to make at least a small profit if they were going to support the start-up, offering knowledge that was both practical and informed by Western values. As the NGO invested more, including erecting a building on their grounds that they offered to rent to the women as their workplace, the women's interest diminished. Although the women spoke of feeling neglectful of their families because of the time spent at the center making soap, it also appeared that they were caught between cultures. A different approach would have been to work closely with the women, who were certainly not opposed to making a profit, to see what Indigenous knowledge they brought that could have helped both groups meet their goals. Each of the women was able to list multiple skills and strengths and understood their value to the project. With facilitation by an organizer committed to IKS, those skills and strengths could potentially have been harnessed to build the soap making business and deepen IKS.

Ethical and methodological dilemmas

Research methodologies that are appropriate for local Indigenous communities should employ cultural competence and apply culturally sensitive research methods, which are applicable to diverse participants. Qualitative research, in particular, of those methods employing participatory approaches offers essential tools for social sciences, bringing scholars into the often private and intimate lives of vulnerable populations, marginalized communities, and people who are misunderstood, ignored, and sometimes villainized (Mkabela, 2005).

Research participant vulnerability is one of the least examined notions in research ethics with Indigenous communities. We explore vulnerability as largely stemming from social determinants and inequalities. Emmanuel et al. (2004) and Kottow (2003) articulate vulnerability as the incapacity to protect one's own interests, being in a subordinate/dependent position. Our argument is that local Indigenous knowledge is often undermined or disregarded by Western knowledge and creates a research vulnerability, which needs to be protected. Kottow clarifies that vulnerability "applies to everyone; what really matters in research ethics is susceptibility, which means being poor, undernourished, and lacking in medical care and therefore predisposed to additional harm" (2003, p. 460).

The problem of research vulnerability is evident in most research conducted in African local Indigenous knowledge. Mabvurira and Makhubele (2018) emphasized that African worldviews are different from Western worldviews and when conducting research it is essential to understand that problems and cultures of both Africans and Westerners differ and may not be effective if applied in each other's contexts. This YouTube video (Eelderink, 13 Feb 2016, *Semi-structured interviewing for Participatory Action Research* https://youtu.be/cGQz8hZQ8fU) is an example of semi-structured in-depth interviewing in Uganda that could be applied to similar communities to negotiate these vulnerabilities and build relationships.

African life is communal and embedded in the Ubuntu philosophy as opposed to the individualistic nature of Western life. Ubuntu implies a sense of humanness, recognizing and caring about the human dignity of others, which should be adhered to in all research involving local Indigenous communities. The South African White Paper on Welfare (Department of Welfare, Republic of South Africa, 1997) distinguishes Ubuntu as more than the principle of caring for each other's well-being and as a spirit of mutual support but "acknowledges it as both the right and the responsibilities of every citizen in promoting individual and societal well-being" (p. 2). Undoubtedly, if Ubuntu is adhered to in research with local Indigenous communities, the potential for increased harmony within Western knowledge exists, offering unity, respect, and mutual co-operation of all the knowledge production.

Participation recognizes the importance of involving all stakeholders, including people who are financially poor and made voiceless by existing power structures, in the research and development process (Cornwall & Jewkes, 1995). People who are custodians of local Indigenous knowledge are creative and have the competence to conduct research.

The permission of a community representative, a mediator or gatekeeper in the local Indigenous community who will also contextualize guidelines for the local setting, should be sought. This partnership will also assist in facilitating community permission and consent. Research participants should know they are taking part in research that benefits the careers of the researchers, but no other benefits can be promised, neither to individuals nor the community. It should be emphasized that the research should be carried out only with their informed consent. Members of local Indigenous communities can be unfamiliar with Western scientific concepts. Attention should be given to the content, languages, and procedures used to obtain informed consent. The consent process has the ability to affect their understanding of information and make informed decisions in conducting research.

There are various challenges and ethical concerns that can be experienced in undertaking participatory research. Though some challenges can be anticipated due to the participatory nature of the study, some can be beyond the control of researchers and co-researchers. Since some challenges could not be controlled, they may create many delays in the study. In a study conducted by Shokane (2017) with people in the community of Naphuno, Greater Tzaneen in the Limpopo province of South Africa affected by natural disasters, the scheduled community meetings and focus group discussions and meetings with the community members were at times postponed. The co-researchers could not meet with the researcher as planned due to service delivery protests experienced in the community of Naphuno during the period of fieldwork. The service delivery protests resulted in barricaded roads, causing delays in the scheduled fieldwork. The data collection process, as part of the fieldwork visits, which could have been conducted in six months, had to be postponed and rescheduled. This made the study labor-intensive, time-consuming, and exhaustive, as the researcher had prolonged and extensive engagement in the field.

Through participatory methods, researchers maintain various positions in relation to the community participants that provide them opportunities to achieve optimal contact and relationships with research participants and community stakeholders. These positions have been described (Cornwall & Jewkes, 1995) as (a) contract (or passive) participation, where researchers' contract with stakeholders, local leaders, and/or services needed for the research; (b) consultative participation, where researchers consult stakeholders on problems/questions and develop solutions; (c) collaborative participation, where researchers and stakeholders work together as partners in the research process; and (d) collegiate (empowering) participation, where researchers work with and support research, development systems, and capacities of stakeholders.

Shokane's (2017) research offers an example of how researchers and communities can work together as partners in the research process to ensure the capacities of stakeholders. A reflexive approach was used, which involved training research participants as co-researchers to assess if skills transfer had taken place as a result of being co-researchers with the researcher. To overcome the challenge of bringing the research participants to the level of the co-researchers, Shokane started with training the research participants/co-researchers, and this was conducted at the grassroots level appropriate for the community members. The training was also used as a learning strategy that was aimed at empowering participants as co-researcher of the study. Schenk, Nel, and Louw (2010) affirm that it is essential for a researcher to facilitate the training process which helps "to access and release people's knowledge and skills (their assets)" (p. 116).

The findings of the study confirmed that indeed skills transfer took place. Thus, the community members possessed capacity and skills, mostly technical such as data gathering, recording, and analysis required to conduct the study. In following the participatory process, the community members were guided to become co-researchers to actively participate in the formulation of the research plan and strategy. The process has encouraged community members (research participants) to prioritize their needs and problems by conducting an analysis of their problems and coming up with solutions through a participatory process of using their own skills and knowledge. Though there are many approaches in community development that can ensure and promote participatory research, in this case, the Asset Based Community Development (ABCD) (Kretzmann & McKnight, 1993) approach was also applied in guiding the gathering and analysis of qualitative and participatory data. The ABCD framework emphasized that coping and withstanding any community challenge primarily lies in the hands of the community itself. The ABCD approach sanctioned the utilization of existing community resources, assets, skills, and abilities of community members, which were used to explore ways of addressing and coping with the challenges of being affected by natural disasters in rural communities. In this regard, the people affected by natural disasters relied on the limited resources (assets) available to them and had galvanized them to develop a participatory community development model.

Though the implementation, ABCD promoted a bottom-up approach in community development, it has also encouraged the incorporation of resources outside the community which warranted the involvement of external stakeholders such as government, the municipality, and NGOs, who usually intervene in issues of disaster management in communities. The process which was followed was in line with the participatory nature of the study, and it promoted the inside out approach of the ABCD. The strengths of the ABCD center on believing that the community members possess strengths and have solutions to the challenges they experience.

Conclusions and recommendations to promote Indigenous approaches and participatory research methods

Looking at the above discussions, we are able to relate our work to le Grange's (2016) model of "emerging" following the five phases he delineates. (1) Rediscovery and recovery: colonized people rediscover and recover their own history, culture, language, and identity. Rediscovery and recovery models and conducting research become necessary. Theories and methods should expose the hurt caused and recover the history using the local languages in this regard. (2) Mourning: lamenting the continued assault. All research should be accompanied by theories of change. The latter should expose and condemn the distractors and damagers of the histories, cultures, languages, and identities of local communities. (3) Dreaming: Imagining the alternative. All research has to offer hope and assurance to communities whose histories, cultures, languages, and identities have been trampled upon. (4) Commitment: having a sense of urgency, agency, and agitation for change. Our research values and mission should be centered around change. This relates to the point about lamenting the continued assault. (5) Action: translating dreams into action, ensuring that the "underdog knowledge" is protected, improved, and represented for and with truth and honor. Models of change and implementation become necessary. This demand should challenge institutions such as universities to rethink their research policies. In essence, universities should self-criticize their existence and presence. Truth and honor should guide their thinking and practice.

Social science researchers have a moral responsibility to ensure that local communities are recognized and benefit from the research, including building capacity to use local knowledge to alleviate poverty, regain dignity, and improve education. The local Indigenous communities should not only be participants in the research activities but should receive benefits and incentives from the results of research of equal partners. There is a concern that most research conducted in local communities does not regard or view local communities as equal partners and that the people are not equally informed on what is to be done. How the process is to be approached and executed, including the outcome and benefits of that outcome, must honor the local Indigenous communities and their people (Dondolo, 2005). Other issues such as the equitable distribution of both burdens and benefits of research should be considered to recognize and compensate for time, inconvenience, cost (expenses), or other concerns.

The IKS practitioners can also be included in family and community engagement efforts to build and enhance relationships among schools and the community to further ground IKS in early education. Building these relationships promotes a vision of a sustainable future because African IKS practitioners have lived in harmony with the environment and have utilized local resources without impairing nature's capacity to regenerate (Gumede, 2016). The use of cultural items through IKS practitioners as resources in the formal educational curriculum can be very effective in bringing Indigenous knowledge alive for students (Ndlovu-Gatsheni, 2018). Young learners may already be familiar with some aspects of Indigenous culture and, therefore, may find it interesting to learn more about it through these cultural forms and the community knowledge holders. This will promote a new educational paradigm whereby learners and youth could themselves be actively involved in the collection of folk stories, songs, legends, and proverbs that are retold in their community, thus helping to preserve IKS.

The process of interaction must be based on equality between the researcher and the community members who are the holders and producers of knowledge in their daily activities. In by far most cases, the situation is that the researcher sets the agenda and members of the community remain passive. Participatory research methods that build partnerships with community members offer some solutions. In this model, the community is not just there to be studied, but members are active as necessary partners in framing research questions, delineating methods, carrying out the study, and analyzing findings (Cornwall & Jewkes, 1995). Even this, however, cannot fully disengage from power imbalances between researcher and participant. Differences in motivation for the project, access to resources, physical comforts, and other factors result in researcher and participant having very different experiences of the process and must be addressed.

We propose the following five considerations. First, researchers and scholars need to develop and promote collaborations with local communities. Being validated by a community of knowledge becomes critical in this regard. This in a way changes how ethical clearances are done. The question is, who should provide ethical clearance. It should not be left to institutions of higher learning or research institutions alone; Indigenous communities have a crucial role. Masoga's (2018) experience conducting research in the Limpopo Province of South Africa and our work in Malawi had to be cleared and validated by the local communities and their leaders in addition to human subjects review boards from our institutions.

Second, research in Indigenous knowledge should be approached in a participatory way, that is, by emphasizing the involvement of the community in the whole research process. Indigenous knowledge researchers in communities need to be sensitive in applying the techniques of interaction and data collection processes with local communities (Mkabela, 2005). Local communities must never be passive in any research process. These local communities have a great deal to contribute, and their voice should never be stifled.

Third, there is a need to develop a code of conduct governing interaction between researchers and the local communities themselves. It is maintained that a code of conduct should ensure that the intellectual property rights of local communities as producers and holders of Indigenous knowledge are not abused and exploited and that local communities themselves gain some benefit from research (Masoga & Kaya 2013).

Fourth, science and scientific thinking need to be looked at in a broader sense. Scientific thinking is a contested terrain. Local communities have the capacity to think scientifically and their language of scientific thinking has to be deciphered in a negotiated space by both researchers and local communities involved in the research. It cannot be taken that researchers are the only custodians of scientific thinking while excluding the ability to think scientifically located in local communities. The example given earlier of Mma Maake becomes appropriate in this case. As in the light of the first consideration, codes of conduct in research should be revised and involve the place of local communities. Language and languaging, a "form of verbalization used to mediate the solution(s) to complex problems and tasks" (Swain et al., 2009, p. 5), in this regard becomes critical. Questions such as: How, what, and who should frame the codes for conducting research should never be taken for granted. There is more to language than the construction of words and sentences. Language is constructed in a space where, for example, rituals are performed and interpreted. Languaging specifically looks at the social context of language, looking at language in the life of a community.

Fifth, the dynamism of communities should be accounted for in all research. Communities are not homogenous, nor do their people have a singular perspective in looking at life. This dynamism provides opportunities for researchers to consider variations in their interpretations of knowledge domains located in local communities. Communities have their own dynamics and are never static. Their dynamism helps enhance the quality and substance of what is being researched. The heterogeneities of local communities should enrich this dynamism and reflexibility in conducting research in such spaces.

For Indigenous knowledge to have a significant bearing on sustainable development, African societies must gain some currency in schools, the social institutions officially chartered to organize learning, certify knowledge, and train the next generation of citizens (Nel, 2005). In view of its potential value for sustainable development, it is necessary to preserve and promote Indigenous knowledge for the benefit of future generations. Local knowledge, embedded in communities of practice, becomes critical in helping one to emerge out of the state of either blindness or dizziness.

References

Asante, M.K. (2003). *Afrocentricity: A theory of social change* (2nd edition). Chicago, IL: African American images.

Berger, R. (2015). Now I see it, now I don't: Researcher's position and reflexivity in qualitative research. *Qualitative Research, 15*(2), 219–234. doi: 10.1177/1468794112468475

Blitz, L.V., Yull, D., Kufeyani, P., & Wapinski-Mooradian, J. (2018). *Akuluakulu? Sapasidwa kanthu* (grown-ups? They get nothing): Informing an international community-University Partnership in Malawi. *Social Development Issues, 40*(1), 5–16.

Boven, K., & Morohashi, J. (Eds.) (2002). *Best Practices Using Indigenous Knowledge*. Joint publication of The Hague: The Netherlands Nuffic, and Paris, France, UNESCO/MOST.

Breidlid, A. (2009). Culture, indigenous knowledge systems and sustainable development: A critical view of education in an African context. *International Journal of Educational Development, 29*, 140–148. doi:10.1016/j.ijedudev.2008.09.009

Capra, F. (1988). *Uncommon Wisdom. Conversation with Remarkable People*. London: Flamingo.

Chilisa, B. (2012). *Indigenous Research Methodologies*. Los Angeles, CA: Sage.

Chukwuokoko, J.C. (2010). Afrocentrism or Eurocentrism: The dilemma of African development. *OGIRISI: A New Journal of African Studies, 6*, 24–39.

Cornwall, A., & Jewkes, R. (1995). What is participatory research? *Social Science & Medicine, 41*(12), 1667–1676.

Department of Welfare, Republic of South Africa. (1997). *Principles, guidelines, recommendations, proposed policies and programmes for developmental social welfare in South Africa*. Last viewed on 24 January 2020 Retrieved from: https://www.gov.za/sites/default/files/gcis_document/201409/whitepaperonsocialwelfare0.pdf

Dikko, M. (2016). Establishing construct validity and reliability: Pilot testing of a qualitative interview for research in Takaful (Islamic Insurance). *The Qualitative Report, 21*(3), 521–528.

Dondolo, L. (2005). Intangible heritage: The production of indigenous knowledge in various aspects of social life. *Indilinga African Journal of Indigenous Knowledge Systems 4*(6), 110–126.

Eelderink, M. (2016, February 13). *Semi-structured interviewing for Participatory Action Research*. Last viewed on 24 January 2020. Retrieved from: https://youtu.be/cGQz8hZQ8fU

Emmanuel, E.J., Wendler, W., Killen, J., & Grady, C. (2004) What makes clinical research in developing countries ethical? The benchmarks of ethical research. *Journal of Infectious Diseases, 189*, 930–937.

Eno, M.A., Ingiriis, M.H., Haji, J.M., Eno, O.A., & Eno, M.A. (2012). Slavery and colonialism: The worst terrorism on Africa. *African Renaissance, 9* (1), pp. 9–26.

Grenier, L. (1998). *Working with Indigenous Knowledge: A Guide for Researchers*. Ottawa, ON: International Development Research Centre (IDRC).

Guba, E. (1981). Criteria for assessing the trustworthiness of naturalistic inquiries. *Educational Communication and Technology, 29*, 75–91.

Gumede, V. (2016). Towards a better socio-economic development approach for Africa's renewal. *Africa Insight, 46*(1), 89–105.

Kanji, N., & Greenwood, L. (2001). *Participatory Approaches to Research and Development in IIED: Learning from Experience*. London: International Institute of Environment and Development (IIED).

Kapborg, C., & Berterö, I. (2002). Using an interpreter in qualitative interviews: Does it threaten validity? *Nursing Inquiry, 9*(1), 52–56.

Kottow, M.H. 2003. The vulnerable and the susceptible. *Bioethics, 17*(5–6): 460–471.

Kretzmann, J., & McKnight, J. (1993). *Building Communities from the Inside Out: A Path Toward Finding and Mobilizing a Community's Assets*. Chicago, IL: Asset-Based Community Development Institute, ACTA Publications.

Larkin, P.J., Dierckx de Casterlé, B., & Schotsmans, P. (2007). Multilingual translation issues in qualitative research: Reflections on a metaphorical process. *Qualitative Health Research, 17*(4), 468–476.

Le Grange, L. (2016). Decolonising the university curriculum. *South African Journal of Higher Education, 30*(2), 1–12.

Lincoln, Y.S., & Guba, E.G. (1985). *Naturalistic Inquiry*. Beverly Hills, CA: Sage.

Mabvurira, V., & Makhubele, J.C. (2018). Afrocentric methodology: A missing pillar in African social work research, education and training. In: A.L. Shokane, J.C. Makhubele & L.V. Blitz (Eds.), *Issues Around Aligning Theory, Research and Practice in Social Work Education (Knowledge Pathing: Multi-, Inter- and Trans-Disciplining in Social Sciences Series Volume 1*), (pp. 11–26). Cape Town, SA. AOSIS. https://doi.org/10.4102/aosis.2018.BK76.01

Makhubele, J. (2008). The impact of indigenous community-based groups towards social development. *Indilinga: African Journal of Indigenous Knowledge Systems*, 7(1), 37–46.

Mamdani, M. (2018). The African University. *London Review of Books, 40*(14), 29–32.

Masoga, M.A. (2002). *Contesting space and time: Intellectual property rights and the indigenous knowledge systems research in South African universities*. Paper presented at the International Symposium CODESRIA/Illinois under the Theme: African Universities in the 21st Century, April 25-27, 2002, Campus Numeric Franchophone de Dakar, Agence Universitaire de la Franchophone, Dakar – SENEGAL.

Masoga, M.A. (2017). Critical reflections on selected local narratives of contextual South African indigenous knowledge. In: P. Ngulube (Ed.), *Handbook on Indigenous Knowledge Systems in Developing Countries* (pp. 310–333). Hershey, PA: USA International Publisher of Progressive Information Science and Technology Research.

Masoga, M.A. (2018). Making the fish understand its water: Reflecting on Africanisation, Indigenous knowledge, and decoloniality of our time. In: E.R. Mathipa, S.D. Matjila, & T. Netshitangani (Eds.), *Indigenous Proverbs, Idioms, Folktales, Riddles, Poems, Songs, Stories and Metaphors: The Bedrock of the Ubuntu Philosophy* (pp. 127–148). Noordwyk, SA: Mosala-MASEDI Publishers Booksellers.

Masoga, M.A. (2018, 28 June). *Address to the National Institute for Humanities and Social Sciences*. Northern Corridor Doctoral School in Tzaneen, Limpopo Province, South Africa.

Masoga, M.A., & Kaya, H. (2011). Building on the indigenous: An appropriate paradigm for sustainable development. In: G. Walmsley (Ed.), *Africa in African Philosophy and the Future of Africa*, (pp. 154–169). Washington, DC: The Council for Research in Values and Philosophy.

Mkabela, Q. (2005). Using the Afrocentric method in researching indigenous African culture. *The Qualitative Report, 10*(1), 178–189.

Mogorosi, L.D. (2018). Ethics in research: Essential factors for consideration in scientific Studies. In: A.L. Shokane, J.C. Makhubele & L.V. Blitz (Eds.), *Issues Around Aligning Theory, Research and Practice in Social Work Education (Knowledge Pathing: Multi-, Inter- and Trans-Disciplining in Social Sciences Series Volume 1* (pp. 69–93). AOSIS, Cape Town, SA. https://doi.org/10.4102/aosis.2018.BK76.04

Mogorosi, L.D., & Thabede, D.G. (2017). Social work and indigenisation: South African perspective. *South African Journal of Social Work and Social development, 29*(2), 1–18.

Moreno Sandoval, C.D., Mojica Lagunas, R., Montelongo, L.T., & Juárez Diaz, M. (2016). Ancestral knowledge systems: A conceptual framework for decolonizing research in social science. *AlterNative: An International Journal of Indigenous Peoples, 12*(1), 19–31.

Muhammad, M., Wallerstein, N., Sussman, A.L., Avila, M., Belone, L., &, Duran, B. (2015). Reflections on researcher identity and power: The impact of positionality on community based participatory research (CBPR) processes and outcomes. *Critical Sociology (Eugene)*, *41*(7–8), 1045–1063. doi:10.1177/0896920513516025

Ndlovu-Gatsheni, S.J. (2018). *Epistemic Freedom in Africa: Deprovincialization and Decolonization*. Abingdon, Oxon: Routledge

Nel, P. (2005). Indigenous knowledge: Contestation, rhetoric and space. *Indilinga African Journal of Indigenous Knowledge Systems*, *4*(1), 2–14.

Nel, P. (2008). Indigenous knowledge systems: Conceptualization and methodology. Unpublished lecture (presented 21 October), University of the Free State, Africa Studies Centre Roundtable, Bloemfontein, South Africa.

Nyong, C.T. (2007). Indigenous knowledge and sustainable development in Africa. Case study on Central Africa. In: Emmanuel K. Boon and Luc Hens (Eds), *Indigenous Knowledge Systems and Sustainable Development: Relevance to Africa. Tribes and Tribals*, Special Issue No. *1*, 121–139.

Owusu-Ansah, F.E., & Mji, G. (2013). African indigenous knowledge and research. *African Journal of Disability*, *2*(1), 1–5.

Pop, T. (n.d.). From Eurocentrism to hybridity or from singularity to plurality. Partium Christian University, Oradea, Romania. Viewed 05 March 2019, from: https://www.scribd.com/document/246328470/Titus-Pop-From-Eurocentrism-to-Hibridity-or-From-Singularity-to-Plurality

Prah, K.K. (2017). The centrality of the language question in the decolonization of education in Africa. *Alternation*, *24*(2), 226–252.

Schenk, R, Nel, H., & Louw, H. (2010). *Introduction to Participatory Community Practice*. Pretoria, SA: Unisa Press.

Shizha, E. (2007). Critical analysis of problems encountered in incorporating indigenous knowledge in science teaching by primary school teachers in Zimbabwe. *The Alberta Journal of Educational Research*, *53*(3), 302–319.

Shokane, A.L. (2017). Development of a participatory community development practice model for rural communities affected by natural disasters. Ph.D. thesis (Unpublished). Retrieved from: http://hdl.handle.net/10210/226391 (accessed: 15 May 2019).

Shokane, A.L., & Masoga, M.A. (2018). African indigenous knowledge and social work practice: Towards an Afro-sensed perspective. *Southern African Journal of Social Work and Social Development*, *30*(1), 1–18. https://doi.org/10.25159/2415-5829/2320

Swain, M., Lapkin, S., Ibtissem, K., Suzuki, W., & Brooks, L. (2009) Languaging: University students learn the grammatical concept of voice in French. *The Modern Language Journal*, *93*, 5–29.

United States Institute of Peace (2019, 14 March). Youth-led peacebuilding: Participatory action research. Last viewed on 24 January 2020. Retrieved from: https://youtu.be/pvsNeKlbbss

wa Thiong'o, N. (1986). *Decolonizing the Mind: The Politics of Language in African Literature*. Nairobi, Kenya: East African Educational Publishers; Portsmouth, NH: Heinemann.

Chapter 5

Methodological challenges and ethical dilemmas

Research on domestic violence in Greece

Sheetal Ranjan and Vasiliki Artinopoulou

Introduction

As the women's movement has advanced globally, there has been an increasing interest in research related to women's lives around the world. The *2030 Agenda for Sustainable Development* adopted by all United Nations Member States in 2015 includes targets for gender equality which includes the elimination by 2030 of all forms of violence against women and girls and all harmful practices such as child, early, and forced marriage and female genital mutilation (Sustainable Development Goal #5). Worldwide, one in three women has experienced physical or sexual violence – mostly by an intimate partner. When accounting for sexual harassment, this figure is even higher (World Health Organization, 2013). Worldwide, almost three in five women killed were killed by their partners or family in 2017 (United Nations of Drugs and Crime, 2019). Given these startling statistics, presently, almost three-quarters of the world's countries have outlawed domestic violence (Tavares & Wodon, 2017; World Bank Group. 2018). In the past decade, international agencies such as the World Bank, UNWomen, and similar organizations have provided increased research and programmatic funding for gender-based violence. The combination of these factors has led to an increasing need for research to understand the status of women as it relates to domestic violence in different parts of the world. This research typically falls within the broader disciplines of criminal justice, sociology, psychology, public health, and women's studies.

While this chapter is written with the intention of serving as a guide to scholars trying to conduct domestic violence research in Greece, the information and frameworks provided in this chapter can be used for other kinds of criminal justice research as well. Further, even though cross-cultural research is a worthwhile endeavor, it is generally very complex and is often prone to errors. This is especially true of the research related to criminal justice. The main challenges include differing legal frameworks, definitions, concepts, social norms, and cultural stereotypes that debunk assumptions of universality and create difficulties in comparative analysis. It is therefore important to raise crucial questions about these issues at each stage of the research for it to be both reliable and valid. Focusing on the culture being researched is important, as are the legal constructs operational within the country. One of the first steps in conducting research related to criminal justice is to understand its structure in the country of question. Therefore, the next section provides a general framework of research in Greece, highlighting some national strategies aimed at improving research both in terms of quantity and quality.

Research in Greece: A general framework

In the last decade, there has been significant development toward a wider legislative framework to strengthen and promote research in Greece. The *National Strategy for Research, Technological Development and Innovation*, established in 2014, was followed by a series of laws, roadmaps, action plans, and interventions all aimed at promoting innovation through increased national and international research. Yet, conducting research in Greece is a rather difficult task and is still plagued with many problems and challenges, leading to reduced effectiveness and a lack of efficiency for academies, research institutions, and the researchers themselves to propose and conduct quality research projects. The financial crisis in the country, starting in 2009, had a significant impact on the academically qualified and talented individuals fleeing the country for better opportunities, leading to a significant "brain drain." This was further exacerbated by the lack of national resources to support research institutions and researchers. The financial and structural weakness for the institutional funding of research organizations led to a "research crisis" in the universities and other institutions in Greece. Nevertheless, and somewhat paradoxically, Greek researchers have responded to this national "research crisis" by seeking increased participation in research projects funded by European and international organizations instead of the traditional national avenues for research funding. However, these well-intentioned attempts are often thwarted by many challenges. Criminal justice research in Greece is particularly challenging as it involves interaction with a range of organizations. Therefore, in the next section, we provide a brief description of the Greek criminal justice system, which will offer some perspective in planning your research.

The Greek criminal justice system

The Greek criminal justice system is based on the Continental tradition. The stages of the criminal justice process in Greece are prosecution, preliminary examination, trial, and implementation/execution of the penal decision. The Prosecutor supervises the whole process as well as the actions of the rest of the authorities (police, prisons, and the officers in the justice system); during these stages, he/she acts as an independent judicial authority in the name of the State to ensure both the constitutional rules and the proper operation of the application of the law. Moreover, the Prosecutor conducts the penal prosecution and the preliminary investigation and is responsible for checking the imposition of the decisions of the court.

For the past ten years or so, the Greek criminal justice system has been facing two main problems: the excessive length of proceedings and extremely limited use of information and communication technologies (ICT). Both problems have an impact on limiting access to justice for citizens and researchers (Sakellaropoulou et al., 2019). During the financial crisis in Greece between 2014 and 2016, the public budget for the functioning of the Greek Criminal Justice system was reduced by up to 33 percent – reducing the number of judicial employees and judges that are needed for an effective criminal justice system. According to the research data of the World Bank, the estimated time of solving a judicial case in Greece is 1580 days (World Bank, 2016). In 2010, Greece ranked among the five "slowest-moving" judicial systems in the EU member states (Rass-Masson & Rouas, 2017). As stated in the EU Justice Scoreboard (2017), electronic submission of claims is not in place in Greece. Electronic means are currently available solely to monitor the stages of a proceeding, and these are offered by only half of the courts in Greece. Other aspects, such as the possibility to submit a case or to relay summons, do not appear to be available in Greece. Consequently, the judicial statistical data either do not provide enough information or are not well elaborated. These issues are further exacerbated by recent legislation related to data protection and the code of ethics in criminal justice research. In the next two sections, we provide a general overview of the new legislation and regulations related to data protection, followed by those related to morality and ethics in research.

Data protection legislation in Greece

A corpus of European legislation on protecting the personal data came into force on all member states in 2018, they are: (i) the *General Data Protection Regulation* (GDPR); (ii) the *Data Protection Law Enforcement Directive* (EU/2016/680); and (iii) the establishment of the *National Data Protection Authorities*, the *European Data Protection Board*. The combination of these legislations and directives are concerned with a citizen's fundamental right to data protection whenever personal data is used by criminal law enforcement authorities for law enforcement purposes. In particular, it ensures that the personal data of victims, witnesses, and suspects of crime are duly protected and will facilitate cross-border cooperation in the fight against crime and terrorism. Greece is bound by these legislations like all other EU member states resulting in the increased protection of personal data. Since these legislations and directives are rather new, they have immediately impacted criminal justice-related research activities in higher education institutes, research centers, and other organizations in the civil society. Given the slowness of pace in Greece, it will be a long while before clarity emerges about which data is accessible for research purposes and in what format.

Committee for Morality and Ethics in Research in Greece

Recently, Law 4521/2018[1] in Articles 21 to 27 mandated the formation of *Ethics Committees* at all *Institutes of Higher Education* (IHE) and provided clear guidelines about the purpose of the ethics committee, its composition, the qualifications of its members and their term limits, operation of the committee, and outlines conflicts of interest. This law requires both the applicant and the ethics committee to ensure that the research proposals meet the ever-changing laws, regulations, and treaty agreements of Greece and the European Union. This committee is charged with the responsibility to approve the research protocols and advise the researchers for any project revisions needed to meet legislative mandates. The decision of this committee is binding, and no research can be executed without their permission.

In addition to the Ethics Committees at each IHE, the *Greek Society of Criminology* has been engaged in a dialog since 2009 to develop its own code of ethics (Spinelli and Kranidioti, 2009) to bring it in line with the code of ethics of international academic societies such as the American Society of Criminology,[2] British Society of Criminology,[3] Australian and New Zealand Society of Criminology,[4] and similar organizations. However, this task is yet to be completed. Issues such as informed and/or signed consent, permission procedures, and the protection of vulnerable groups and children are still challenging at both the practical and empirical level (Frohock et al., 1988; Edens et al., 2011; Gallagher et al., 2016). Research ethics in Greek criminological research is still in the fledgling stages, and researchers typically follow a basic standard to protect the anonymity of the research sample, gaining consent and avoiding plagiarism. Most often, they try to meet the hurdles of the research as and when they encounter them in the process of gaining access to the research sample. Given this context, the next section provides a discussion about getting access to the Greek criminal justice system for research.

Getting access to research in the Greek criminal justice system

Depending on the criminal justice-related topic and research methodology, researchers in Greece have to ask for formal permission from the supervising authority, usually the *Ministry of Justice* (https://www.ministryofjustice.gr/) or the *Ministry of Citizen Protection* (http://www.mopocp.gov.gr/). Websites of both these ministries do not include any information about procedures for gaining research access. Typically, a researcher would have to directly contact either agency to determine which one has the authority to grant permission based on the specific nature of the research project. Once that has been determined, researchers from academia, research centers, NGOs, post-graduate or PhD students, and other experts submit the request for permission, based on the instructions received from the concerned ministry. This request typically includes documentation on the aims of the research, the certification of the affiliated research institution, the methodology and survey/interview tools, the research protocols, the ethics of the research, and the expected results. The ethics section of the research application is significant in gaining permission. It should describe measures that will be taken to protect the anonymity of the research participants and the personal data of individuals. It should also include sample consent forms for the research participants. The other criteria that are considered before research approval is granted include the safety of the researchers (especially in prison settings) and the protection of the everyday tasks of the staff and institutions where such research will be conducted. The *Central Scientific Board for Prisons* (a national advisory council in the *Ministry of Citizen Protection*) is responsible for examining the research request, depending on the topic and the nature of the research. Prison staff, probation officers for adults and juveniles, security staff, and other professional categories of employees in the Ministry are not allowed to participate in any research procedures/projects without the previous official approval of the research protocol. For research concerning criminal justice topics beyond prisons and the penitentiary system, the *General Prosecutors Office in the Supreme Court* (Areios Pagos) (https://www.eisap.gr/) is the proper authority for submitting the research request and granting permission. This office typically handles research requests for interviews with judicial staff and public servants (prosecutors/judges). For the independence of justice, the research request would be forwarded by them to the *Director of the Courts of First Instance* and/or the *Court of Appeals*. In general, for judicial participation in a research project, senior judicial agreement and permission are required.

As detailed in the paragraphs above, there is not one centralized place for seeking criminal justice-related research permissions in Greece. The processes are not detailed on any of the ministry websites either. However, the *General Secretary for Criminal Justice Policy* in the Ministry of Justice released an internal circular (dated January 21, 2018, bearing reference #8201) on the procedures of getting access and permission for all agencies and organizations supervised by the General Secretary. This document was circuited exclusively within the agencies of the Ministry and was not published widely for academics and researchers. This document came up from the obligation of the Greek government to harmonize the national law and rules with the EU binding legislation on the protection of personal. Given the authors' knowledge about this document, we have created a separate section at the end of this chapter which can serve as a guide for future scholars interested in gaining research access to the criminal justice system in Greece.

The challenges of the Greek criminal justice system, legislations, and lack of clarity about the codes of ethics described in the previous sections, as well as the challenges of gaining access to data described in this section, have an impact in doing quantitative criminological research and affect the comparability of statistics with other countries. However, qualitative research has been more feasible on issues related to the Greek criminal justice system. Legal research (especially related to case law) and criminological and sociological research using qualitative methodologies such as case studies, interviews, narratives, and focus groups are well developed in Greece, throwing light on different aspects of the criminal justice system, such as the prison settings, the victims' participation in the criminal proceedings, the rights of the accused, and other similar issues.

While these processes and lack of clarity may seem intimidating and challenging for a newcomer, the general impression of the authors of this article, based on their own and colleagues' experiences, has been that the ministries usually approve research requests that are well documented, meet the mandates, and are channeled through the proper sources. Based on the experience of the authors, a research application may take about two months for processing and decision. More often, the concerned authority may ask for further clarification on the research project before a final decision, thereby increasing the processing time.

Because there are no published data on examining how many requests for research have been submitted in the ministries and other authorities, how many of them were finally approved or rejected, what was the nature of the research request, and the justification of potential rejections, the authors contacted various ministries to request this information. We were able to get pertinent information from the *Directorate-General of Detention and Crisis Management*, which is a department in the *Ministry of Citizen Protection*. This information is specific to detention facilities in Greece. In personal communication, they confirmed that their department follows the Greek Constitution and the State's obligations to European Law regarding access to information and the development and promotion of the research which are under articles 5A and 16 of the Greek Constitution. They also take into consideration the *General European Regulation on Personal Data Protection* in approving the requests for research. All requests for research received in their department are examined using two criteria: (i) whether the research is aligned with the national and European legislation; and (ii) can the research be conducted without disrupting the function and rules of the prison. This department is also charged with the responsibility of keeping records for the requests and making decisions about research access. Tables 5.1 and 5.2 present data of the research requests they have been received from May 2018 to December 2019 and the research topics of the requests.

Table 5.1 Research Requests Received by the Directorate of Detention and Crisis Management

	2018 (from 5/24/18)	*2019 (1/1/19 to 12/20/19)*
Total number of research requests	10	37
Number of research requests approved	10	28
Number of requests under review with clarifications requested	0	3
Number of requests pending for review	0	6

Table 5.2 Request Approved based on Research Topic Areas by the Directorate of Detention and Crisis Management

Research topics	*2018 (from 5/24/18)*	*2019 (1/1/19 to 12/20/19)*
Education of convicted	2	11
Health issues	3	2
Mental health	1	1
Addiction and criminality	0	4
Conviction and parentship	2	2
Human Rights and conviction	0	5
Case study/conditions of imprisonment	2	3
Total	10	28

In Box 5.1, we present a practical guide on questions to ask and suggested solutions for research challenges in Greece based on the internal circular (dated January 21, 2018, bearing reference #8201) on the procedures of getting access and permission for all agencies and organizations supervised by the *General Secretary for Criminal Justice Policy* in the *Ministry of Justice*. Individuals who are involved with the criminal justice system are considered protected, and the individuals (as well as data about them) are not easily accessible to researchers without the official permission of the *National Regulation Authority on the Protection of Personal Data*. The aims of this document are: (i) to clarify the procedures of applying for research in the Greek Ministry of Justice; (ii) to ensure that there is a consistent way of dealing with all applications for getting access and permission for conducting scientific research in all agencies and services supervised by the *Ministry of Justice*; and (iii) for the promotion and regulation of scientific research aligned with the ethical guidelines on the protection of personal data in alignment with new national legislation and European binding agreements to safeguard the subjects of the research. It is fair to assume that all criminal justice agencies will be subject to similar guidelines, and therefore this guide may be useful for anyone interested in criminal justice research in Greece. This guide is framed in a question and answer format for clarity and ease of use.

WHO CAN APPLY TO THE *MINISTRY OF JUSTICE* TO CONDUCT RESEARCH?

Independent researchers or team of researchers who write essays/thesis (in undergraduate, post-graduate, doctoral, post-doctoral level) and/or implement projects have the right to apply. However, for the team of researchers who implement projects, the head/director of the research team must hold a PhD title.

Comment/suggestions:

- There appears to be a lack of clarity in the case of project implementation. It is not clarified what projects need to be supervised by a PhD holder. For example, it is not clear whether this directive is just for academic research within Greece or also applies to international and EU funded research.
- This precondition reflects an academic strictness on conducting research and seems to be favorable toward PhD holders, while disadvantaging potential researchers who are experienced in the field who may not hold a PhD degree.
- The document does not provide any pathways for foreign researchers to apply for permission to conduct research.
- Given the lack of clarity, it seems beneficial for a foreign researcher(s) to partner with a Greek scholar holding a PhD degree, preferably one who is employed within an institution of higher education and can navigate the internal ethics procedures. Having a Greek academic as a research partner also helps in mitigating language barriers.

Where should the research application be submitted?

The Head of the Department in the *General Secretary of Criminal Justice Policy* has the responsibility to receive the application for research. The department examines the claim and sends the justified response on the approval or rejection of the claim to the *Central Directorate of the Ministry* with notification to the researcher(s). Then, the *Central Directorate of the Ministry* examines if special permission from the *National Authority on the Protection of the Personal Data* is required. If this special permission is required, the *National Authority for the Protection of Personal Data* either agrees and gives permission to the *Ministry of Justice* to elaborate the personal data and to the researcher for permission to create a file on that data or rejects the claim. The *Central Directorate of the Ministry of Justice* makes the final decision of the claim (approval /rejection).

Comment/suggestions:

The whole procedure seems bureaucratic, complicated, and problematic. The main problems are:

- There are two or more agencies/departments/directorates in the ministry who deal with the research application. One agency receives the application and another decides. In between the two agencies, another authority out of the *Ministry of Justice* – which is an independent regulation authority – intervenes having a crucial role in the final decision of the claim. Thus, there are no clear guidelines on the responsibilities not only in terms of agencies and organizations but also internally within the same ministry.
- Accordingly, the researcher is not aware of the proper agency to submit the claim/application for research and in which cases/fields of research/ methodologies the permission of the National Regulation Authority on the Protection of Personal Data is needed.

In which type of application is the approval of the *Authority for the Protection of Personal Data* needed?

The official permission of the *Authority for the Protection of Personal Data* is required in the following cases:

- If the application asks for access to the file(s) of individuals who are kept in any prison institution (medical institutions for prisoners are also included).
- If the application asks for permission to conduct interviews with prisoners, convicted, or juveniles who are supervised by Probation Officers.

Comment/suggestions:

- For applications related to statistical data held by the *Ministry of Justice*, official approval by the *Authority for the Protection of Personal Data* is not needed.

What are the documents to be submitted?

A number of documents need to be submitted. Minimally, they include:

- The application with a document describing the topic, the type and the methodology of the research, the timetable, the expected results, and the protocols to be used.

- Certification of the Research Manager or the Research Supervisor of the members of the research team (the names and expertise of the research team) and the framework of the research as well.
- A personal written legal statement of the researcher and/or the head of the research team to keeping the ethical standards on the protection of the sensitive personal data, the anonymity of the subjects, and the non-disclosure of any personal data in third parties. This statement should include an undertaking to send a copy of the research results to the responsible department of the *Ministry of Justice*.

What about consent forms?

A clear, written consent form is needed for the participation of juveniles (over the age of 18) and adults in the research.

What about research that involves children?

Applications for interviews with children (up to 18 years old) are not accepted in general.

What about research that involves professionals and staff of the agencies in the *Ministry of Justice*?

Interviews with the professionals take place within the available working time and without interrupting the daily tasks and the effective function of the agency.

Domestic violence research in Greece

Having discussed the general framework of criminal justice research in Greece and issues related to ethics and gaining permission in the previous sections, we now focus on domestic violence research in Greece, highlighting legislative frameworks, national research priorities, and existing data sources related to domestic violence.

Overview

Domestic violence (DV) in Greece has been researched for the past three decades. National data indicate that there are no substantial differences in the prevalence and frequency of the phenomenon compared with other EU countries (European Union Agency for Fundamental Rights 2014). Women and children are the most vulnerable groups for domestic violence victimization, and the risk of victimization increases in migrant, refugee, and asylum seeker communities. The social recognition of the problem came up rather late in Greece despite recommendations by international organizations to raise awareness and promote research on the topic (Artinopoulou, 2006, Chatzifotiou, 2005). This outcry of early feminist activists and scholars, coupled with the pressure to conform to European Union agreements, led to the passing of the Greek Domestic Violence Law in 2006 (Law 3500/2006).[5] This law was further strengthened by LAW 4356/2015[6] to include same-sex couples and Law 4531/2018[7] to bring it in line with the *Ratification of the Council of Europe Convention on the Prevention and Combating of Violence Against Women and Domestic Violence* more commonly known as the *Istanbul Convention* of the Council of Europe.[8]

These laws regulate several issues related to domestic violence including marital rape, dating violence, and the prohibition of children's corporal punishment. Further, they recognize the vulnerable situation of pregnant women, children, and persons with special needs, either as victims or as witnesses of violence. The laws provide for civil consequences derived from criminal law provisions. Primarily, the law recognizes that violence is evidence of the breakdown of a marriage breakdown and has negative consequences for children and juveniles. Law 3500/2006 foresees the need for social and psychological support services for both victims and offenders. To this effect, it includes an innovative provision called "penal mediation" or "victim-offender mediation" in domestic violence cases. Law 3500/2006 came into full force in 2007 and was the result of the harmonization of Greek legislation with EU directives on the standing of victims in criminal proceedings (Council Framework Decision 2001/220/JHA). Within this law, penal mediation is foreseen only for misdemeanors, either before or after prosecution. Artinopoulou (2010) argues that the regulation of penal mediation in the Hellenic legal tradition is seen as an innovation and a step toward negating the traditional punitive system.

Ranjan (2019) says that the penal mediation clause is theoretically advanced and has the potential to advance the field of domestic violence internationally. However, she urges for its provisions to be clarified and implemented uniformly across Greece with adequate training for prosecutors, police, and victim service agencies. Ranjan (2019) further advocates for the use of concerted national data collection efforts to measure the effectiveness of penal mediation in Greece, providing a set of recommendations for both purposes, which include the creation of a national working group to review penal mediation in Greece. She suggests the formation of two sub-groups under the direction of the ministry: (i) a legal subgroup to review legal frameworks and clarify them; and (ii) a research subgroup to collect data and measure the success of the program in reducing reoffending. She suggests that the work of these sub-groups should inform each other and should later work with the ministry to develop common policies, protocols, guidelines, and training so that the penal mediation program can be uniformly implemented across Greece (Ranjan, 2019).

The institutional landscape of DV data in Greece

National data on DV in Greece can be obtained from different sources. Administrative and criminal data sources are collected by the police, public prosecutors, courts of the first instance (criminal and civil courts), healthcare services, social service agencies, etc. Administrative data and crime statistics are usually gathered on a regular basis and are mostly comparable over time, even though the data presented might not fully reflect the real incidence of women affected, as only registered/official numbers are presented (Tsiganou, 2016). The second relevant source of data are population-based surveys: population-based household surveys are considered the most reliable method for obtaining information on DV and for measuring the extent of violence in the general population. These surveys can be of two types: (i) large-scale surveys related to broader issues (such as poverty, crime, or reproductive health), which include special modules on DV perpetration and victimization; and (ii) dedicated surveys, which gather detailed information on specific aspects of DV, such as on causes of violence, circumstances, and consequences of violence and information on perpetrators. These surveys attempt to collect information that cannot be obtained from administrative or criminal data sources. Such large-scale surveys are typically conducted by high-level institutions or governmental bodies like ministries or national statistical institutes. Sometimes, these surveys can be initiated by independent agencies or NGOs. The third source of DV data is from non-governmental organizations, such as shelters, support services (such as lawyers' associations, legal aid services, and advocacy organizations), and NGO umbrella organizations that maintain records of incidents they are involved with. Their records can provide qualitative information as well as data on the prevalence and incidence of DV, such as the number and nationality of women living in shelters or requiring support.

The political structure for DV research in Greece

Permission from the authorities is needed depending on the aims, objectives, and research methodology. If the target group is women victims of DV hosted in the support services of the *General Secretary for Gender Equality*, then the claim/request for the research should be submitted to the Head of the Secretary. Until July 2019 and before the national elections and the political change in Greece, the *General Secretary for Gender Equality* was placed in and supervised by the *Ministry of Home Affairs*. After the political and institutional changes (July 2019), the *General Secretary for Gender Equality* moved to the *Ministry of Labour and Social Affairs* and was renamed as *General Secretary of Family Policy and Gender Equality*. Consequently, policy priorities and the individuals at the top of the hierarchy have changed. The researchers have to be well informed on the institutional changes and the persons in the hierarchy in order to find out the proper sources for submitting the research application.

The other target groups for DV research within the Greek criminal justice system have typically focused either on the offenders who are convicted for DV related crimes (homicides included) or the prosecutors and judges who work on DV crimes in the country. Access in the criminal justice system is as detailed above in the section titled *Getting access for research in the Greek criminal justice system*. Regardless of where one is seeking to conduct research, details on the aims and objectives of the research and the methodology are needed with the application. Direct access to the victims of domestic violence themselves is usually not approved for reasons of safety and the victim's protection, especially if the victims are hosted in shelters and counseling centers of the General Secretary. While we do not have official data about the number of research requests received, research access to staff at these organizations and indirect information from the professionals have generally been approved in the past as indicated by published research by the authors of this paper as well as others (Artinopoulou, Mamai, & Papkitsou, 2015; Petropoulos, Fotou, Ranjan, Chatzifotiou, & Dimadi, 2016; Pitsela, & Theofili, 2013; Ranjan, 2019; Wasileski, 2017).

Conclusion

Sotiropoulos (1995) argues that bureaucracy as a state structure has both a coercive and a service function and both functions need to be fulfilled under certain legal and constitutional constraints, which may vary by time and place. The theoretical legitimacy and administration of the criminal justice system include hierarchy, formality, organization, and bureaucracy, as described by Sotiropoulos (1995). The current criminal justice systems in Greece and many other countries of the world are still traditional, monolithic (Artinopoulou, 2010), rigid, old-fashioned. and bureaucratic (Dias & Vaughn, 2006). The fear of crime, insecurity, and lack of trust in institutions have all increased in Greece during the years of the financial and social crisis (Lazarides, 2016; Cheliotis & Xenakis, 2011), and therefore, new political responses are needed. It is essential for the criminal justice systems to shift from the traditional Weberian structural and mechanistic perspective of bureaucracy to an updated, efficient, and flexible model that is more open to citizens and allows for research and the generation of evidence-based policies that advance the justice system and democratic principles.

The guidelines for submitting an application for criminal justice research are vague and unclear. Specific forms for the application and documentation needed for the application are not to be found on the websites of various ministries. These are further complicated by the constant change in the Greek political structure in recent years. For example, after the recent elections in 2019, there were significant political changes in the Greek government. Many responsibilities shifted from the *Ministry of Justice* to the *Ministry of Citizen Protection* (by Presidential Decree 81/2019). The authority for detention centers, criminal justice policy, reentry, rehabilitation, and social inclusion policies and departments has moved to the *Ministry of Citizen Protection*. The *Central*

Scientific Board for Prisons (the advisory body for approving applications for academic research) has also moved to the *Ministry of Citizen Protection*. The current social context for doing research in Greece is additionally challenging because of migrant and refugee issues, the protection of victims' rights in the criminal justice system, and the need for effective criminal justice policy.

Recommendations to the government

We suggest an integrated guide on data collection and research in the Greek criminal justice system describing the detailed procedures for submitting the claim/request, steps of approval, and providing the templates for the documentation of the request. This would be both useful and practical. Only in a few countries are there published guidelines for researchers in the ministries of justice. For example, the UK Ministry of Justice has a certain procedure for conducting research and distinguishes three fields of research: prison research, court research, and other justice-related research.[9] In Australia, not only the procedures and the templates are published, and the guidelines, but also a code of conduct for researchers has to be signed by the researchers after the approval and before commencing their research.[10] Further, for domestic violence research, there is no readily available information. We strongly recommend publishing this information on the website of the *General Secretary for Family Policy and Gender Equality*. A step-by-step guide for the researchers, procedures of submitting the research request, and ethical guidelines for the safety of the victims will help researchers plan their activities and advance the field of domestic violence research in Greece.

Recommendations for criminal justice-related organizations

Academic societies (such as the Greek Society of Criminology), departments within IHE, and criminal justice research institutions need to partner together for the advancement of the discipline of criminology and practice of criminal justice in Greece. Not just for operational reasons, but also for strengthening criminological research in Greece and encouraging evidence-based policies a collaborative approach is necessary. The code of ethics needs to be developed and implemented by academic societies at the earliest. Using that code as a framework, the ethics and logistics of criminal justice research in Greece need to be put on the agenda of higher institutions and research centers for dialog and discussion. These discussions should include balancing the national and EU legislative frameworks with the need for data to drive evidence-based policy. These discussions need to be specific to the safety of researchers and subjects in criminal justice settings. Once these guidelines and codes are developed, collaborative national training programs need to be developed and training opportunities need to be made available for criminal justice researchers. These institutional changes will need to reflect the political transition in criminal justice and the need for the system's efficiency.

Final words

Criminal justice research in Greece is getting increasingly complicated and difficult. Therefore, evidence-based policies that are sorely needed to improve the criminal justice system may become increasingly difficult and lack a research-oriented focus in the near future if measures are not taken to rectify the situation. At the macro-level, it appears that institutional and legal changes in the government, bureaucracy, and lack of guidelines for the researchers and of procedures to be followed for getting access to the Greek criminal justice system are major challenges for conducting criminological research in Greece. At the micro-level, the pathway of finding the appropriate contact person in respective agencies to submit the research application is also complicated. However, these issues are not unique to Greece; these issues are common across the world in both developing and developed countries. Therefore, this chapter aims to provide a clearer picture than ever before about the challenges of navigating the system for criminal justice and domestic violence research in Greece.

Reflecting on the suggestions offered in this chapter from an insider–outsider perspective, it is quite remarkable to note that the experiences of the local researcher (Artinopulou) and the foreign researcher (Ranjan) are well-aligned. We believe that this is mainly because of their common expertise in gender-based violence. In writing this chapter, both authors had similar viewpoints on the needs of the victims and the prevention of secondary victimization by the criminal justice system. The foreign researcher (Ranjan) did not speak Greek and often utilized the help of colleagues as interpreters. While she encountered some red tape in navigating the Greek systems for her ongoing research, her own experiences with similar bureaucratic processes in India mitigated any potential frustrations. Despite differing methodologies used in their research projects and differences in their own educational training and cultural backgrounds, a victim-centered perspective was essential to both researchers in guiding their respective research projects.

Notes

1 https://www.kodiko.gr/nomologia/document_navigation/345491
2 https://www.asc41.com/ASC_Official_Docs/ASC_Code_of_Ethics.pdf
3 https://www.britsoccrim.org/ethics/
4 https://anzsoc.org/about/ethics/
5 https://www.kodiko.gr/nomologia/document_navigation/154457
6 https://www.kodiko.gr/nomologia/document_navigation/140974
7 https://www.kodiko.gr/nomologia/document_navigation/354118
8 https://www.coe.int/en/web/istanbul-convention/home?

9 https://www.gov.uk/government/organisations/ministry-of-justice/about/research#apply-to-conduct-research (accessed September 12, 2019).
10 https://department.justice.wa.gov.au/S/students_researchers.aspx (accessed September 12, 2019).

References

Artinopoulou, V. (2006). *Women's Abuse Within the Family*. Nomiki Bibliothiki, Athens, Greece (in Greek).

Artinopoulou, V. (2010). *Restorative Justice. The Challenge of the Current Criminal Justice Systems*. Nomiki Bibliothiki, Athens, Greece (in Greek).

Artinopoulou, V., Mamai, A. & Papkitsou, V. (2015). *Restorative Justice in Cases of Domestic Violence – Country Report Greece*. European Public Law Organization, Greece. Retrieved September 17, 2019, from https://www.verwey_jonker.nl/doc/2015/7388_Restorative_Justice_Compilation_countryreports_addendumCR2.pdf

Chatzifotiou, S. (2005). Family violence in Greece and the police response. In Malsch, M. & Smeenk, W. (Eds.), *Family Violence and Policing in Europe: Learning from Research, Policy and Practice in European Countries*. Ashgate, Aldershot, England.

Cheliotis, L. & Xenakis, S. (2011). Crime, fear of crime and punitiveness in contemporary Greece. In Cheliotis, L. & Xenakis, S. (Eds.), *Crime and Punishment in Contemporary Greece: International Comparative Perspectives*, pp. 1–43. Peter Lang, Bern.

Dias, C. F. & Vaughn, M. S. (2006). Bureaucracy, managerial disorganization, and administrative breakdown in criminal justice agencies. *Journal of Criminal Justice*, *34*, 543–555.

Edens, J. F., Epstein, M., Stiles, P. G. & Poythress Jr, N. G. (2011). Voluntary consent in correctional settings: Do offenders feel coerced to participate in research? *Behavioral Sciences & the Law*, *29*(6), 771–795.

European Commission. (2017). *The 2017 EU Justice Scoreboard*. Publications Office of the European Union, Luxembourg. Retrieved September 17, 2019, from https://ec.europa.eu/info/sites/info/files/justice_scoreboard_2017_en.pdf

European Union Agency for Fundamental Rights. (2014). *Violence against Women: An EU- Wide Survey*. Main results, Publications Office of the European Union. Retrieved September 17, 2019, from https://fra.europa.eu/sites/default/files/fra_uploads/fra-2014-vaw-survey-main-results-apr14_en.pdf

Frohock, F., Faden, R. & Beauchamp, T.. (1988). A History and Theory of Informed Consent. *The American Political Science Review*, *82* (1), 271–273.

Gallagher, B., Berman, A. H., Bieganski, J., Jones, A. D., Foca, L., Raikes, B. & Ullman, S. (2016). National human research ethics: A preliminary comparative case study of Germany, Great Britain, Romania, and Sweden. *Ethics & Behavior*, *26*(7), 586–606.

Lazarides, G. (Ed.). (2016). *Security, Insecurity and Migration in Europe*. Routledge, Farnham.

Petropoulos, N., Fotou, E., Ranjan, S., Chatzifotiou, S. & Dimadi, E. (2016). Domestic violence offenders in Greece. *Policing: A Journal of Policy and Practice*, *10*(4), 416–431.

Pitsela, A. & Theofili, C. (2013). Domestic violence and mediation in Greece: Findings from the implementation of the restorative procedure. *Internet Journal of Restorative Justice*, 1–38.

Ranjan, S. (2019). Domestic violence legislation in Greece: Analysis of penal mediation. *Women & Criminal Justice*, *30*(1), 1–27.

Rass-Masson, N. & Rouas, V. (2017). *Effective Access to Justice*. European Parliament Policy Department for Citizens' Rights and Constitutional Affairs, Belgium. Retrieved

September 17, 2019, from https://www.europarl.europa.eu/RegData/etudes/STUD/2017/596818/IPOL_STU(2017)596818_EN.pdf

Sakellaropoulou, K. N., Pikranos, M. N., Symeonidis, I., Androulakis, V. P., Nicolaides, T., Tsogas, L. & Alikakos, P. (2019). *Justice in Greece: Suggestions for a Modern Judicial System*. diaNEOsis, Athens. https://www.dianeosis.org/

Sotiropoulos, D. A. (1995). The remains of authoritarianism: Bureaucracy and civil society in post-authoritarian Greece. *Cahiers d'Etudes sur la Méditerranée Orientale et le monde Turco-Iranien, 20*. Retrieved September 17, 2019, from http://journals.openedition.org/cemoti/1674

Spinelli, C. & Kranidioti, M. (2009). Code of ethics for the Greek criminologists: Priority for the 21st century. In Maria Kranidioti (ed.) *Criminology and European Crime Policy. Essays in Honour of Aglaia Tsitsoura*, pp. 549–589. Sakkoulas Publications, Greece.

Tavares, P., and Wodon, Q. (2017). Global and regional trends in women's legal protection against domestic violence and sexual harassment. *Ending Violence against Women Notes Series*. Washington, DC: World Bank. Retrieved September 17, 2019, from http://pubdocs.worldbank.org/en/140781519943384134/EndingViolenceAgainstWomenandGirlsGBVLawsFeb2018.pdf

Tsiganou, I. (2016). Statistical surveying of crime in current Greece. *The Art of Crime*, November 2016. Retrieved September 17, 2019, from https://theartofcrime.gr/η-στατιστική-αποτύπωση-του-εγκληματι/

United Nations Office of Drugs and Crime. (2019). *Global Study on Homicide 2019 Gender-Related Killing of Women and Girls*. Retrieved September 17, 2019, from https://www.unodc.org/documents/data-and-analysis/gsh/Booklet_5.pdf

Wasileski, G. (2017). Prosecutors and use of restorative justice in courts: Greek case. *Journal of Interpersonal Violence, 32*(13), 1943–1966.

World Bank. (2016). *Doing Business 2016: Measuring Regulatory Quality and Efficiency*. Washington, DC: World Bank. doi: 10.1596/978-1-4648-0667-4. License: Creative Commons Attribution CC BY 3.0 IGO. Retrieved September 17, 2019, from http://documents.worldbank.org/curated/en/240331468197990497/pdf/100884-PUB-Revised-PUBLIC.pdf

World Bank Group. (2018). *Women, Business and the Law 2018*. Washington, DC: World Bank. License: Creative Commons Attribution CC BY 3.0 IGO.

World Health Organization. (2013). *Global and Regional Estimates of Violence Against Women: Prevalence and Health Effects of Intimate Partner Violence and Non-Partner Sexual Violence*. World Health Organization. Retrieved September 17, 2019, from https://apps.who.int/iris/handle/10665/85239

Chapter 6

Co-opting voice and cultivating fantasy

Contextualizing and critiquing the *A Gay Girl in Damascus* hoax blog

Gordon Alley-Young

Introduction

> The hoax not just expresses a fantasy but also records a fantasy sold, and most importantly bought, even by hoaxer herself, as true. It's not just a wish, but a cure for that wish – a curse – it's facepaint you wear, if only for a while.
>
> (Young, 2017, p. 146)

Fanon argues, "The European faced with the [veiled] Algerian woman wants to see" (1967b, p. 44). Westerners' desire to lift the veil resulted in public veil bans (e.g., France, Belgium, and The Netherlands) that are said to help establish individual freedom. Saïd (1979, p. 207) cites Western-colonial depictions of Eastern women as "creatures of a male power-fantasy" with "unlimited sensuality." Abu-Lughod (2002) frames early Western feminists' relationships with Muslim women as akin to missionaries from the 1800s. This imagined, exotic, vulnerable, veiled, but available Eastern woman manifested in Syrian activist Amina Abdallah Arraf al Omari and her blog *A Gay Girl in Damascus* (*AGGiD*). Western media followed Amina from February to June 2011, when she was revealed to be American graduate student Tom McMaster.

AGGiD demonstrates how journalists embraced Amina through a Western lens that perceives Eastern women as exotic others to be desired and possessed, if only in the imagination. Syria's dictatorial rule and civil war helped the hoax by limiting safe access to the country and necessitating that activists and others communicate anonymously via social media. *AGGiD* sounded true, it was perhaps an appropriation of real experiences, and journalists chose to believe a woman named Amina reporting harassment, violence, and oppression under the Assad regime. This critical cultural case study argues that the *AGGiD* was accepted as true because it fitted mainstream Western journalism's perceptions of Muslims/the Middle East and also LGBTQ+ people, it allowed journalists to safely report on war-torn Syria, and it satisfied news audiences' increasing appetite for first-person perspectives. This case study will provide historical context on cultural representations and also on journalistic hoaxes in order to address how *AGGiD* exploited blind spots in Western media's perception of Muslim/LGBTQ+ subjects and how *AGGiD's* creator likely co-opted the voices/stories of actual Middle Eastern and North African (MENA) women. This case study will also address how journalist safety and cultivating the immediacy/first-person perspectives of new and digital media led the news media to accept and promote *AGGiD*. This case study focuses on mistakes made by Western media in reporting on the *AGGiD*/Amina phenomenon and is not meant to be a wholesale condemnation of the media. In other words, because the media used Amina to speak for all Syrian/Muslim/MENA women, it is important to note that this case study represents one individual's critique of the media's handling of one news story and is by no means the only perspective on this matter.

Literature review

Amina and *AGGiD* occurred in a media context that has never adequately represented the diversity of modern Muslim womanhood. Al-Mahadin (2011) identifies a dichotomy where Arab media stereotype Muslimahs (Muslim women) as overtly sexual and Western media stereotype her as oppressed and burka-clad. Some Muslim women have thus taken to new media to self-represent (Bastani, 2000). Award-winning Iraqi blogger Riverbend (i.e., *Baghdad Burning*) provided readers with an insider's account of the impact of the Iraqi war on her professional and personal life that helped legitimize anonymous citizen journalists (McCauliff, 2011; Riverbend, 2005 & 2006). Harris (2008) also argues that anonymous online communication allows Muslim women to evade cultural prescriptions (e.g., on coed conversation). A Muslim woman might discuss changing gender roles and/or women's rights in Islam online (Piela, 2010). Western audiences are drawn to both hoaxes (i.e., *Saudi Girl*, *AGGiD*, Gulsumoy Abdujalilova) and real Muslimahs (i.e., Riverbend, Bana al-Abed, and Neda Agha-Soltan) online suggesting a Western hunger for glimpses into Middle Eastern women's lives.

Amina's blog enticed Western audiences' by describing a lesbian salon. Amina also conducted covert online romances. Both traditional and new media stayed committed to the Amina hoax. When Amina's cousin reported her as kidnapped via *AGGiD*, some continued to suppress their doubts. Audiences identified with Amina ideologically, as a Syrian American Muslim with a US education and outlook who was irreverent and also politically bold in her advocacy of Western democracy and women's and LGBTQ+ rights.

Amina is part of a long tradition of hoaxes. Smith (2009) argues the first generation of journalistic hoaxes occurred in the penny presses of the early 1800s. Robinson (1975) cites reports of Englishman Roger Dodsworth who purportedly came back in 1826 after freezing in a 1629 avalanche. The second generation of journalistic hoaxes (mid-1800s–1970s), relegated the hoax to April Fools' Day (e.g., the BBC's 1957 Swiss spaghetti tree harvest report)

(Smith, 2009). The third era brought journalists and business together on hoaxes (1970s to present; e.g., *The Guardian's* 1977 feature on fake tropical island San Serriffe included fake ads by real companies) (Smith, 2009). Journalists (e.g., BBC, CNN, and Forbes) unwittingly collaborated with fake Canadian company AptiQuant in 2011 by spreading news of a phony study that linked internet browser choice to intelligence (Lowe, 2012). April Fools' type hoaxes differ from those seeking illegitimate gain (e.g., fame-seekers, forgers, plagiarists, history deniers, criminals who scapegoat fake perpetrators) (Lichtenstein, 2018; Smith, 2009). Journalists sharing the AptiQuant hoax on social media pointed to disclaimers on their accounts (i.e., distinguishing their vetted journalism from content shared on social media but not vetted) but critics question whether this is enough (Lowe, 2012: Wyatt, 2012). McMaster sought to launch a writing career (Bell & Flock, 2011) but his hoax potentially wasted government resources and likely desensitized the public to future LGBTQ+, women's, and political rights activists seeking support. Regardless of the type or the media platform used to promote it, hoaxes teach us that all news is socially constructed and thus should be questioned (Smith, 2009).

Academia is not immune to hoaxes. In 2018, three scholars submitted 20 hoax research articles on the invented discipline of grievance studies to a variety of journals and seven were accepted (Lichtenstein, 2018). Some attribute the acceptances to the papers being presented as the work of famous scholars and/or the rapid assembly-line nature of digital editorial processes (Lichtenstein, 2018). Previously, in 1996, physicist Alan Sokal published a fake article in the journal *Social Text* as a parody of the quality of articles published by the journal (Witkowski, 2011). In October 2007, Witkowski (2011) replicated Sokal and published an article under a pseudonym about a faked new type of psychotherapy in the popular psychology magazine *Charaktery*. Similarly, journalist and biologist Dr. John Bohannon tricked 304 fee-charging open-access (OA) journals in 2013 with a fake study about the anti-cancer benefits of a chemical extracted from lichen, and over half accepted the flawed manuscript (Al-Khatib & Teixeira da Silva, 2016). Bohannon subsequently paired with a German reporter studying the junk-science diet industry, created a flawed study promoting the weight loss benefits of high cocoa chocolate, published the study in a fee-charging OA journal in 2015, and, with a press release, Bohannon's study made the front page of German tabloid *BILD* and made headlines in the US, UK, Ireland, India, and Australia (Al-Khatib & Teixeira da Silva, 2016). Witkowski's (2011) and Bohannon's work shows how readers of health journals/magazines who believe hoaxes can face potential health risks (Al-Khatib and Teixeira da Silva, 2016).

McMaster is not the first person to lie to enhance their career. *Washington Post* journalist Janet Cooke's fake news story, "Jimmy's World," about an eight-year-old heroin addict, grabbed international headlines (Cooke, 1980). City leaders searched for Jimmy, and Cooke, an aspiring African American journalist educated at elite white prep schools, both earned and lost a Pulitzer Prize (Sager, 2016). Neglected, addicted, and ghetto-trapped Jimmy reified white society's racist stereotypes of African Americans just as Amina spoke to a Western fantasy of sexually oppressed Muslimahs. Additionally, from 2003–2005 Jamie Reynolds and Mike Brenner allegedly created Kodee Kennings, an eight-year-old daughter to soldier Dan. Kodee's sympathetic letters about Dan's service in the Iraq war were published in Southern Illinois University's student paper *The Daily Egyptian*. Kodee's creators allegedly enlisted actors to play Kodee and Dan (later said to be killed in combat), actors who reportedly thought they were acting in a hidden camera, reality-style film (Heinzmann, Casillas, & Huppke, 2005; Kapur, 2007).

Hoaxes foster public mistrust. When seven-year-old Bana al-Abed tweeted against Russia's military support of Assad, some journalists argued al-Abed was a hoax or a propaganda tool (Russia Today, 2016). After al-Abed's identity was verified (i.e., the al-Abed's family left Syria for Turkey), the media sympathetic to Russia questioned her credibility (Bartlett, 2018). Efforts to disprove/discredit al-Abed and other social activists are more likely to gain traction because of widespread journalistic hoaxes.

The issue of hoaxes aside, framing journalistic stories to focus on one single individual's story can also prove problematic. Specifically, van Krieken and Sanders (2017) note that journalism focused on individual personal narratives (i.e., narrative journalism) may overemphasize storytelling techniques and reader involvement and thus challenge journalistic objectivity and credibility. Boesman and Meijer (2018) distinguish that while all news is storytelling in a broad sense, that storytellers, who might prefer being called a reporter, narrator, or documentary maker, approach subjects/stories with open attitudes and listening ears and thus differently from journalists, who might take a more critical stance and approach subjects/stories with a hypothesis they are seeking to confirm. Yet while media scholars might recognize the difference, the public might not see this distinction.

The popularity of digital media means that journalism increasingly frames news stories via an individual's lived experiences and increasingly highlights citizen journalism. Baresch, Hsu, and Reese (2012) argue that in the digital era there is a shortened editorial process and many new texts demanding attention (i.e., often by citizen journalists outside of newsrooms). Yet Chadha and Steiner (2015) argue that citizen journalism is often characterized by extreme, unsubstantiated assessments and unusual one-time cases (e.g., disasters). Conversely, Cunningham (2003) argues that the problem is not journalist's personally investing in news stories, for instance, Ron Martz's personal Iraq war diary for NPR, for Cunningham argues that the alternative, complete objectivity, makes us "passive recipients of news, rather than aggressive analyzers and explainers of it" and prevents journalists from achieving deeper understandings of what is true and false in the stories that they report.

Methodology

This case study uses Scholes's (1985) textual power method. This method is suited to analyzing *AGGiD*/Amina as Scholes is an English literature scholar interested in critically reading texts in context. Scholes (1985) argues that examining the codes a text is built from allows us to expose and criticize the power structures of that text. This analysis will draw on a variety of texts (i.e., family history, blogs, journalism, viral videos, documentaries, and Middle Eastern and North African [MENA] scholarship) and this fits with how Scholes (1998) defines a text as a site of meaning (i.e., oral, imprinted, electronic) created through an interweaving of cultural codes. Textual power also requires the tasks of interpreting and criticizing the text.

Interpretation considers what the choice of certain cultural codes and the absence of other codes means in terms of social power dynamics and the meanings within texts (Scholes, 1985). This chapter argues that *AGGiD* was convincing because McMaster drew source material from other lives/texts. Scholes (1985) calls these connections intertextuality, meaning how texts speak to each other based on similar meanings/themes. For example, why does Amina describe beauty culture being a refuge for feminists and LGBTQ+ people? Similar themes also appear in other MENA women's/popular cultural narratives. Amina's career teaching literature also resembles McMaster's mother's early life. When Amina describes the government officers who threaten her family, they resemble tropes presented as part of popular representations of MENA. Interpretation examines symbols, narratives, tropes, or genre conventions as choices that reflect one's beliefs about who does and who does not exercise power and privilege in society.

Criticism then challenges these meanings and power structures from a critical perspective (Scholes, 1985). Criticism, in this particular case study of the *AGGiD* phenomenon, will use postcolonial, orientalist, and feminist scholarship to challenge *AGGiD's* problematic and co-opted representations of the MENA region and its people. Criticism will also consider how knowledge generation can safely, ethically, and truthfully operate in the context of a diverse digital media society that blurs the lines between media audiences, consumers, and producers.

Findings

Qualitative analysis included multiple types of texts including the now-deleted *AGGiD* blog posts (i.e., screen captures, archived posts, media quotes/paraphrases), comparable blogs, examples from those living and working in the MENA region, media coverage of Amina/Tom McMaster and *AGGiD*, and critical orientalist, postcolonial, and media/journalism scholarship. The analysis focused on discovering the cultural codes and socio-cultural influences that allowed Amina/*AGGiD* to develop a following. The analysis sought to expose the problematic ideologies and power structures underlying the *AGGiD* phenomenon. The analysis will also examine contextual factors that potentially contributed to the initial success of *AGGiD*/Amina with the goal of achieving greater veracity and more balanced cultural representations in the future.

A qualitative analysis of this case study yielded three sites of meaning where meanings coalesced. The first site of meaning examines how Tom McMaster, aided by aspects of media and society, was able to sell *a Western fantasy of a lesbian Muslimah activist.* This site of meaning is not meant to excuse McMaster's lying, but as Meyer (2010) argues, lying is a cooperative act (i.e., the hoax worked because the media/society accepted the lie). The second site of meaning argues that McMaster actively participated in *co-opting MENA voices/identities* and one such voice/identity might be Neda Agha-Soltan. Critics dispute whether Agha-Soltan's is an activist but foregrounding her and others directly affected by the events of the MENA region speaks to the deficit of McMaster's co-opted perspective. The final site of meaning considers issues of *truth, ethics, and the rise of the citizen journalist* raised by *AGGiD.* This site of meaning considers issues, especially those related to power and privilege that complicated and delayed the discovery of this hoax with an eye to foreseeing similar complicating factors in the future. These sites of meaning are not exhaustive and are shaped by both the researcher's perspective, the lenses provided by Scholes' (1985; 1998) textual power method, and the critical scholarship brought to bear in the implementation of this method.

A Western fantasy of a lesbian Muslimah activist

AGGiD reflects the Western desire to symbolically possess the East through participation in the lives and the events of the region. Amina described growing up in rural Virginia among Mennonites and nature on her blog (Bell & Flock, 2011). Women have stereotypically been associated with nature both positively, as a life force, and negatively, as the lesser counterpart to man (i.e., culture) (Ortner, 1972). Amina's early life contrasts with her later life as an educated Damascene urbanite seeking independence from patriarchal domination. The feminist ideologies/agendas that McMaster and other males-posing-as-females hoax bloggers attribute to their female alter-egos would be an interesting direction for future study.

Amina blogged about a Damascus hair salon populated by lesbians where she reported finding camaraderie (Marsh, 2011). Amina seemingly reflected a third-wave feminist agency for beauty beyond the male gaze. Cahill (2003) argues that the practice of beauty for the delight and pleasure of women alone (i.e., excluding the male spectator), can foster feminist empowerment. Yet Amina intertwines the orientalist fantasy and the heterosexual fantasy of lesbians because the salon is where an observant Muslimah can let down her veil and headscarf, for a Western audience that Fanon (1967b, p. 44) argues, "wants to see." Abdi and Calafell (2017, p. 366), discussing two Muslim women banding together in the film *A Girl Walks Home Alone at Night*, argue, "The shared intimacy of Otherness in a world in which [Muslim] women's bodies are commodities that they must continue to fight for control over, is significant as is the lack of sex in favor of Other or queer intimacies." McMaster cultivates a queer intimacy in his salon of queer Damascenes who preen, not for the patriarchy, but seemingly for each other's pleasure. Yet it was McMaster, and readers like him, who delighted in the lesbian salon imagery. The lesbianism that McMaster performs online as hoax personas is perhaps best defined as what Wirthlin (2009) calls the fad lesbian. This is when the heterosexual culture appropriates the lipstick lesbian fantasy often as a fleeting performative act designed for the straight male gaze so as not to threaten heterosexual identity (i.e., lacking agency and power) (Wirthlin, 2009).

Irish writer Oscar Wilde is popularly credited as saying, "Everything in the world is about sex except sex, sex is about power," and McMaster was able to wield a great deal of power. Amina had online relationships with blogger Paula Brooks (US) and Sandra Bagaria (Canada). Bagaria, who exchanged 500 emails over six months before learning that Amina's headshot was fake (i.e., allegedly taken from Londoner Jelena Lecic's Facebook page), replied when questioned by journalists, "Of course I have doubts of: Is it true? What's not true? But, again, I'm quite certain that there's really someone writing. Now the face she has, I don't know" (BBC News Middle East, 2011). Bagaria's support of Amina perhaps speaks to the strength of their online bond at one point in time.

Paula Brooks was later exposed as Bill Graber, a straight-identifying, retired military officer and construction worker who claims to advocate for LGBTQ+ equality. Graber promoted Amina and her blog while posing as lesbian blogger Paula Brooks on blog *Lez Get Real* (*LGR*); Graber was allegedly one of Amina's online romantic partners (Flock & Bell, 2011). Amina met Brooks when the former was recruited to write for *LGR* around the time of the fall of the Tunisian president (i.e., January 2011) at the beginning of the Arab Spring (Peralta, 2011). *LGR*'s editors would later publish an apology for the 135 pieces Amina published on *LGR* and for helping to start *AGGiD* (Carbonell, 2011; Mackey, 2011). *LGR*'s editors grew suspicious when all of Amina's work came from Scottish, not Syrian, computers (Mackey, 2011). However, initially, when *LGR* political editor Melanie Nathan questioned Amina's veracity, Brooks accused Nathan of being anti-Arab and Nathan subsequently resigned (Advocate, 2011).

Tom McMaster, as Amina, and Bill Graber, as Paula, were two heterosexual identified males engaged in lesbian role-playing, the way other heterosexual males might engage in a fantasy football league. Paula Brook's alleged rebuke of Melanie Nathan was an attempt to preserve a fantasy relationship, a bid to preserve the fantasy of a Syrian activist, and self-preservation, as Paula and *LGR* were also a hoax. All three goals were interrelated. The attraction of heterosexual males to spectate on lesbians and lesbian culture is well documented. Duncker (1995, p. 9) shares the fascination of a male French film crew who she observed filming a lesbian doing mundane daily routines who told her,

"We know nothing about you. You're so hidden. All we have are pornographic images." Cooper (1994) cites the example of Canadian photographer Nina Levitt who used photo exhibitions to critique how suggestive images of lesbians on book covers encouraged a heterosexist gaze and fascination with lesbians. Similarly, Stanley (2004) argued that the popular TV series *The L Word* actively sought straight males' viewership with its frank depictions of lesbian sex. Sex scholars argue that lesbian erotica attracts straight men who are aroused by visual cues that emphasize youth and downplay drama and emotional complexity (Ogas cited in Khazan, 2016). Amina was geographically distant, physically absent, and emotionally simplistic as her interactions online were text-based (i.e., not visual/auditory) and thus emotional cues and relational drama were likely minimized. As Amina's communication was text-based (i.e., email, blog), it was asynchronous allowing others to choose when to interact, thus further de-complicating her.

Eventually, Tom McMaster, a Virginia-born graduate student at the University of Edinburgh, came forward as Amina. On Sunday, June 10, 2011, one day shy of four months after starting *AGGiD*, McMaster wrote on his now-deleted blog, "While the narrative voice may have been fictional, the facts on this blog are true and not misleading as to the situation on the ground" (*AGGiD* screenshot cited in Mallinson, 2011). He continues, "I do not believe that I have harmed anyone – I feel that I have created an important voice for issues that I feel strongly about" (*AGGiD* screenshot cited in Mallinson, 2011). McMaster's mother argued, "He was raised in a family that has a warm feeling for the Middle East" (Bell & Flock, 2011).

McMaster's repeated use of "I" evokes a sense of the Western individualist economic, cultural, and discursive perspectives that historically fueled colonization of the MENA region. McMaster's multiple assertions of "I" evoke colonial discourses by which white, male Westerners attempt to dominate political/protest discourses of the East by presenting events from their perspective. Eide (2006) argues that this perspective appears in newspaper reports of Egypt's 1919 national uprising that presuppose that readers will side with the British Empire. McMaster shirks blame by purporting to have created voice when in reality he deprived others of voice. The "warm feelings" that McMaster's mother claims prompted McMaster's actions are likely to be more aptly described as paternalistic benevolence, or how imperialist nations historically made decisions for and directed the life and norms of colonized people both abroad and domestically (Black, 2007; Shresth, 2009). McMaster's "warm feelings" could also be sexual, arising from the online lesbian relationships he conducted as Amina, or duping delight, meaning the pleasure he felt initially with getting away with lying publicly (Meyer, 2010), and/or a passion for his own self-interests, as writing under an assumed identity proved more lucrative.

McMaster's last post accuses the media of superficial coverage of the MENA region and Western society of liberal Orientalism. McMaster argues, "The events are being shaped by the people living them on a daily basis. I have only tried to illuminate them for a western audience. This experience has sadly only confirmed my feelings regarding the often superficial coverage of the Middle East and the pervasiveness of new forms of liberal Orientalism" (McMaster cited in Mallinson, 2011). McMaster's criticism of Western media's liberal Orientalism is valid but the critique should be self-reflexive as McMaster reflects paternalistic benevolence in framing himself, as a white Western savior, in the best position to illuminate the Middle East and its issues, rather than the people living these issues on a daily basis.

McMaster intimated that the West was a safe haven, in contrast to the potential violence Amina faced in the Middle East. McMaster constructed this dichotomy when Amina expressed fear over having her fingernails ripped off by a faceless Syrian government brute (Sly, 2011). McMaster's fingernails detail is meant to shock and horrify Western audiences who are meant to conjure mental images of Muslim men as violent terrorists wielding instruments of torture upon Amina. Razack (2005) argues that since 9/11, Western feminists have capitalized on a discourse of Muslim men as violent as a justification for the West's "War on Terror." Similarly, critics have accused early Western feminists of being fixated on saving the non-Western woman from the non-Western man (Fanon, 1967a; Mohanram, 1999). McMaster, as Amina, canceled a meeting with a UK reporter claiming that she was followed (Addley & Hassan, 2011). Again, McMaster's fictional discourse conjures a shadowy figure, a Muslim boogeyman lurking just steps behind Amina and threatening to pounce. This critique is in no way is meant to diminish the very real, disproportionate, and gender-based violence directed at women by men worldwide.

In an April 26, 2011, *AGGiD* post titled *My Father the Hero*, McMaster reifies the Muslim boogeymen as two government officers who threaten Amina and her father with sexual violence. Amina describes one as having an "Oily smile that doesn't extend to the eyes," and another who touches Amina's breast and says, "'Maybe if you were with a real man,' he lears [sic], 'you'd stop this nonsense and lies; maybe we should show you now and let your pansy father watch so he understands how real men are'" (McMaster, 2011). Fanon (1967a) argues that attack fantasies have been historically cited by white women as a reason to mistrust Black men. Criminals have been shown to blame their own crimes on fictional bushy or shaggy-haired strangers (i.e., coded racial references), for instance, convicted child murderer Dianne Downs (Corvallis Gazette-Times, 2010; Rule, 1988).

The Syrian boogeymen McMaster describes were enough to make the US State Department inquire into Amina's kidnapping (Flock & Bell, 2011). The post *My Father the Hero* prompted an individual claiming to be Lebanese pro-democracy activist, Fouad Hamdan, past Executive Director of the Arab Human Rights Fund, to offer support to Amina in his response to the post (McMaster, 2011). News of kidnapping shifted the press from advocate to protector. Though they questioned Amina's veracity, the media opted to keep her in the public eye, perhaps hoping to protect her. The media and State

Department's actions speak to the orientalist critique of the West as only caring about the Middle East in so far as its interests/citizens are concerned, even when those citizens are no more real than the fictional bogeyman that Amina constructs.

The Amina persona was fearless, evoking what Inness (1999) identified as the tough girl persona in second/third-wave feminist popular culture texts (e.g., blogging that she would keep her nails cut short to curtail torture). When government officers accuse her, Amina describes talking back and standing her ground, "I clamp down hard on the urge to flee. If I run, I know that they will shoot. I can see weapons, the bulge of pistols and likely knives under their jackets" (McMaster, 2011). Though dramatic, this scene is merely an action TV/film trope called "stand your ground" (TV Tropes, n.d.). Fictional Amina risks nothing while Syrian activists and journalists have paid for similarly bold actions and words with their freedom/lives.

Syrian activists and journalists have reason to fear the Assad regime even as McMaster's fictional imagery draws upon popular cultural repertoires and the imaginary. Syrian blogger Kamal Sheikhou was arrested for "publishing information liable to defame the nation" before disappearing, journalist/blogger Jehad Jamal (using the pseudonym Milan) was arrested from a café, journalist Myriam Haddad spent 12 days in custody before being released, and an anonymous 28-year old woman was reported as being tortured for a week before dying near Khan Shehoun, one of an estimated 2200 Syrians killed by August 2011, the same year *AGGiD* rose to prominence (ABC News, 2011; BBC Worldwide Monitoring, 2011; Reporters Without Borders, 2011). The deaths of over 100 journalists are attributed to the first six years of the Syrian conflict; journalist kidnappings peaked in 2013 with almost one occurring per week (Dlewati, 2016). This paper lacks the space to list all of the journalists, bloggers, and activists arrested in Syria before, during, and after the Amina hoax and one can only speculate as to the role of McMaster's hoax in prompting any of these arrests, tortures, and/or disappearances. A subsequent section of findings will discuss further how media can better respond to situations like those posed by the *AGGiD* phenomena in the future. Western journalists have, subsequent to *AGGiD*, investigated the extent to which LGBTQ+ people are persecuted within Syria. Harkin (2016) interviewed LGBTQ+ Syrians, including a soldier, and they reported social attitudes toward homosexuality ranging from begrudging acquiescence of unexpressed homosexuality to reports of murders by the Islamic police.

Co-opting MENA voices/identities

McMaster manipulated the media, oversimplified human rights struggles in the MENA region, and co-opted MENA region activists' voices as his own. Creating change through social pressure becomes increasingly more difficult when society is desensitized to/or skeptical of human suffering because of hoaxes like *AGGiD*. McMaster argued publicly that Amina was creative fiction yet her story resembles that of public figure Neda Agha-Soltan who died in the streets of Tehran, Iran, in June 2009 after being shot by a sniper while present at a protest of controversial Iranian presidential election that returned Mahmoud Ahmadinejad to power. McMaster might have taken details from Agha-Soltan's life as her story was documented in a film by Abraham and Thomas (2010).

Flock and Bell (2011) demonstrate that as early as 2006 McMaster used Yahoo! Groups (2006) to connect to Amina and establish her backstory using his Virginia upbringing, his mother's life (i.e., as a former teacher in Turkey), and his wife's knowledge (i.e., a PhD scholar in Syrian economic development) as source material. McMaster's wife Britta Froelicher would later say in an interview, during which she also denied prior knowledge of Amina, "I knew he had a blog and we talked about Syrian politics all the time, but I never checked it" (Bell, 2011). McMaster also studied Arabic Studies at Emory University and traveled to Syria in 2008 (Flock & Bell, 2011). Any narrative needs probability as to sound likely to have happened, and fidelity, meaning to have a ring of truth (Fisher, 1989). Amina's story secures these qualities likely by co-opting elements of Neda Agha-Soltan's and other's lives.

Research into Neda Agha-Soltan as a media phenomenon shows that McMaster is not the only one to create a new text from Neda's life story. Immediately after Agha-Soltan's death, short videos that documented her dying went viral online where audiences juxtaposed the video images with writings, texts, original drawings, and music. Gyori (2013) argues that these competing and complimenting discourses are online media users' attempts to make sense of the life and death of the woman they call Neda. Gyori's (2013) research captures how new and digital media audiences are not passive observers, they are active participants in meaning-making.

At the height of *AGGiD's* notoriety, a fictional cousin persona used the blog to report that Amina was captured (Hassan, 2011). It is around this time that Amina's story began to unravel. A reporter's meeting with Amina was canceled for safety reasons despite Amina's prior claims to care more for the cause than for her own safety (Addley & Hassan, 2011). Amina's profile picture was then traced to an unrelated Facebook account and belonging to an unsuspecting Londoner Jelena Lecic. Amina's blog was then traced to a computer in Scotland. Supporters resolved their cognitive dissonance by reasoning that Amina's inability to meet and faked picture were meant to protect her safety. Computer experts in 2011 were advising activists, with an emphasis on Middle Eastern countries due to the Arab Spring, to use VPN's (i.e., virtual private networks) to protect themselves by masking their country of origin (Messieh, 2011). This did not quell the hoax suspicion that would quickly grow and eventually overtake McMaster.

While peaceful protestors assembled worldwide wearing Neda masks and proclaiming publicly, "We are all Neda!" Tom McMaster revived Amina, his

2006 chat group persona, with narrative details similar to Neda Agha-Soltan's or another activist's life story. That said, Semati and Brookey (2014) question the public framing of Neda as an activist and a feminist while others like Alley-Young (2014) accept how Agha-Soltan's family/friends have publicly framed her life. For similarities, consider how each narrative represents the feminist potential of beauty culture. Neda is said to have fought Iranian authorities to become the first young woman not to wear the chador in her high school and to have created distractions at university, thus allowing other young women to slip through clothing, hair, and makeup checkpoints despite infractions (Abraham & Thomas, 2010). Likewise, Amina's love of beauty culture and women led her to find a Damascus hair salon populated by lesbians, a place where she also found support and camaraderie amidst a shared love of beauty culture.

Feminism opposes beauty culture when it is an extension of the male gaze (Cahill, 2003), when it is the sole source of women's agency, or in the case of Amina, when it fuels a heterosexist fantasy. As a woman in the Islamic Republic of Iran, Neda's hair, face, and body are subject to modesty restrictions, so makeup and fashions are risky choices with potential consequences. Davis (1991) argues that beauty choices can empower women who do it to reassert control over their lives. Similarly, Delano (2000) argues that women's makeup can be a form of women's empowerment such as how it disrupts the hyper-masculinized culture adopted in World War II America. One could argue that any patriarchal society, whether a religious, secular, Muslim, Christian, Eastern, or Western, wages war against its female citizens through the restrictions it places on women's bodies. Thus, evading these restrictions by uncovering, covering, and/or taking charge of one's own body can be acts of individual choice, resistance, and empowerment.

Fanon (1967b) describes how Algerian women resistance fighters wore hijabs to hide bombs/messages and to move freely to fight their French colonial rulers. As a student of Arabic Studies at Emory University, and as the spouse of a PhD student in Syrian economic development, it is highly likely that McMaster was familiar with Neda Agha-Soltan and with Fanon's (1967b) germinal writings. Amina makes allusions to the Algerian resistance movement when she jokes that the hijab is useful for protests. Neda has to cover her hair to venture into certain public spaces and a documentary of her life speculates that defying modesty rules (e.g., letting her hair covering slip) and challenging beauty display rules (e.g., wearing makeup) on the day of the protest ultimately led to her death at the hands of a sniper (Abraham & Thomas, 2010). Thus, for both women, religious garb figures into their lived experiences of opposition.

Amina and Neda both marry, divorce, and find new love in a changing or new context. Amina's first gay kiss happens against the upheaval of 9/11 and she finds love online (i.e., Sandra Bagaria, Paula Brooks). Neda's first marriage similarly ends in divorce and she unexpectedly meets boyfriend Caspian Makan on vacation in Turkey, where she enjoyed traveling to escape Iran's restrictions on women (Abraham & Thomas, 2010). Makan has opposed Iranian government propaganda as authorities have claimed that Neda's death videos are fake and that Neda is really a foreign actress or that Neda was shot when she was believed to be the sister of a terrorist (CNN, 2009; Farber, 2009). Similarly, as Amina's story unraveled, Paula Brooks (aka Bill Graber) publicly defended Amina. Caspian Makan is an advocate for Neda's activism and memory while Sandra Bagaria initially defends Amina when her identity is questioned. Paula Brooks (i.e., Bill Graber) likely seeks pleasure and notoriety from his online lesbian role-playing (i.e., as a disabled, feminist lesbian blogger) and also self-protection, because by protecting Amina, Graber also protects his alter-ego and thus himself.

Amina and Neda's relationships with their audiences reflect what Walther (1996) calls hyperpersonal communication, wherein ideal perceptions are created, the actors highly edit their self-presentations, and others felt intensified intimacy with each woman as a result. Amina romances American blogger Paula Brooks (i.e., Bill Graber) and Canadian Sandra Bagaria online and perhaps many others. As a result, Brooks and Bagaria vouch for Amina being real even when her pictures are proven to be false. Bagaria exchanged 500 emails with Amina in just over six months (BBC News Middle East, 2011). Yet when questions are raised about Amina's Facebook picture, Bagaria initially held onto her idealized vision of Amina.

Similarly, online audiences bond very quickly and intensely with Neda after only knowing her initially through three short viral videos of her death. In the videos, Neda is shown after having been hit by the bullet, on the ground, and finally bleeding and dying. The videos frame Neda's head and upper body and a man close to her, perhaps her music teacher, urges her to not be afraid and to stay with him. Audiences feel so close to Neda via her videos and online pictures of her that they stage mass "We are all Neda!" rallies worldwide. Neda's supporters create social media tribute pages in Neda's name to recognize her contributions to activism and her life in the face of those who would challenge, erase, or forget her. People who will never know Neda face-to-face speak to her as though they are addressing a sister or best friend.

Many people post and share poet Shams-e Langaroodi's poem where he addresses her as a daughter saying, "Ah, my dear Neda the red rose of your throat blossomed swelled and engulfed in the song of its petals the face of Iran. And those who have heralded are a million nightingales circling a flower singing your name" (TransProject, 2009). On Neda tribute Facebook pages people unknown to Neda feel that they know her and repost selections of this poem along with reporting online pictures of Neda on the anniversary death much in the same way as Facebook users post memorials to friends and family. The intimacy that social media users feel with Neda relies upon her death videos and social media information. This care and concern for Neda by strangers resembles the concern for and inquiries made on behalf of Amina upon initial reports that she had been kidnapped

Further evidence that McMaster draws on Neda's life as a support text for Amina is how both women similarly describe their attendance at a protest. In one of Neda's last messages to her mother she reports, "They fired tear gas and we're inside a laboratory. We put cigarettes on but our eyes are burning so much" (Media 4 Free Iran, 2010). Amina similarly locates herself in the action writing, "Teargas was lobbed at us. I saw people vomiting from the gas as I covered my own mouth and nose and my eyes burned [...] if this becomes standard practice, a niqab is a very practical thing to wear in future" (Marsh, 2011). Amina thinks of niqabs and coverings as activist tools while Neda's relaxing of her headscarf at the election protest is argued to have led to her shooting.

Neda and Amina's stories both demonstrate invulnerability and vulnerability. The Women's Forum Against Fundamentalism in Iran (WFAFI) (2005a & b) argues that the laws of the Islamic Republic of Iran make women vulnerable and deprive them of the most basic rights from their status within a family to the wider society where they face economic discrimination to political suppression. Neda's vulnerability to the sniper's bullet arguably speaks to WFAFI's assessment. Amina, if a real Syrian woman, would also be vulnerable as a second-class citizen under the law according to Freedom House (2005). Neda is so revered in death by people who know her only through her viral videos that her family in Tehran reports feeling that this public support protects them (i.e., makes them invulnerable) (Abraham & Thomas, 2010). Neda's family also worried about the life of a documentary filmmaker telling Neda's story (Abraham & Thomas, 2010). The family conspires with this filmmaker to provide a fictitious cover story for visiting Iran. So the telling of Neda's story, like the telling of Amina's story, also includes some deception, albeit justified.

Similar to Neda's life, Amina's story initially claims invulnerability, as her family's government connections initially protect her from persecution, as detailed in blog posts like *My Father the Hero* (McMaster, 2011). However, Amina presents as vulnerable when her cousin claims Amina has been kidnapped despite her family's connections. Amina's US followers cite her dual citizenship to urge the US State Department to act (Flock & Bell, 2011). US government intervention would afford a degree of invulnerability to Amina if she were real.

Neda and Amina's stories both have fictionalized elements. The Amina persona was a complete work of fiction built from lifelike elements. The Iranian government also claims that Neda's death is a hoax, created by an actor living in Greece to incite protests (Abraham & Thomas, 2010). Yet Neda's death was real, and it devastated people who both knew her as well as those who only knew her online. Neda's actual death is mirrored by media reports that frame the uncovering of the Amina hoax as death as Swaine's (2011) headline states, "Death of a gay girl." The symbolic death of Amina speaks to the death of the faith that so many would at one time place in her and how the support of her would die and turn into skepticism. Amina's figurative death could result in more actual death as the public becomes desensitized to the real-life struggles faced by activists who struggle to find support, to be believed, or just to survive.

Truth, ethics, and the rise of the citizen journalist

The *AGGiD* blog likely attracted a largely Western and male audience as scholars have long critiqued how Western, male, English-speakers dominate the Internet. Wilson (2005) argues that there is a cyber-leisure gap that allows men more free time to pursue blogs. Skalli (2006) argues that MENA women's online activity may be limited by economic disadvantages, reduced literacy, and patriarchal censorship. Yet MENA's women bloggers have made significant inroads (e.g., Riverbend, *Weblogestan*) despite women facing more online harassment, threats, and cyber-attacks (Friedman, 2008). Nelson (2006) argues that blogs draw third-wave feminists by being interactive, political, and discussion generating. These were, arguably, characteristics of *AGGiD*. Bennett (2011) argues that *AGGiD* "highlights how journalists and readers alike can be seduced by the mirage of the 'authentic voice' online" and argues that the verification processes that eventually would expose the hoax were lacking when *AGGiD* was becoming popular (p. 188).

The traditional media's inability to report the full story of the war in Iraq safely led Riverbend to create her eponymous 2003 blog, later published as two critically praised volumes (i.e., volume one earned a Lettre Ulysses Award and was long-listed for the Samuel Johnson Prize) (Riverbend, 2005 & 2006). Shirkey (2008) reminds us that bloggers do sometimes cover newsworthy events but at the end of the day they are not journalists. This is easy to forget as the lines between the storytelling and journalism have blurred and the desire for first-person news content has grown. Shirkey (2008) cites how Bangkok blogger Gnarlykitty covered September 2006's bloodless Thai coup at a time when the traditional media was silenced. When Gnarlykitty's blog shifted to discuss clubbing and her new Hello Kitty phone, followers asked her to provide more coup information at which time she reminded them that she alone, not her followers, determined Gnarlykitty's content.

Blogging's first-person voice makes it a desirable medium in an individualistic era. Twenge and Campbell (2009) argue, "The minimal filtering of blogs lets in lots of information – lots of noise, but also some interesting signal. But this lack of filtering serves as a gateway for lots of narcissistic noise masquerading as signal" (p. 119). *AGGiD* reflects how the blog can be a gateway for narcissistic noise. McMaster both distracts from the plight of real Syrian activists (i.e., noise) while arguing that his blog helped others to better understand (i.e., narcissism).

Twenge and Campbell (2009) cite two key characteristics of narcissism, devaluing close relationships and overconfidence, that are fueled by a culture of self-admiration arguing, "This teaches it is important to see yourself as much better – bigger, stronger, more capable – than you actually are" (p. 14–15). Similarly, McMaster's apology overuses the "I" pronoun, not to claim responsibility, as "I" language should, but to advance the self. Extreme over-confidence shows when McMaster's apology claims he served to "illuminate" Middle Eastern events for Western audiences (*AGGiD* screenshot cited in Mallinson, 2011). To contextualize McMaster's comment, Jesus is oft-cited as referring to himself or being referred to as light, for instance, "I am the light of the world. Whoever follows me will never walk in darkness, but will have the light of life" (John 8:12, New International Version). Evidence of devaluing others comes in an interview with McMaster's wife who, though she claimed she was innocent of the hoax, still felt the need to apologize for him (Bell, 2011) because, despite a six-month romantic relationship with Sandra Bagaria, McMaster argued, "I do not believe that I have harmed anyone" (*AGGiD* screenshot cited in Mallinson, 2011). McMaster later said he would apologize personally to Bagaria after being queried on this point (Peralta, 2011). Yet his activities were serious enough that the University of Edinburgh required McMaster to confirm in writing that he would not engage in similar activities in the future (Doherty, 2011).

McMaster reflects how online narcissism is growing at the same time that journalism is increasingly featuring citizen journalism and first-person experiences. The correlation of these two phenomena is the perfect storm for those whose job it is to verify facts. McNeill (2018) argues that judging the truth of a post is more complicated online because it depends on who we perceive as the source (i.e., the creator, the endorser, or the sharer). If a trusted journalist from the traditional media is sharing the post, this will certainly affect our perceptions of truth. For this reason, Wyatt (2012) argues that journalists have a responsibility to let followers know the difference between them reporting news/sharing their reflections from when they have verified the information. Scholars have called social media platforms like Facebook echo chambers that surround us with like-minded thinkers (McNeill, 2018). A journalist then faced with an *AGGiD*-type phenomenon must both verify site content and also examine how the content sharing processes and platforms affect theirs and others' perceptions of truth and factuality.

The Western media actively followed *AGGiD*, and Gnarlykitty and Riverbend before that, using its content to augment their journalists who were limited by their outsider-looking-in perspectives on Syria, Thailand, and Iraq. The danger facing journalists sometimes means that relying on citizen journalism sometimes is the only safe option. In January 2011, photojournalist Lucas Dolega (France) was shot and killed in Tunisia and in February 2011 reporter Ahmed Mohamed Mahmoud (Egypt) was shot and killed in Egypt covering the Arab Spring. Cameraman Ali Hassan al-Jaber (Qatar) and blogger Mohammed Nabbous (Libya) died covering Arab Spring protests in Libya in March 2011. Photojournalists Anton Hammerl (South Africa), Timothy Hetherington

(Great Britain), and Chris Hondros (United States) were likewise killed while reporting from Libya in April 2011. Camera operator Wael Mikhael (Egypt) and blogger Mina Daniel (Egypt) were killed in October 2011 while covering Egyptian protests. In February 2011, reporter Lara Logan (South Africa – United States) was gang-raped and beaten by a mob while reporting from Cairo (Logan, 2011).

Communicating via social media is useful beyond self-affirmation or protecting one's physical safety. For marginalized groups in society, who lack access to traditional media, it can be a means to a voice and thus to social power. Thorbjørnsrud and Figenschou (2016) argue that social outsiders lack access to media and control over how the media defines them (e.g., as idealized victims) so publicity stunts and protests can be a means to access the media. For example, when France passed laws banning public veiling, the activists the NiqaBitches produced a viral video of them posing in niqabs (i.e., upper body and face veils), hot-pants, and high heels in front of French government buildings, where wearing the veil would be banned under the new law (Billal, 2010). The NiqaBitches were able to engage the traditional media in a discussion about opposition to the law and comment on French perspectives on women's bodies.

Eide argues that the media treats marginalized groups as too irresponsible to speak on issues beyond their own experiences (Eide, 2011 cited in Thorbjørnsrud & Figenschou, 2016). Western journalism, and society at large, has been criticized for claiming to speak for Muslim women (i.e., prescribing dress codes) and/or only speaking of Muslims, often men, in the context of violence and security (i.e., stories on Muslim extremists or the good Muslim who fights community extremism) (ISPU, 2018; Obama, 2009). *AGGiD* further demonstrates that the West thinks it can speak for and define Muslims.

The media has a legacy of doubting marginalized individuals who come forward to report abuse, harassment, violence, and oppression. The challenge with a blog like *AGGiD* is that it must be thoroughly vetted but not to the effect of silencing a potential survivor. For Western women reporting sexual harassment and violence, the MeToo# movement did not end their mistreatment by the media. For instance, the *New York Times* faced criticism for publishing actor Mayim Bialik's editorial in which she appeared to urge women to dress modestly in Harvey Weinstein's Hollywood to avoid unwanted sexual pressure and attention (Bialik, 2017). The picture with the editorial was not of 43-year old Bialik but her as a 15-year old.

There is no simple solution to the issues posed by media representation, but a way forward should include the diversification of our traditional and new media workforce to include more women and people of color. Pew Research (Grieco, 2018) reports that newsroom employees are less diverse today than US workers overall. Research reveals that 77 percent of reporters, editors, photographers, and videographers in the newspaper, broadcasting, and internet publishing are non-Hispanic whites and 61 percent of newsroom employees are men (Grieco, 2018). Bodinger-de Uriarte and Valgeirsson (2015) argue journalism has not changed in this regard over the last three decades. It is not enough to diversify the journalistic workforce as we must cultivate climates that embrace diversity where all journalists have the power to investigate, question, and speak out. This could have helped in the case of *AGGiD,* as one-time *LGR* political editor Melanie Nathan was accused of being anti-Arab for questioning Amina's veracity; she subsequently resigned (Advocate, 2011).

Public indignation at McMaster's hoax was immediate. He was attacked for capitalizing on the suffering of Syrians, activists, and/or bloggers. Yet the same media that attacked McMaster, from newspapers to feminist blogs, also greatly profited from their coverage of *AGGiD* content. Criticism of the media was buffered by focusing more on McMaster's deception rather than on the lack of follow through by journalists. Reporters Bell and Flock were credited with "old-fashioned detective work" when in fact they simply used a computer to check the blog's origins and check basic facts relating to Amina's story (Kristine, 2011). Bell and Flock, along with others credited with breaking this story, are notable for their commitment to journalistic integrity and their effective practice of digital media literacy skills.

Amina/*AGGiD* allows for the consideration of participants' blind spots and biases. Orientalist and heterosexist ideologies of the exotic other underlie Amina's construction and yet her popular reception suggests that her creator is not alone in his mindset. Making Amina an internet icon requires that society relax its standards for critical thought and factuality. Amina's widespread support speaks to globalized information industries that place profit over public interest. *AGGiD* underscores the increasingly blurry line between blogging and journalism as both are for-profit businesses that implicitly or explicitly advance political ideologies. Feminist blogger Crosley-Corcoran (2012) argues that profit margin is the one topic that is off-limits even for otherwise forthcoming bloggers. This is certainly true in McMaster's case as he publicly expressed his hopes to launch a fiction-writing career through Amina. Questions about the motivations, psychological, financial, and/or otherwise for pursuing a public voice through new (or traditional) media should be asked at the outset and not be questions that get asked in hindsight.

Discussion

After McMaster's outing, press coverage initially criticized and condemned him. Following this was a wave of suspicion and criticism directed at social media. Finally, only then did the press gently wag its finger at itself. Hesse (2011) writes, "Where does [McMaster's] creativity begin to bleed into conning? … Is it the moment when famous journalist strangers become emotionally invested?" McMaster's description as "conning" sits in juxtaposition to the generic, and thus un-implicated, "journalist strangers," who, in addition to going unnamed unlike the perceived perpetrator, are, by contrast, not at fault because their only mistake was becoming "emotionally invested."

In reality, increasing newspaper circulation and furthering journalistic careers, not just emotional investment, is what led journalists to seize upon and promote *AGGiD*. Kristine (2011) applauds Bell and Flock, the two *Washington Post* journalists who helped expose McMaster, for "old-fashioned detective work." The praise is deserved but by constructing the journalists as detectives, it symbolically shifts the responsibility for critical thinking and media literacy to the investigative journalist. In reality, this is the mindset we should all manifest in our engagement with the media in everyday life. Additionally, media is so seamlessly integrated into our everyday lives, relationships, and conversations with others that it is not always clear where human engagement ends and media engagement begins. Schwarz, Newman, and Leach warn that it is those places that information flows smoothly that people need to be most concerned with because it is at these places that people tend to accept information uncritically, for alternately when information is harder to process or unfamiliar that is when people engage more critically (Schwarz, Newman, & Leach cited in McNeill, 2018). This idea of information flow is particularly relevant for the *AGGiD* case because it speaks to audiences challenging themselves by engaging with diverse and marginalized subjects in ways beyond Western cultural tropes and preconceptions.

Amina and her platform, *AGGiD*, are still relevant, not for the activist narrative that we now know to be fictional, but for what it reveals about the changing face of journalism. Journalism must draw audiences who are increasingly turning to new media for first-person content on current and relevant issues. Audiences are seeking immediacy and investment between themselves and the events and people that are shaping their worlds, and as a result, the line between traditional media and new media, journalists, and audiences, as well as those between content producers and content consumers is blurring. Society wins in this equation when this blurring gives marginalized individuals access to a public voice and thus a chance to advance inclusive pro-social perspectives (e.g., Iraqi war-era blogger Riverbend's and Syrian education activist and blogger Marcell Shewaro). The cost of this diversification includes hoax blogs (e.g., *Saudi Girl*, *AGGiD*, and fake Uzbek activist Gulsumoy Abdujalilova) and the increased skepticism that such hoaxes breed that then leads audiences to be more willing to accept that factual reportage could be fake news.

Conclusion

It is interesting to note the similarity between McMaster and the media's responses to the Amina hoax. Both parties shift the blame to each other or scapegoat the public or social media. Social media did not create the journalism hoax as one of the most famous hoaxes in US journalistic history, the story of a fictional eight-year-old African American heroin addict named

Jimmy, appeared in *The Washington Post* in 1980. This was also a case where a hoax succeeded because it appealed to white Western misperceptions of a marginalized social group. That said, it is not wrong for journalists to spotlight real individuals' stories within the context of a larger social phenomenon in order to cut through public apathy and make world events intelligible and/or relatable. For instance, Demick's (2012) journalism during the Bosnian War (1992–1995) focusing on the effects of war on the lives of individual residents of Logavina Street in Sarajevo, a multicultural microcosm of the larger Bosnian society, was nominated for a Pulitzer Prize in 1995 for international reporting. The problem is when the individual narrative simplifies and/or obscures, or in the case of *AGGiD*/Amina falsifies, the larger social reality. At this time it bears repeating the caveat at the beginning of this case study, namely that this case study is but one individual's perspective on the *AGGiD*/Amina phenomenon, among others, and that criticism of the handling of this one story is not meant as an indictment of journalism/the media as a whole.

The entirety of *AGGiD*'s blog content is no longer online thus researchers searching for reporting on Amina might find that some of the media history of this case has been altered (i.e., factually revised, subsequently edited, and/or removed). Yet if accuracy is the goal then the stories should remain intact and hoaxes should be archived when possible as this will allow scholars to study and draw an understanding of such incidents more easily. Phenomena like *AGGiD* will resurface and evolve in the future ways that will make them harder to detect, so rather than trying to erase an event from public consciousness, we need to approach it like an object lesson for interrogating our capacity for critical thought and media/cultural literacy. Unfortunately for those seeking to forget about and erase Amina/*AGGiD* from public discourse, the permanence of digital information is a defining characteristic of new media. Unfortunately for those seeking to collect, compile, and study information of *AGGiD* and similar media phenomena, the idea of information permanence in a digital age does not take into account the time, tools, and resources required by scholars seeking to unlock this permanence.

References

ABC News. (2011). Syrian woman 'tortured to death'. *ABC News*. Retrieved from http://www.abc.net.au/news/2011-08-25/seven-killed2c-150-arrested-in-syria3a-activists/2854620

Abdi, S., & Callafel, B.M. (2017). Queer utopias and a (feminist) Iranian vampire: A critical analysis of resistive monstrosity in A Girl Walks Home Alone at Night. *Critical Studies in Media Communication*, *34*(4), 358–370.

Abraham, N. (Producer), & Thomas, A. (Director). (2010). *For Neda* [Motion picture]. United States: HBO Documentary Films. Retrieved from http://www.youtube.com/watch?v=F48SinuEHIk

Abu-Lughod, L. (2002). Do Muslim women really need saving? Anthropological reflections on cultural relativism and its others. *American Anthropologist, 104*(3), 783–790.

Addley, E. & Hassan, N. (2011, June 9). Middle East: Syria: Mystery surrounds lesbian blogger feared abducted [includes *AGGiD* blog screenshot – "Update on Amina"]. *The Guardian*, p. 22.

Advocate. (2011, September). Reporter imposters. *Advocate*, 1052, p. 8.

Al-Khatib, A., & Silva, J. (2016). Stings, hoaxes and irony breach the trust inherent in scientific publishing. *Publishing Research Quarterly, 32*(3), 208–219. doi: 10.1007/s12109-016-9473-4

Al-Mahadin, S. (2011). Arab feminist media studies. *Feminist Media Studies, 11*(1), 7–12.

Alley-Young, G. (2014). Whose niqab is this? Challenging, creating and communicating female Muslim identity via social media. *Journal of Media Critiques*, 2, 71–90.

Baresch, B., Hsu, S., & Reese, S. (2012). Studies in news framing. In S. Allan (Ed.), *Routledge ompanion to news and journalism studies* (pp. 637–647). New York: Routledge.

Bartlett, E. (2018, June 28). Bellingcat & Atlantic Council join to award exploited Syrian child & American mass murderer. *Russia Today*. Retrieved from https://on.rt.com/98ns

Bastani, S. (2000). Muslim women on-line. *The Arab World Geographer, 3*(1), 41.

BBC News Middle East. (2011, June 9). Syrian mystery of Amina Arraf: 'A gay girl in Damascus.' *BBC News*. Retrieved from http://www.bbc.com/news/world-middle-east-13719131

BBC Worldwide Monitoring. (2011). RSF condemns woman blogger's abduction, continuing crackdown on media. *BBC Worldwide Monitoring*. Retrieved from http://www.lexisnexis.com.kbcc.ezproxy.cuny.edu:2048/hottopics/lnacademic

Bell, M. & Flock, E. (2011, June 12). A gay girl in Damascus comes clean. *The Washington Post*. Retrieved from http://www.washingtonpost.com/lifestyle/style/a-gay-girl-in-damascus-comes-clean/2011/06/12/AGkyH0RH_story.html (31 March 2012).

Bell, M. (2011, June 13). Britta Froelicher, wife of a gay girl in Damascus, caught in her husband's hurricane. *The Washington Post*. Retrieved from http://www.washingtonpost.com/blogs/blogpost/post/britta-froelicher-wife-of-a-gay-girl-in-damascus-talks-about-being-caught-in-her-husbands-hurricane/2011/06/13/AGPJrETH_blog.html

Bennett, D. (2011). A 'gay girl in Damascus', the mirage of the 'authentic voice' - and the future of journalism. In J. Mair & R. L. Keeble (Eds.), *Mirage in the desert? Reporting the Arab Spring* (pp. 187–195). Bury, St Edmunds: Abramis Academic Publishing.

Bialik, M. (2017, October 17). Opinion: Mayim Bialik: Being a feminist in Harvey Weinstein's World. *The New York Times*. Retrieved from https://www.nytimes.com/2017/10/13/opinion/mayim-bialik-feminist-harvey-weinstein.html

Billal, M. M. (2010, October 3). *Niqabitch* [Original full video]. Retrieved from https://www.youtube.com/watch?v=5GmYRTTbN7g

Black, J. (2007). Remembrances of removal: Native resistance to allotment and the unmasking of paternal benevolence. *Southern Communication Journal, 72*(2), 185–203. doi: 10.1080/10417940701316690

Bodinger-de Uriarte, C., & Valgeirsson, G. (2015). Institutional disconnects as obstacles to diversity in journalism in the United States. *Journalism Practice, 9*(3), 399–417.

Boesman, J., & Meijer, I. C. (2018). "Don't read me the news, tell me the story": How news makers and storytellers negotiate journalism's boundaries when preparing and presenting news stories. *The Journal of the International Symposium on Online Journalism, 8*(1), 13–32.

Cahill, A. (2003). Feminist pleasure and feminine beautification. *Hypatia, 18*(4), 42–64.

Carbonell, L. S. (2011, June 10). An apology to our readers about Amina Abdallah [archived]. *Lez Get Real*. Retrieved from https://ict4peace.files.wordpress.com/2011/06/an-apology-to-our-readers-about-amina-abdallah-lez-get-real.pdf

Chadha, K., & Steiner, L. (2015). The potential and limitations of citizen journalism initiatives. *Journalism Studies, 16*(5), 706–718. doi: 10.1080/1461670X.2015.1054179

CNN. (2009). Iran says Neda's death may be tied to 'terrorist' group. *CNN World*. Retrieved from https://www.youtube.com/watch?v=1nydxbGhgv8

Cooke, J. (1980, September 28). Jimmy's world. *The Washington Post*. Retrieved from https://www.washingtonpost.com/archive/politics/1980/09/28/jimmys-world/605f237a-7330-4a69-8433-b6da4c519120/?utm_term=.ff93e23ed4d4

Cooper, E. (1994). *Homosexuality in art in the last 100 years in the West*. New York: Routledge.

Corvallis Gazette-Times. (2010, December 10). Beware myth of bushy-haired stranger. *Corvallis Gazette-Times*. Retrieved from http://www.gazettetimes.com/news/opinion/beware-myth-of-bushy-haired-stranger-dec/article_5901aa90-9405-51d4-9521-895416a52559.html

Crosley-Corcoran, G. (2012). How much do bloggers really make? *The Feminist Breeder*. Retrieved from http://thefeministbreeder.com/how-much-do-bloggers-really-make/

Cunningham, B. (2003, July/August). Re-thinking objectivity. *Columbia Journalism Review*. Retrieved from at https://archives.cjr.org/feature/rethinking_objectivity.php

Davis, K. (1991). Remaking the she-devil: A critical look at feminist approaches to beauty. *Hypatia, 6*(2) 21–43.

Delano, P. (2000). Making up for war: Sexuality and citizenship in wartime culture. *Feminist Studies, 26*, 33–68.

Demick, B. (2012). *Logavina street: Life and death in a Sarajevo neighbourhood*. New York: Spiegel & Grau.

Dlewati, H. (2016). Fewer journalist deaths in Syria – Because there aren't many left. Retrieved from https://www.newsdeeply.com/syria/articles/2016/08/31/fewer-journalist-deaths-in-syria-because-there-arent-many-left

Doherty, B. (2011, December 29). Whatever happened to Tom MacMaster, the "Gay Girl in Damascus" hoaxer? *The Electronic Intifada*. Retrieved from https://electronicintifada.net/blogs/benjamin-doherty/whatever-happened-tom-macmaster-gay-girl-damascus-hoaxer

Duncker, P. (1995). Bonne excitation, orgasme, assure. The representation of lesbianism in contemporary French pornography. *Journal of Gender Studies, 4*(1), 5–15.

Eide, E. (2006). The Empire and the Egyptians. *NORDICOM Review, 27*(2), 153–167. doi: 10.1515/nor-2017-0236

Fanon, F. (1967a). *Black skin white masks* (trans. Charles Markmann). New York: Grove Press.

Fanon, F. (1967b). *A dying colonialism* (trans. Haakon Chevalier). New York: Grove Press.

Farber, D. (2009). Neda: More than an icon. *CBS News*. Retrieved from http://www.cbsnews.com/8301-503543_162-5106343-503543.html

Fisher, W. (1989). *Human communication as narration: Toward a philosophy of reason, value and action*. Columbia, SC: University of South Carolina Press.

Flock, E. & Bell, M. (2011, June 14). Another 'lesbian' blogger is a man. *The Washington Post*, p. C1.

Freedom House. (2005). Women's rights in the Middle East and North Africa – Syria. UNHCS: The UN Refugee Agency. Retrieved from https://www.refworld.org/docid/47387b70c.html

Friedman, J. (2008). Wack attack. *Bitch Magazine: Feminist Response to Pop Culture, 39*, 44–49.

Grieco, E. (2018, November 2). Newsroom employees are less diverse than U.S. workers overall. Pew Research Center. Retrieved from https://www.pewresearch.org/fact-tank/2018/11/02/newsroom-employees-are-less-diverse-than-u-s-workers-overall/

Gyori, B. (2013). Naming Neda: Digital discourse and the rhetorics of association. *Journal of Broadcasting & Electronic Media, 57*(4), 482–503.

Harkin, J. (2016, February). We don't have rights, but we are alive: A gay soldier in Assad's army. *Harper's Magazine*. Retrieved from https://harpers.org/archive/2016/02/we-dont-have-rights-but-we-are-alive/

Harris, A. (2008). Young women, late modern politics, and the participatory possibilities of online cultures. *Journal of Youth Studies, 11*(5), 481–495.

Hassan, N. (2011, June 7). Correction appended: Middle East: Kidnapping: Armed gang abducts gay blogger. *The Guardian – Final Edition*. Retrieved from http://www.lexisnexis.com/hottopics/lnacademic

Heinzmann, D., Casillas, O., & Huppke, R. W. (2005, August 26). Gripping wartime tale was hoax. *The Seattle Times*. Retrieved from https://www.seattletimes.com/nation-world/gripping-wartime-tale-was-hoax/

Hesse, M. (2011, June 14). Online, everyone has a voice – even if it's not his own. *The Washington Post*, p. C1.

Inness, S. (1999). *Tough girls: Women warriors and wonder women in popular culture*. Philadelphia, PA: University of Pennsylvania Press.

ISPU. (2018). Covering American Muslims objectively + creatively: A guide for media professionals. Institute for Social Policy and Understanding. Retrieved from https://www.ispu.org/journalists/#security

Kapur, J. (2007, Spring). Shock and awe: The aesthetics of war and its confrontations with reality. *Jump Cut: A Review of Contemporary Media, 49*. Retrieved from https://www.ejumpcut.org/archive/jc49.2007/kapur-shockAwe/text.html

Khazan, O. (2016, March). Why straight men gaze at gay women. *The Atlantic*. Retrieved from https://www.theatlantic.com/health/archive/2016/03/straight-men-and-lesbian-porn/472521/

Kristine. (2011). Another blogging hoax revealed with old-fashioned detective work. *MamaPop*. Retrieved from http://www.mamapop.com/2011/06/another-blogging-hoax-revealed-with-old-fashioned-detective-work.html

Lichtenstein, A. C. (2018). From the editor's desk: Making it up. (2018). *American Historical Review, 123*(5), xv–xix. https://doi.org/10.1093/ahr/rhy381

Logan, L. (2011, May 1). Lara Logan breaks silence on Cairo assault. *CBS News*. Retrieved from http://www.cbsnews.com/news/lara-logan-breaks-silence-on-cairo-assault/

Lowe, H. (2012). An online hoax reminds journalists to do their duty. *Journal of Mass Media Ethics, 27*(1), 62–64. https://doi.org/10.1080/08900523.2012.644146

Mackey, R. (2011, June 13). Gay girl in Damascus blogger admits to writing fiction disguised as fact. *New York Times*. Retrieved from https://thelede.blogs.nytimes.com/2011/06/13/gay-girl-in-damascus-blogger-admits-to-writing-fiction-disguised-as-fact/

Mallinson, T. (2011, June 13). The story of a gay girl in Damascus or, a straight guy in Edinburgh [*AGGiD* blog screenshot of "Apology to Readers"]. *Daily Maverick*. Retrieved from https://www.dailymaverick.co.za/article/2011-06-13-the-story-of-a-gay-girl-in-damascus-or-a-straight-guy-in-edinburgh/

Marsh, K. (2011, May 6). Syrian revolt finds an unlikely heroine - an outspoken, half-American lesbian blogger: Amina Abdullah shoots to online prominence after father prevents her arrest. *The Guardian International*, p. 24.

McCauliff, K. L. (2011). Blogging in Baghdad: The practice of collective citizenship on the blog Baghdad Burning. *Communication Studies*, *62*(1), 58–73.

McMaster, T. (2011, April 26). My father the hero [archived]. *A Gay Girl in Damascus*. Retrieved from http://webarchive.loc.gov/all/20110428090825/http://damascusgaygirl.blogspot.com/2011/04/my-father-hero.html

McNeill, L. S. (2018). My friend posted it and that's good enough for me!: Source perception in online information sharing. *Journal of American Folklore*, *131*(522), 493–499. doi:10.5406/jamerfolk.131.522.0493.

Media 4 Free Iran. (2010). Neda Agha-Soltan's mother in interview with Rooz: Neda's open eyes drove me mad. *Media 4 Free Iran*. Retrieved from https://www.facebook.com/note.php?note_id=123885057622053

Messieh, N. (2011, June 2). A basic mobile apps arsenal for activists. *The Next Web*. Retrieved from https://thenextweb.com/apps/2011/06/02/a-basic-mobile-apps-arsenal-for-activists/

Meyer, P. (2010). *Liespotting: Proven techniques to detect deception*. New York: St. Martin's Press.

Mohanram, R. (1999). *Black body: Women, colonialism and space*. Minneapolis, MN: University of Minnesota Press.

Nelson, J. (2006). Blogs, wikis, e-zines, and women's herstory. *Feminist Collections: A Quarterly of Women's Studies Resources*, *27*(2/3), 20–21.

Obama, B. (2009, June 4). Text: Obama's speech in Cairo. *The New York Times*. Retrieved from https://www.nytimes.com/2009/06/04/us/politics/04obama.text.html

Ortner, S. (1972). Is female to male as nature is to culture? *Feminist Studies*, *1*(2), 5–31.

Peralta, E. (2011, June 13). Man behind Syrian blogger hoax: Something 'innocent ... got out of hand.' *National Public Radio*. Retrieved from https://www.npr.org/sections/thetwo-way/2011/06/14/137148644/man-behind-syrian-blogger-hoax-something-innocent-got-out-of-hand

Piela, A. (2010). Muslim women's online discussions of gender relations in Islam. *Journal of Muslim Minority Affairs*, *30*(3), 425–435.

Razack, S. (2005). Geopolitics, culture clash, and gender after September 11. *Social Justice*, 32(4), 11–31.

Reporters Without Borders. (2011). Myriam Haddad kidnapped. *Reporters Without Borders*. Retrieved from http://en.rsf.org/+myriam-haddad-kidnapped+.html

Riverbend. (2005). *Baghdad burning: Girl blog from Iraq*. New York: Feminist Press at the City University of New York.

Riverbend. (2006). *Baghdad burning II: More girl blog from Iraq*. New York: Feminist Press at the City University of New York.

Robinson, C. E. (1975). Mary Shelley and the Roger Dodsworth Hoax. *Keats-Shelley Journal: Keats, Shelley, Byron, Hunt, and Their Circles*, *24*, 20–28. Retrieved from http://search.ebscohost.com/login.aspx?direct=true&db=mzh&AN=1975106292&site=ehost-live

Rule, A. (1988). *Small sacrifices*. New York: Signet Books.

Russia Today. (2016, December 8). Doubts raised over Aleppo girl Bana al-Abed's Twitter account. *Russia Today*. Retrieved from https://on.rt.com/7x99

Sager, M. (2016, Spring). The fabulist who changed journalism. *Columbia Journalism Review*. Retrieved from https://www.cjr.org/the_feature/the_fabulist_who_changed_journalism.php

Saïd, E. (1979). *Orientalism*. New York: Vintage Books.

Scholes, R. (1985). *Textual power: Literary theory and the teaching of English*. New Haven, CT: Yale University Press.

Scholes, R. (1998). *The rise and fall of English: Reconstructing English as a discipline*. New Haven, CT: Yale University Press.

Semati, M. and Brookey, R. A. (2014). Not *For Neda*: Digital media, (citizen) journalism, and the invention of a postfeminist martyr. *Communication, Culture & Critique*, 7(2), 137–153. doi:10.1111/cccr.12042

Shresth, S. (2009). Sahibs and Shikar: Colonial hunting and wildlife in British India, 1800–1935 [Doctoral dissertation]. Duke University. Retrieved from https://dukespace.lib.duke.edu/dspace/bitstream/handle/10161/1647/D_Shresth_Swati_a_200912.pdf?sequence=1&isAllowed=y

Shirkey, C. (2008) *Here comes everybody: The power of organizing*. New York: Penguin Press.

Skalli, L. H. (2006). Communicating gender in the public sphere: Women and information technologies in the new MENA. *Journal of Middle East Women's Studies*, 2(2), 35–59.

Sly, L. (2011, June 8). Syrian American blogger is detained in central Damascus. *The Washington Post*, p. A13.

Smith, M. (2009). Arbiters of truth at play: Media April Fools' Day hoaxes. *Folklore*, *120*(3), 274–290. https://doi.org/10.1080/00155870903219714

Stanley, A. (2004). Women having sex, hoping men tune in. *New York Times*, p. 16.

Swaine, J. (2011, June 14). Death of a gay girl; A Syrian lesbian's thoughts on life turn out to be an American student's lies. *The Daily Telegraph*, p. A3.

Thorbjørnsrud, K., & Ustad Figenschou, T. (2016). Do marginalized sources matter? A comparative analysis of irregular migrant voice in Western media *Journalism Studies*, *17*(3), 337–355. doi: 10.1080/1461670X.2014.987549

TransProject. (2009). Translation of Iran slogans and poems – 3. *CNN*. Retrieved from http://ireport.cnn.com/docs/DOC-285635

TV Tropes. (n.d.). Stand your ground. *TV Tropes*. Retrieved from https://tvtropes.org/pmwiki/pmwiki.php/Main/StandYourGround

Twenge, J. M., & Campbell, W. K. (2009). *The narcissism epidemic: Living in the age of entitlement*. New York: Free Press.

van Krieken, K., & Sanders, J. (2017). Framing narrative journalism as a new genre: A case study of the Netherlands. *Journalism: Theory, Practice, and Criticism*, *18*(10), 1364–1380. Retrieved from https://journals.sagepub.com/doi/full/10.1177/1464884916671156

Walther, J. B. (1996). Computer-mediated communication: Impersonal, interpersonal, and hyperpersonal interaction. *Communication Research*, *23*(1), 3–43.

Wilson, T. (2005). Women in the blogosphere. *Off Our Backs*, *35*(5/6), 51–55.

Wirthlin, K. (2009). Fad lesbianism: Exposing media's posing. *Journal of Lesbian Studies*, *13*(1), 107–114. doi: 10.1080/07380560802314243

Witkowski, T. (2011). Psychological Sokal-style hoax. *Scientific Review of Mental Health Practice*, *8*(1), 50–60. Retrieved from http://search.ebscohost.com/login.aspx?direct=true&db=a9h&AN=57737926&site=ehost-live

WFAFI: Women's Forum Against Fundamentalism in Iran. (2005a). Official laws against women in Iran. *Women's Forum Against Fundamentalism in Iran*. Retrieved from http://www.wfafi.org/laws.pdf

WFAFI: Women's Forum Against Fundamentalism in Iran. (2005b). On the occasion of the International Women's Day, Iranian women call for an end of fundamentalist regime in Tehran. *Women's Forum Against Fundamentalism in Iran.* Retrieved from http://wfafi.info/wfafistatement14.htm

Wyatt, W. (2012). Ground rules for musing journalists. *Journal of Mass Media Ethics, 27*(1), 64–66. doi: 10.1080/08900523.2012.644147

Yahoo! Groups. (2006). *Alternate-history. Yahoo!* Retrieved from http://groups.yahoo.com/group/alternate-history/message/18736

Young, K. (2017). *Bunk: The rise of hoaxes, humbug, plagiarists, phonies, post-facts, and fake news.* Minneapolis, MN: Graywolf Press.

Chapter 7

"Hindu nationalism" or "Hinduphobia"?

Ethnocentrism, errors, and bias in media and media studies

Vamsee Juluri

Introduction

In 2017, the question of how Indian people, cultures, and traditions are depicted in American media captured public attention on two different occasions. The first of these was a pop-spiritual-travelogue program on CNN called "Believer" hosted by the author Reza Aslan. The program was severely criticized by public figures and the Indian American community for its sensationalism, xenophobia, and orientalist depiction of a non-Western people as cannibals and shit-eaters. Congresswoman Tulsi Gabbard of Hawaii (who is of non-Indian lineage but is a Hindu, and the first Hindu member of Congress) said the program felt "as if touring a zoo" (Safi, 2017). My article in the *Huffington Post* calling the program "reckless, racist and dangerously anti-immigrant" was widely quoted by *The Washington Post*, *The Guardian*, and other publications (Juluri, 2017). The chief concerns about CNN's program were not only its egregious factual errors and distortions (for example, CNN labeled Varanasi, the sacred Indian city featured in the program as the "City of Death" although Hindus refer to it as the "City of Light") but also its timing. Less than a week before the CNN program aired, a young Indian engineer was shot dead in Kansas City amidst widespread concerns about how the Trump campaign rhetoric may have led to a climate of hostility toward immigrants in America ("The United States," 2017).

If hundreds of Indian Americans protested outside CNN offices around the country for the channel's callous disregard for the safety and dignity of a minority immigrant community, another form of protest over media misrepresentations captured the attention of the public a little later in the same year: the release of the American stand-up comedian Hari Kondabolu's scathing documentary entitled "The Problem with Apu." Featuring veteran and newer media figures such as Whoopi Goldberg, Aziz Ansari, Kal Penn, and others, the documentary explored the ethics and politics of a white actor (Hank Azaria) assuming a "Brownvoice" (Dave, 2013) in order to portray a South Asian "Brown" character in the popular TV show The Simpsons. Kondabolu spoke, in the movie and elsewhere, about the bullying he and other Brown children were often subjected to in school since Apu of The Simpsons was probably the most well-known example of a South Asian character (or stereotype) in the American media. Kondabolu, along with Goldberg and others, argued that the character of Apu essentially represented a racist American trope, "minstrelsy," and sought (unsuccessfully) to get a response from Azaria as a way of addressing the problem.

At the center of these two moments of public contestation and struggle over the representation was a community that is often described as a "model minority" and celebrated for its very high success compared with other immigrant groups to the United States. While Indian Americans are believed to be among the most educated and wealthiest ethnic groups in the United States (Desilver, 2014), such celebratory facts also tend to distract from a more fundamental cultural and political question about representation stemming from the real-life demographics of minorityhood in religious, racial, and ethnic terms in the United States. Indian Americans constitute a little over 1 percent of the total population, with about 3.9 million people as of 2015 ("Indian Population in," 2017). This population is by no means only Hindu and consists of Muslims, Sikhs, and others. The actual percentage of Hindus in America remains an extremely small one, with about 2.2 million people or about 0.7 percent of the total American population ("Fueled by immigration," 2015).

Given these facts, it is important for researchers to go beyond self-censoring stereotypes about privilege and the like and ask the questions one would about any minority community's depictions in the media. Does this community control its own representations or does it remain subjugated to mainstream media stereotypes and myths despite its seeming privilege? Does the American media enable the participation of Indian American voices and views, particularly on their own cultural heritage and traditions or does it perpetuate a more dated colonial, orientalist, and racist discourse?

Specifically, where does the label "Hindu" fit in the intersection of various discourses of race, class, gender, and religious and cultural identification in the community? When The Simpsons depicts a South Asian character as both a bumbling, dishonest businessman *and* also explicitly as a practicing Hindu, or when a global media outlet like CNN uses brazenly inaccurate labels and hurtful racist tropes to paint a sordid picture of a sacred Hindu subculture as a violent, barbaric sect, what is the discourse that is being normalized around what it means to be a Hindu in America today? Is there validity to the claim of the protestors who stood outside CNN's offices that CNN's programs were guilty of Hinduphobia (along the lines of Islamophobia and anti-Semitism), or is the approach of Kondabolu, who studiously avoided any discussion of stereotypes of Hinduism in The Simpsons (and there are many, from corpses in the Ganges to randomly configured blue-toned gods) more appropriate to the debate at hand?

My thesis in this debate is that a very specific history of American media misrepresentations, myths, and stereotypes about a cultural formation commonly known to its members and others as "Hinduism" has been largely excluded from the academic conversation until now due to, essentially, "error and ethnocentrism" in South Asian and South Asian American media studies. Although scholars of religious history like Altman (2017) have tried to show how the "Hindu" was imagined in American media discourses, his approach also tends to follow current academic fashion in terms of seeking to demonstrate the constructed-ness of Hindu identity, rather than to advance a critique of colonialism from the perspective of an Indigenous Hindu position. I believe that a systematic study of key moments, texts, and contexts in the construction of the American media figure of "the Hindu" is a necessary step in expanding our understanding of the causes and consequences of misrepresentation. In this chapter, I outline a rationale and method for media researchers to study such misrepresentations.

"Hindu nationalism" or "Hinduphobia"? The polarized debate

I use the phrases in quotes to suggest that they are both contested. I use them in the first instance but will not use them after for clarity, except in cases where a source is directly being cited.

Academic researchers of media tend to approach the question of Hindu representation in media (or Hindu identity more generally) largely through concerns about a phenomenon labeled in academic discourses as "Hindu nationalism." The term gained currency in academia in the late 1980s and 1990s as a label to describe the rise of the Ram Janmabhoomi movement, a political mobilization of Hindus by the BJP (Bharatiya Janata Party, or Indian Peoples' Party) in India centering around the question of whether a Hindu sacred site in Ayodhya upon which an imperial-era mosque was built by the Mughal leader Babur ought to be returned to Hindus for the restoration of the destroyed temple. Media researchers carefully examined popular media phenomena of the 1980s, such as the popular Doordarshan TV serials Ramayan and Mahabharat, to argue that popular culture had enabled the rise of religious-nationalist identifications that threatened the secular conception of India and possibly the future of religious minorities in the country (Rajagopal, 2001; Mankekar, 1999) in the context of then Prime Minister Rajiv Gandhi's decision to offer a favorable temporary concession to Hindus in the Ayodhya temple/mosque dispute as a balancing act for his government's move to override the Indian Supreme Court on a judgment favorable to Muslim women but opposed by some Muslim men, a case of multiple appeasements as it were (Singh, 2016). The idea of Hindu nationalism as a threat to India's future also spilled over into Western news media coverage, with the *New York Times* and other publications evoking concerns about Hindu nationalists in events unrelated to the supposedly Hindu nationalist parties, such as the assassination of former Prime Minister Rajiv Gandhi at an election rally by the Sri Lankan Tamil Tigers in May 1991 (Crossette, 1991 May). Concerns about Hindu nationalism acquired further currency in Western commentaries on India in the early 2000s shortly after the 9/11 attacks on the United States by Islamic terrorists. Leading commentators argued that Hindu nationalism was a grave threat to South Asia (Sen, 2005; Nussbaum, 2007), and formulated a set of claims and concerns that would also gain formidable currency through repetition in mainstream media as noted in some of the examples later in this chapter.

In the United States, leading voices in South Asian American studies repeated these concerns about Hindu nationalism in a different context, that of immigrant Hindu American community concerns in America, coining phrases like "Yankee Hindutva" to describe, and often dismiss, such concerns (Prashad, 2000; Prashad, 2012). The broad concerns expressed about Hindu nationalism by these writers included a frequently repeated fear that followers of an organization called the Rashtriya Swayamsevak Sangh (RSS) in India believed in an exclusive notion of India as a Hindu nation; begrudged equal rights to Muslims and Christians; had gained political power through their political arm, the BJP; and sought to turn India from a secular nation into a Hindu nation. Other fears repeated about Hindu Nationalism included the charges that the early founders of the RSS admired Hitler, and that a Hindu nationalist had assassinated Mahatma Gandhi for being inclusive toward Muslims. In addition, some of these commentators wrote frequently in the early 2000s that Hindu nationalists were also engaged in unscholarly and politically motivated intrusions into history writing, alleging that textbooks were being rewritten in India under the 1998–2004 BJP government to reflect unscientific myths and beliefs. The allegation about Hindu nationalists rewriting history textbooks also surfaced in the United States in 2006, in a community-initiated protest about colonial-era errors and biases in children's sixth-grade history textbooks (Thapar and Witzel, 2006; Juluri, 2006). The discourse about Hindu nationalism acquired much greater intensity in media and academia in that period also because of a violent outbreak of Muslim-Hindu and Hindu-Muslim violence in the Indian state of Gujarat in early 2002. I use the two phrases "Muslim-Hindu" and "Hindu-Muslim" here to offer a more precise representation of the violent events of this time. The first phrase refers to the burning of a passenger train carrying Hindu pilgrims including women and children by a Muslim mob in the town of Godhra, and the second one to the violent attacks that followed against Muslim civilians by Hindus elsewhere in the following days. The then Chief Minister of Gujarat, Narendra Modi, was widely condemned in the international media as a "Hindu extremist" who encouraged a "pogrom" against Muslims in his state by Hindus. Although he was cleared of all allegations of inaction by several inquiries in India by a government led by a different party than his, the discourse of concern about Hindu nationalism continued to follow around his figure and his subsequent rise as Prime Minister of India. From 2015 until the time of writing (2019), Western news media and many academic commentators continue to maintain that Modi has launched a program of Hindu nationalism in India that is seeking to make the country more Hindu through violence, exclusion, and silencing directed at Muslims and Dalits. In 2019 alone, for example, the American public broadcaster NPR featured as many as 45 reports that mention "Hindu nationalism" out of a total of 73 stories with the keyword "Hindu" (as of September 2019; Juluri, 2019).

My comments on the media depiction of the RSS and related organizations should be viewed as a comment on the rigor, precision, and at times honesty of such depictions rather than as an endorsement or an equation of the RSS and related organizations with the broader Hindu community. I do not believe these organizations speak for all Hindus or for what Hinduism ought to be. However, even an informed critique of the RSS and Hindu nationalism requires better information than media reporting dominated by Hinduphobic tropes as I attempt to show in this essay. To this end, especially in regards to the RSS's positions and actions on a variety of issues ranging from Indian identity, temples, caste, Muslims and Christians, women, and sexual minority rights, it is important to go beyond commentaries that focus on the nineteenth and early twentieth-century intellectual genealogies of Hindu nationalism (for example, Sharma, 2003) and also focus on studies that engage with current practices of the RSS (for example, Andersen & Damle, 2018).

Hindu nationalism is clearly the dominant lens through which India is reported in the media, and, as my research so far indicates, the dominant lens through which anything "Hindu" is talked about in the media as well. It enjoys academic credibility and journalistic normativity as well. What this term refers to specifically, who coined it and why, whether it indicates Hindu views of the phenomenon or is a largely exogenous one, and whether it is used consistently with any academic or journalistic rigor are all questions that would be worth asking in a discussion on error and ethnocentrism in research. My view based on the reading of this literature, as well as the emerging literature from community activists and to an extent from within academia on the alternative concern about Hinduphobia, and most importantly, on the growing evidence of bias, exclusion, silencing, and rampant ethnocentrism, racism, and colonial-style religious supremacism in media discourses on Hindus is that Hindu Nationalism is not a stable, self-evident, or objective conceptualization at all. Its usage demands and deserves interrogation, and so do what its usage in media and academia conceal as well, which may well be described as propaganda in the case of media depiction of Hindus today, and sheer academic orientalism, in the case of social research on Hindus today.

I first outlined several problems with the way in which Hindu nationalism was being constructed in academic and journalistic writing in a review essay entitled "Hinduism and its Culture Wars" (Juluri, 2014). Briefly, my position was that the distinction between secularism in India as presented by authors like Sen, Nussbaum, and others, and Hindu nationalism, was suspect for the manner in which it excluded the notion of Hinduism. These writers followed a dominant trend in academic discourses on Hinduism based on

Western Indological traditions that viewed the use of the word "Hinduism" as somewhat interchangeable with what they called "Hindu nationalism." They argued that there essentially was no Hinduism till the Hindu nationalists invented it in the nineteenth century, a cruel, calculated elite collaboration between the Brahmin "priests" of India and the British colonial rulers. It should be noted that I call out the word "priests" in quotes to contest the uncritical Indian-context application of this Eurocentric Protestant-Christian label as if it were a universal term following the important interventions on this term by Adluri and Bagchee discussed elsewhere in this chapter. As a result of this conflation, it was clear in my view that the "secularism" that these critics of "Hindu nationalism" were offering was nothing less than the existential annihilation of Hindu identity itself; the name, belonging, value, and most of all the everyday legitimacy associated with that name in the world today. This normative, destructive academic delusion nearly acquired profound real-world influence in 2016 when South Asia studies scholars subscribing to this paradigm persuaded the California Board of Education to erase the words "India" and "Hinduism" in the school history curriculum and to replace them with the words "South Asia" and "religion of ancient India," respectively (Juluri, 2016). The board initially agreed to such changes, but then backtracked following a strong counterargument led by other scholars and a vociferous community protest including a public petition signed by 25,000 people.

The frame of Hindu nationalism, however, continues to be a dominant assumption in academic writing, and in journalistic writing on Hindus and India, though it is clearly not uncontested. Challenges to these received views have come not only from the community in cases of public debate like the California textbooks issue but also from a small group of professional and independent scholars who have demonstrated several problems in the very foundations of the paradigms in which the Hindu nationalism flag-waving scholarship operates. Koenraad Elst (2001), for example, has argued for a more anti-colonial interpretation of the Hindu uprising of the 1980s in India, showing that the aspiration for justice and equity among Hindus in India is more comparable to anti-colonial Indigenous movements around the world rather than any European right-wing sort of nationalism as believers in Hindu nationalism often claim. I have also argued that a generational view of Hindu identity engaging in decolonization offers a more productive view of Narendra Modi's rise rather than the monolithic Hindu nationalism notion alone (Juluri, 2015b).

More recently, Vishwa Adluri and Joydeep Bagchee (2014) have engaged with the core historical, political, and epistemological claims of this whole paradigm itself by turning their critical attention to the source of the whole received idea of India as an invention of Brahmin priests and British elites in the nineteenth century; the writings of the nineteenth-century German Protestant missionaries engaged in the very colonial-orientalist enterprise of translating Sanskrit texts for the purpose of conversion, domination, and control. Adluri and Bagchee show that many of the *assumptions* on which the Hindu nationalism scholarship in academia today (and many political formations in Indian democracy too, such as certain identity-based movements and parties) are simply colonial concoctions with no basis in Indian social or epistemological reality. The figure of the Brahmin that dominates the imagination of even contemporary Western academic experts of Hinduism such as Wendy Doniger (2009) in her clever phrase "Dead Male Brahmins" (derived from the Western idea of the "Dead White Male") for example, needs to be understood as a possible re-iteration of nineteenth-century projections by German Indologists of their own anti-Semitic and anti-Catholic prejudices about Rabbis and priests. As Adluri and Bagchee write: "for all that German Indologists claimed to be concerned with Brahmanic oppression of the lower castes, they made no serious efforts at its abatement. Their Brahmans were creatures of their own imagination, caricatures of Rabbis drawn with brown chalk" (306).

The Hindu nationalism paradigm is on shaky ground in academic discourses (also see Adluri & Bagchee, 2019), but continues to be rampant in journalistic, particularly Western-journalistic depictions of India today and, increasingly, in fiction too, as seen in several productions available on Netflix such as *Sacred Games*, *Ghoul*, *Leila*, and *Family Man*, and in movies like *Slumdog Millionaire*. The notion that Hindus are best known mainly through this particular trope of a violent, Islamophobic, intolerant mob wearing orange scarves and red tilaks (red markings) is a widespread one in Western media today. It is in this context, primarily as a tool for media research, that I now introduce the second key term of my analysis, namely, the idea of Hinduphobia.

Hinduphobia, as the term implies, is similar in usage and intent to earlier names for specific forms of bigotry and violence faced by excluded or targeted minority groups such as Homophobia and Islamophobia. Jeffery Long (2017), in his essay laying out a road map for distinguishing between Hinduphobia and merely academic criticism of Hindu thought and practices, credits the UK based Hindu Human Rights (HHR) group and the USA-based independent scholar Rajiv Malhotra for the recent popularization of the use of this term. The HHR has found that the term "Hinduphobia" was in usage in anti-colonial writing in England and India as early as 1883 and describes it as a "modern term for a far more ancient practice" (Malini, 2020). In recent times, the term has been used by community activists engaged in human rights work such as securing the lives of Hindu minorities in places like Pakistan, Bangladesh, Kashmir, and elsewhere, and also in reader responses to media depictions of Hinduism, Hindus, and Hindu nationalism. Hinduphobia has widely come into usage as a way of describing systemic bias or prejudice against Hindus in the media and surfaced into popular anger most recently in September 2019 when an NPR reporter and producer in India, Furkan Khan, tweeted that Hindus ought to convert out of their "piss and cow-dung worshipping religion" to solve India's problems (Rajghatta, 2019). Khan apologized and resigned, but NPR's inaction prompted a public petition signed by over 7000 people which has now elicited the promise of further study by their Vice President for News. The deeper context to this tweet's Hinduphobic nature is the fact that "urine" has become a widely used smear against Hindus in recent months not only by journalists and scholars but also in one instance by a suicide bomber prior to his murder of 40 Indian policemen, mostly Hindus, in Kashmir this year.

The term "Hinduphobia" has also been used prominently in American public conversation by the first Hindu Congresswoman and one of the candidates for the Democratic Presidential nomination, Tulsi Gabbard. Rep. Gabbard was attacked viciously by her Republican opponent in Hawaii through poster campaigns accusing her religion of being a "devil-worshipping" one. The interesting complement to this right-wing bigotry, however, is the fact that it was followed up by smear campaigns against Gabbard's Hindu family background (her mother is a Vaishnava and her father a Catholic) from activists and publications on the supposedly progressive left as well. In early 2019, the online publication *Intercept* published an article claiming to have investigated donors with "Hindu-sounding names" and later backtracked for the xenophobic statement, but never really apologized. In the summer of 2019, *New York* magazine published a long essay exoticizing and demonizing Tulsi Gabbard's Vaishnava Hindu childhood as some kind of a "cult" background. This tendency of depicting a Hindu public figure's background as something sinister reached an inquisitional peak in September when an interviewer on NPR affiliate WBUR Boston repeatedly ignored Gabbard's statement that she was a Vaishnava Hindu to repeatedly ask if she came from a cult background. It would appear that Tulsi Gabbard's use of the term "Hinduphobia" to describe the media's treatment of her and her American Hindu supporters does raise a broader question of whether American democracy is truly accepting not only of gender and racial diversity but religious diversity as well. For her part, Gabbard wrote an op-ed calling for an end to all forms of religious bigotry, including Hinduphobia (Gabbard, 2019). One point of criticism of Gabbard's early views about gays and lesbians needs to be understood clearly in relation to the broader issue of Hinduphobic attacks on her. While Gabbard has disowned and apologized for her earlier participation as a youth in her family's conservative positions, it is important to recognize that the allegations of homophobia pertain more to her Catholic family background rather than the Hindu part. Additionally, it is imperative to separate individual views and interpretation of any religion from the religion itself; an understanding that the scholars, activists, and media personnel seem to have while covering any news of terrorist attacks carried out in the name of Islam, and emphasize not to equate it with the religion itself and to avoid Islamophobia. However, the same logic and commonsense are not afforded to Hindus and Hinduism, and thus, it warrants the need to recognize and study Hinduphobia.

Researching media Hinduphobia: Beyond the South Asian and Hindu nationalist frameworks

Media researchers have for the most part not yet recognized, despite growing concerns expressed by the Hindu community and by prominent Hindu political figures like Gabbard that Hinduphobia must be named, studied, and contested as any other form of religious and racial (considering that most, though not all, Hindus are also people of color) bigotry would. There is no study of "Hindu" depictions in Western media to the best of my knowledge, although there have been at least two important studies of "South Asian" depictions in Western media (Dave, 2013; Thakore, 2016). The only scholarly study of media Hinduphobia published so far seems to be Sachi Edward's examination of Christian websites and the different tropes used by them against Hindus (Edwards, 2018), although scholars and activists have written about Hindu representation and decolonization more broadly and extensively elsewhere. This is a notable absence in the media research literature considering how extensively the representation of other postcolonial and/or immigrant cultural and ethnic groups' depictions have been studied and contested (Said, 1981; Hamamoto, 1994; Kilpatrick, 1999; Shaheen 2012; Pennington & Kahn, 2018).

Media researchers need to go past the current canonical dismissal of Hindu identity as one that is coterminous with dominance, oppressiveness, and moral opprobrium under the label of Hindu nationalism, and broaden the emerging discussion about South Asian representation to include questions specifically of Hindu representation as well. After all, to use the example of The Simpsons once again, there is only so much one can pretend that the specifically religious tropes evoked in the series about Hindus such as arranged marriages, octuplets, gods with many hands, corpses in the river Ganga, and so on, do not exist and have no bearing on the racial tropes surrounding a comical "Brown" figure of this discourse. To put this need in the context of the famous mantra of "race, class, gender, and sexuality" often invoked in critical media and cultural studies classes, we might add that religion also needs to be addressed explicitly as a site of struggle, oppression, and contestation in cultural politics today; and all the more so considering that the colonial sources of much of what is described as anti-South Asian or anti-Brown bigotry and misrepresentation in media are shaped specifically by imperial, monotheist-intolerant religious views of what we call Hinduism and Hindus.

While the immediate sources of anti-Hindu bigotry and propaganda in the media may not be explicitly religious in nature and are often made by supposedly progressive or even atheistic voices including South Asian writers and scholars themselves in a "re-orientalistic" vein (Lau and Mendes, 2012), what needs to be recognized and studied is the fact that many of the assumptions normalized by such progressive or atheistic voices do come from colonial-religious intolerance of native cultures and peoples.

I propose below a framework drawing on critical postcolonial studies and cultural studies for the study of media Hinduphobia so that media researchers may get past what has essentially been a deeply ethnocentric denial of Hindu self-representation in academia and the media. I propose, broadly, three levels of engagement with media texts so that researchers can begin to map out systematically and objectively how the "Hindu" is depicted in the media, and to begin the important intellectual, ethical, and political work of Hindu anti-colonial writing and teaching in media studies (Table 7.1).

The *first level* of study of the media would involve mapping the quantitative dimensions of Hindu depictions in journalism, film, television, advertising, and other genres. Drawing on research on bias, agenda-setting, framing, and content analysis techniques, researchers might address questions such as: How often does the word "Hindu" appear in news headlines, and in association with what other terms (like "Nationalist," "Extremist," "Mob," and so on)? When are criminals specified as part of a specific religion and when are they not, in the case of news about Hindu-Muslim conflict? How many news reports talk about Hindus as victims of non-Hindu aggressors compared with Hindus as aggressors (in the case, say, of Kashmir coverage)? What illustrations are used to depict Hindu people and customs, and what sort of gender, class, and occupational diversity is shown in such illustrations (are "Hindus" often showed as aggressive males of a certain age or are Hindu children and women also shown in equal measure)? How are sources and voices from different communities presented in terms of credibility and prestige (for example, if a Muslim scholar is cited on an issue, is there a counterview from a Hindu scholar, or is a Hindu politician or criminal quoted instead?)? Are there outright factual errors?

The *second level* of study of media Hinduphobia would involve identifying in the coverage of Hinduism and Hindus what in other contexts have already been identified as colonial-racist tropes. Following critical studies of orientalistic discourses about colonial and formerly colonial subjects (Dorfman and Mattelart, 1975; Said, 1978; Shohat and Stam, 1994), researchers might approach media coverage of Hinduism and Hindus (as a formerly colonized people) as a site of neo-colonial "othering," silencing, dehumanization, and appropriation. Tropes such as backwardness, ritualism, sentimentality, irrationality, lack of individuality, the man of color as a danger to women and children, and most of all, a lack of history and agency, can all be operationalized and identified in media discourses about Hinduism and Hindus.

The *third level* of study of media Hinduphobia would involve engaging with and contesting, as a subset of colonial tropes above, those historically constructed, culturally specific, and politically consequential tropes which are frequently deployed as if they were uncontested facts about Hinduism and Hindus. These tropes might include references to Sati, the caste system, greedy Brahmin priests, "animal worship" as primitivism and superstition, religiously motivated violence along the lines of the infamous "Thuggee" discourse, and others (Rotter, 2000; Sharma, 2018).

Table 7.1 A Coding Framework for Studying Media Hinduphobia

	Analysis level	*Indicators*	*Rationale for indicators*	*Examples*
1	Media bias	"Hindu" word appearances in news reports.	Are the majority of "Hindu" tagged stories neutral, positive, or negative in a publication? If negative associations dominate, it could be seen as a sign of bias or stereotyping.	45/73 articles tagged "Hindu" on NPR in 2019 were about extremism, nationalism, or militant politics (Juluri, 2019, September 16).
2		Labeling of aggressors and victims in inter-religious violence.	If only one religion is named as the aggressor in reports on inter-religious violence, it may be an effort to sanitize violence by another religion's members.	*NYT* reported Islamist serial bomb blasts in South Indian city of Coimbatore without naming culprit ("bomb blasts"), but names Hindus as a source of concern in ten headlines in the following four-week period (February 14 – March 14, 1998) "A rising Hindu tide frightens India's Muslims," "Hindu still proud of role in killing the father of India," "Hindu bloc moves closer to power," etc. On March 1, 2002, *NYT* has a headline saying "Hindu rioters kill 60 Muslims in India" and on March 5, 2002, a headline saying "Hindu justifies [the] killing of Muslims in reprisal riots" but no headline specifies that Muslims killed Hindu women and children on the Godhra train (Juluri, 2019 October 28).

3	Imbalanced sources quoted	Is the "Hindu view" in a report depicted with an Indigenous expert or authority, or by a militant, or fringe source? How does it compare for non-Hindu viewpoints?	*New York Times* reports on the Ayodhya issue in December 1992 quotes for the Muslim view a Tahir Mahmood, head of Islamic and comparative studies at the Indian Institute of Comparative Studies, and Rasheeduddin Khan, director of Indian Institute of Federal Studies, a Hindu view is depicted with quotes from a Jipendar Tyagi, a physician (Gargan, 1992 December 11). NPR has several reports on Kashmir in 2019 in which academic experts are quoted criticizing the Modi government's move, but no experts talking about the Kashmiri Hindu massacre and exile (Juluri, 2019, September 16).
4	Illustrations	Studies like National Geographic show the importance of images in "othering" different cultures. A key question is whether Hindus are depicted as diverse, feminine, old and young, vulnerable, or as masculine, threatening, objectified, etc.	The saffron-colored Hindu "mob" is a common theme in Western newspapers. In 2016, a *Los Angeles Times* tweet on the Islamist fundamentalist preacher Zakir Naik showed a picture of a saffron-Hindu mob instead of him following the Dhaka terror attack (Bengali, 2016 July 10).
5	Factual errors/false statements	In news, making false claims; in fiction, using symbols of one culture to depict another, use of fictitious labels, etc.	Indian English newspapers have frequently used Hindu-cultural terms like "sadhu" in headlines about crimes done by non-Hindu religious leaders. The NBC series Quantico had an episode where a Hindu terrorist (marked with saffron) is said to be a part of a (non-existent in real life) terror group called "Indian Nationalists" ("Priyanka Chopra Apologises," 2018).

(*Continued*)

Table 7.1 Continued

	Analysis level	*Indicators*	*Rationale for indicators*	*Examples*
6		Mistranslations	Many words associated with Hinduism have specific meanings that Sanskrit and Indian language experts would know. Western news media often make up their own versions.	NPR and other sources often translate the Sanskrit word "shuddhi" for temple ceremonies as "purification," which feeds into a broader Hinduism is Nazism trope (see row 21). Another questionable translation seen in BBC reports is that of the phrase "Jai Sri Ram" (Victory to Lord Ram) as "Hail Lord Ram," with its similarity to the German "Heil" associated with "Heil Hitler" (BBC, 2019 April 24).
7	Colonial tropes	Depicting Hindu deaths/suffering as unimportant/erasing mention of Hindu victimhood	Shohat and Stam (1994) say that the "systematic devalorization of life, the dead or dying body" and "refusal of empathy" are a key part of the "grammar of colonial racism."	Hindu victims of violence are rarely named, individualized, or humanized in news reports. The Hindu women and children who died in the 2002 train attack by Muslims are often described as "extremists" to devalue their innocence. After the 2019 Pulwama attack, the *NYT* interviewed the bombers' family and friends but not one of the 40 Indians (mostly Hindus) who were killed by him (Juluri, 2019 March 10).
8		Depicting Hindus as a danger even in reports where they have been victims	"Blaming the victim" is a common colonial trope according to Shohat and Stam (1994).	Note examples from row 2 above

9	Depicting Hindus as oppressors/ privileged in relation to more privileged/powerful groups	The charge of "reverse discrimination" is a common colonial trope according to Shohat and Stam (1994).	Hindus are depicted commonly as a privileged group because of them being a numerical majority in India, and a wealthy minority in the US; several reports in NPR, BBC, Foreign Policy, etc. depict Hindus as akin to whites, and Muslims as similar to Blacks (erasing the history of Hindu suffering under Islamic imperialism, see row 10).
10	Erasing a Hindu view of history, taking a "terra nullius" view of India before Islamic and European colonialism	"Lack of history" and "lack of material civilization" is a common colonial trope according to Shohat and Stam (1994).	NPR reported that "Hindu Nationalists" are erasing Muslim history by changing the name of Allahabad to Prayagraj without admitting that the place was originally called Prayagraj by Hindus (Juluri 2019, May 9).
11	Sexualized characters lacking ethics, self-control	"lack of sexual modesty" is a common colonial trope according to Shohat and Stam (1994).	Mistranslating the "naamam" or forehead-markings worn by Vaishnava Hindus as a "mark of phallus" by Katherine Mayo (Sinha, 2000); depiction of sexual violence as a Hindu religious problem as seen, for example, in a *Daily Beast* article depicting the plant-Goddess Tulsi as a victim of rape by the God Vishnu and the planetary deity Bruhaspati as a rapist who "is still a God in India" (Khan, 2016, March 25).

(Continued)

Table 7.1 Continued

	Analysis level	*Indicators*	*Rationale for indicators*	*Examples*
12	Hinduphobic colonial tropes	"Idols"	Andrew Rotter (2000) identifies "terrifying and hideous idols" as a key part of early colonial missionary writing on Hindus.	Presence of monstrous, non-representative fantasy-images as Hindu gods and goddesses in pop culture (Kali Ma in Katherine Mayo's Mother India, Indiana Jones and the Temple of Doom movie); the presence of temples as ruins (Jungle Book); the absence of living temples and beautiful shrines; mocking Hindu worship as "idolatry" and false belief.
13		"Stagnant religion"	Andrew Rotter (2000) identifies "stagnant religion" as a key part of early colonial missionary writing on Hindus.	Presenting Hinduism as a religion constantly in need of "reform," for example, NPR's coverage of Nepali Hindus removing their home shrines as a solution for women being endangered by snake bites and cold in "menstruation huts" (Preiss, 2019, May 13).
14		Thugs, Sadhus, Priests, Brahmins	Andrew Rotter (2000) identifies "filthy sadhus" as a key part of early colonial missionary writing on Hindus; it also ties into Hinduism depicted as a "cruel and despotic" religion.	The demonization of Hindu gurus and seekers in BBC, *NYT*, NPR, and the CNN program Believer with Reza Aslan on Hindu cannibals and excreta-eaters; arguably the attempt to show the rise of BJP as a Hindu religious "passion" as opposed to a rational political phenomenon.
15		Cows	Andrew Rotter (2000) identifies the "sacred cow" as a classic colonial trope, particularly the notion that "cows were more valued than Christians."	Depiction of crime in India over cattle theft as an irrational Hindu belief and attempt to impose Hinduism on non-Hindus (Hasan Minhaj's Netflix show).

16	Cowardice	Andrew Rotter (2000) identifies "cowardice" as a key part of early colonial missionary writing on Hindus.	Older movie depictions of Hindus; Temple of Doom villagers.
17	Lack of self-control; irrational actions; superstition; the language of over-emotion	Andrew Rotter (2000) identifies a "lack of self-control" as a key part of early colonial missionary writing on Hindus; closely related to illness, it was seen as a mark of a weak race.	UK newspaper cartoon of Gandhi as an infant who soiled his diapers discussed in Rotter (2000).
18	Sati	Arvind Sharma (2017) says the number of "Sati" incidents was widely exaggerated by British colonizers; and self-immolation protests by widows against British rulers who eradicated their widow pensions were lied about as if they were Hindu religious customs (Sharma, 2017).	Gratuitous references such as in Netflix show "Polar" not even set in India where the protagonist tells a group of American schoolchildren about Sati.
19	Inequality	Arvind Sharma (2017)	Inequality is a key theme in the movie Slumdog Millionaire, particularly in the character of the quizmaster who calls the hero a "chaiwala" or tea-boy.
20	Illiteracy/Brahmins as monopolizers of learning	Arvind Sharma (2017) cites Dharampal's (1983) monumental research on the existence of widespread multi-caste schools until the time of British colonialism.	California history workbooks and other educational resources normalize the Eurocentric colonial myth that learning in India was confined to the Brahmin caste.

(Continued)

Table 7.1 Continued

	Analysis level	*Indicators*	*Rationale for indicators*	*Examples*
21	Contemporary neo-colonial Hinduphobic tropes	"Hindu nationalism" or Hinduism as Nazism; appropriation of Swastika to mean Nazism rather than Hindu meanings; mistranslations to imply Nazi-ness	Koenraad Elst, in several books and articles, has argued against the dominant academic view equating Hindu revival with Nazism; he says Deen Dayal Upadhyaya's "Integral Humanism" is the key text followed by the RSS.	Reuters deleting a photo of US diplomat Nikki Haley outside a Delhi temple because there was a Hindu religious symbol on the temple; use of Hindu Swastika (and even Om) by anti-Modi (Indian Prime Minister) protestors in ways suggesting Nazi imagery; use of the Indian word "Swastika" instead of the German name "Hakenkreuz" (Hooked Cross) for the Nazi symbol (Juluri, 2018, July 6).
22		Denial of Hindu indigeneity to India	Intense debates continue about "Aryans."	Depiction of Hindus as "Aryan Invaders/Migrants"; maps in children's history textbooks implying that Hindus are not indigenous to India.
23		Caste system as natural, eternal, four-tiered with Brahmins as richest	See Adluri and Bagchee (2014); Arvind Sharma (2017). Adluri & Bagchee (2014) write: "Merely attacking Brahmans with the same intensity, for the same reasons, in the same language, and for the same religious motivations as attacking Catholics in Germany is not science; it is simply self-righteous enrichment at the price of cultural genocide" (423).	Several media reports since 2014 attempt to present "Hindu nationalism" as an upper-caste movement against Muslims and Dalits (despite obvious contradictions such as Narendra Modi and many of his supporters being from less privileged castes). Use of a European class-system pyramid to represent Indian society's complexities. Use of orientalist academic construct of "Brahmanism" to explain caste violence especially when violence is done by non-Brahmins.

24	Propaganda/ dehumanization/ demonization tactics	Depiction of everyday, popular Hindu symbols, and practices as "extremist" or "Hindu nationalist"	Demonization/scaremongering/"Star of David" type tactic.	*Washington Post* op-ed in 2014 claiming Modi's references to the river Ganga and his fasting for the festival of Navratri in his New York speech were "dog-whistle politics" for "Hindu fundamentalists" (Nair, 2014, October 3); *New York Times* report claiming the sari is a symbol of Hindu nationalism (India Today Web Desk, 2017, November 14); use of the phrase "devout Hindu" by NPR and *Washington Post* as a marker of violent Hindus (Juluri, 2019, September 16).
25		Sewage, filth, lack of hygiene	Classic dehumanization tactic (Smith, 2011) Also noted by Rotter (2000) in colonial missionary literature;	*New York Times* article attributing public defecation to Hindu sacred texts (Juluri, 2014, July 21); Slumdog Millionaire's sewer-diving scene.
26		Use of de-individualizing words like "Mob"	Classic propaganda tactic of dehumanizing the other; see Black Hole of Calcutta (Sharma, 2017) and Thuggee myth (Woerkens, 2002)	"Mob" is a commonly used phrase in writing about Hindus (see the example from row 4 above).
27		Use of animal-like descriptors	Classic dehumanization tactic (Smith, 2011).	Shashi Tharoor used the word "howling mob" to describe Hindus in his 2002 *New York Times* op-ed (Tharoor, 2002 March 6).
28		"Cow piss drinker"/"cow dung worshipper"	Filth and animal tropes deployed together; a classic dehumanization tactic (Smith, 2011).	NPR reporter Furkan Khan tweeted that Hindus should convert out of their cow dung worshipping religion in 2019; the phrase "cow piss drinker" was used by JeM suicide bomber in his manifesto before he killed 40 Indians, mostly Hindus; it is also used commonly on Twitter by many journalists and professors (Juluri, 2019, March 10).

A possible *fourth level* might be recognizing the deployment of well-recognized dehumanization propaganda tactics (Smith, 2011), such as associating Hindus and Hindu customs with ridicule, disgust, and irrational fear.

In Table 7.1, I present a systematic approach toward a content analysis of media Hinduphobia along these lines, sharing several examples from the *New York Times*, NPR, and other media sources from my ongoing research.

Conclusion

It would seem that several tropes commonly recognized as colonialist, racist, and orientalist in nature in the critical media and cultural studies literature appear in Western media depictions of Hindus and Hinduism. Additionally, it seems to be the case that quantitative indicators of diversity of representation and bias indicate that the coverage of Hinduism in major Western news outlets like National Public Radio and the *New York Times* is somewhat narrow, one-sided, and excludes representation of Hindu voices, perspectives, and most importantly, Hindu suffering and victimization by militant religious fundamentalists. The label "Hindu," in other words, tends to appear in Western media mostly in association with aggression, fundamentalism, misogyny, and Islamophobia. The defense for such a situation is usually the argument that the news media is simply presenting facts about events happening in India around the phenomenon they label as "Hindu nationalism," and worse, that charges of "Hinduphobia" do not deserve attention as it is a concept lacking validity.

The core principle (or presumption) underlying this denial is the misunderstanding, or misrepresentation, of the name "Hindu" in the academic canon as a category of dominance, especially in a global context. If the word "Hindu" refers to an identity specific to a group of people with immense privilege relative to those denying their claim to pain, protest, and justice, both in the present and in terms of the past, then there might be some validity to such a position. However, we find in academia and journalism that the denial of Hinduphobia, and the assertion of the word "Hindu" as somehow synonymous with "White," comes not only from a section of South Asian activists and scholars, but also from white, first world intellectuals. The second major point of relevance here is more objective and somewhat independent of the identity-accountability matrices of academic practice (who gets to speak about whom). It is simply the question of how the people of India, who have since fairly recent times come to be legally, culturally, and politically marked as "Hindus," have (regardless of their immense diversity in terms of various demographic factors) fared at the hands of forces of power in the past and the present. It is widely accepted in the scholarly literature that India (or "South Asia") suffered from colonization and is a post-colony. The people of India and of the diaspora are acknowledged in the scholarly community, on the basis of history, to be a postcolonial people affected by imperialism, racism, and so on. However, current academic canons hold that if some of these people identify with their own understanding and subjectivity about this experience of colonization *as Hindus*, then they have somehow assumed a colonial or neo-colonial "Hindu nationalist" consciousness. And whatever empirical evidence we may observe about media depictions of Hindus that would, in the case of any other postcolonial people, generate scholarly consensus somehow becomes irrelevant because, essentially, academic bureaucratic convention believes that the colonized people of India can contest to their misrepresentation under the label of being "South Asian" as in the case of Hari Kondabolu's Apu documentary, but not so under the label of being "Hindu."

There is, ultimately, a material, political, and existential dimension to the debate about media representation that also has to be addressed in order to decolonize current ethnocentric assumptions in the study of Hinduism in the media, and that is the question of Hindu victimization during earlier anti-Hindu imperialist invasions of India, and also in more recent times. One useful line of reasoning on this point is offered by the prolific and sometimes anxiously contested Belgian researcher of Hindu movements and politics, Koenraad Elst. While Elst's numerous writings on various topics are more suitable for debate by scholars in other disciplines, what may be relevant here specifically is his attempt to critically distinguish Hindu rhetoric of grievance from a more rigorous and analytical understanding of the Hindu experience of religious coercion and violence from monotheistic imperial forces in the past. The following evaluation by Elst (2014) of claims by Hindus for the recognition of a "Hindu holocaust" or "Hindu genocide" is useful:

> "Genocide" means the intentional attempt to destroy an ethnic community, or by extension any community constituted by bonds of kinship, of common religion and ideology, of common socio-economic position, or of common race. The pure form is the complete extermination of every man, woman, and child of the group (e.g. Native Tasmanians)... Hindus suffered such attempted extermination in East Bengal in 1971, when the Pakistani Army killed 1 to 3 million people with Hindus as their most wanted target... the second, less extreme type of genocide consists in killing a sufficient number who form the backbone of the group's collective identity and assimilating the leaderless masses into the dominant community (e.g. Tibet)... (p. 99) in antiquity, such partial genocide typically targeted the men for slaughter and the women and children for slavery of concubinage... the third type of genocide consists of preventing procreation among a targeted population... the fourth type of genocide is when the mass killing takes place unintentionally (e.g. Mao, Arab-European slave trade).
>
> (p. 100; examples from original text)

Such a classification scheme might help future researchers separate the less scholarly Hindu rhetoric of grievance, including those slogans which are often viewed skeptically as "Hindu nationalistic," from a more objective way of talking about history and the present. The word "holocaust," for example, is something that Elst believes that should not be appropriated from its painful place in Jewish experience to be used loosely by Hindus for their own pain. The main distinction between the Jewish experience of the "shoah" (and those of other victims of mass violence and extermination) and Hindus, he notes has to do with the impact of such violence on relative demography. In the past, and at present, the large demography of Hindus numbering in the hundreds of millions makes it seem that even large-scale massacres have not reached a situation of substantially mutilating the community as a whole; the percentage of the total population exterminated never seems to be on a scale that threatens the survival of the people as a whole.

However, and this is a key point that Elst notes, the sheer demographic scale of Hindu populations also means that in absolute terms even a small percentage of Hindu populations being exterminated implies a very large number of casualties, mass slaughter by any lens imaginable. According to his framework, Hindus have been subjected to at least two forms of genocide listed in his schema above; the slaughter of the "backbone" or spiritual and cultural leadership, and mass negligence or indifference to deaths due to colonial, racial, or religious bigotry as in the case of the famines under British rule. More recent cases of Hindu genocide, such as their slaughter in East Pakistan in 1971, and the forced displacement of Hindus from Kashmir in the early 1990s, are also rarely acknowledged as a sufficient real-world cause of concern in the scholarly literature to perhaps justify taking the study of media whitewashing of violence against Hindus seriously. However, what media researchers need to engage with in order to further develop the rationale for the scholarly study of Hinduphobia is not only the phenomenon of silencing and exclusion of Hindu victimhood in media discourses but also the deeper question of "epistemicide" (Viswanathan, 2019) and dehumanization that continues through the proliferation and normalization of essentially colonial-era anti-Hindu tropes from the imagination of racist-eugenicists like Katherine Mayo even in present-day entertainment like the movie Slumdog Millionaire. By erasing Hindu views of our own symbols, sacred and secular, by overwriting our own languages and meanings with their own propagandistic terminology such as BBC's translation of "Jai Sri Ram" or "Victory to Lord Ram" as "Hail Lord Ram" with its close insinuation of the Nazi "Heil," media Hinduphobia also involves an act, through brute force of technology and capital investment, of cultural genocide. There are no human rights, essentially, is what this machine seems to say, if you are Hindu. If you erase the name "Hindu," then and only then can one be deemed worthy of human rights discourse, just as Hari Kondabolu sought to do in the space of pop culture.

To continue to avoid talking about Hinduphobia in the scholarly community under the pretext of it somehow being a Hindu nationalist strawman is highly dubious from an academic and from an ethical point of view. Instead, it would be imperative for researchers in various fields in the social sciences to broaden the conversation around the term "Hindu" and stop using the practices of critique within that term where appropriate as a gate-keeping device for silencing a Hindu anti-colonial critique. In my field of media studies, for example, researchers would do well to expand the study of media Hinduphobia by approaching it as essentially a form of propaganda analysis with relevance to the discourse on human rights and justice. Hinduphobia, essentially, is a form of propaganda, a form of persuasive communication that does not reveal itself to be persuasive, aimed at normalizing the erasure of Hindus at representational, epistemic, cultural, behavioral, political, and possibly existential levels. It is a dehumanization device in the service of a genocidal project long contested in its earlier forms as religious imperialism and as modern colonialism and still contested today in its newer form as neoliberal globalization. A sane public discourse, and a reasonable understanding of errors and ethics in the field of social research, would perhaps recognize that Hinduphobia is a valid area of study and contestation for the one billion human beings who are known as Hindus.

Acknowledgments

The author thanks James Sater for pointing out the BBC's mistranslation of "Jai Sri Ram" as "Hail Lord Ram" rather than "Victory to Sri Ram."

References

Adluri, V. & Bagchee, J. (2014). *The Nay Science: A History of German Indology*. New York: Oxford University Press.

Adluri, V. & Bagchee, J. (2019). Cry Hindutva: How rhetoric trumps intellect in South Asia studies. *Academia*. Retrieved February 9, 2020 from: https://www.academia.edu/40082617/Cry_Hindutva_How:Rhetoric_Trumps_Intellect_in_South_Asian_Studies

Altman, M. (2017). *Heathen, Hindoo, Hindu: American Representations of India, 1721–1893*. Oxford: Oxford University Press.

Andersen, W. & Damle, S. (2018). *The RSS: A View to the Inside*. New Delhi: Penguin.

BBC (2019, April 24). Why is a 2,500 year old epic dominating India's polls? BBC News. Retrieved February 9, 2020 from: https://www.bbc.com/news/world-asia-india-47944411

Bengali, S. (2016, July 10). Preacher who called 9/11 an 'inside job' comes under scrutiny after Bangladesh attack. *The Los Angeles Times*. Retrieved February 9, 2020 from https://www.latimes.com/world/la-fg-bangladesh-india-preacher-20160710-snap-story.html

Crossette, B. (1991). ASSASSINATION IN INDIA; A Blast, and Then the Wailing Started. The New York Times, May 22, 1991. Retrieved from https://www.nytimes.com/1991/05/22/world/assassination-in-india-a-blast-and-then-the-wailing-started.html.

Dave, S. (2013). *Indian Accents, Brownvoice, and Racial Performance in American Television and Film*. Chicago, IL: University of Illinois.

Desilver, D. (2014). Five facts about Indian Americans. *Pew Research*. http://www.pewresearch.org

Dharampal (1983). *The Beautiful Tree: Indigenous Indian Education in the 18th Century*. Goa: Other India Press.

Doniger, W. (2009). *The Hindus: An Alternative History*. New York: Penguin.

Dorfman, A. & Mattelart, A. (1975). *How to Read Donald Duck: Imperialist Ideology in the Disney Comic*. New York: International General.

Edwards, S. (2018). #Hinduphobia: Hate speech, bigotry, and oppression of Hindus through the Internet. In M. Balaji (ed.), *Digital Hinduism: Dharma and Discourse in the Age of New Media* (pp. 111–127). Lanham, MD: Rowman and Littlefield.

Elst, K. (2001). *Decolonizing the Hindu Mind: Ideological Development of Hindu Revivalism*. New Delhi: Rupa.

Elst, K. (2014). *Communal Violence and Propaganda*. New Delhi: Voice of India.

"Fueled by Immigration." (2015, May). Hindu population up in U.S. *India Today*. Retrieved February 28 2020 from: https://www.indiatoday.in/world/story/hindu-population-up-in-united-states-becomes-fourth-largest-faith-252755-2015-05-13

Gabbard, T. (2019, January 26). Religious bigotry is unamerican. *Religion News Service*. Retrieved October 13 2019 from: https://religionnews.com/2019/01/26/tulsi-gabbard-religious-bigotry-is-un-american/

Gargen, E. (1992, December 11). The hatreds of India. *The New York Times*. Retrieved February 9, 2020 from: https://www.nytimes.com/1992/12/11/world/hatreds-india-hindu-memory-scarred-centuries-sometimes-despotic-islamic-rule.html

Hamamoto, D. (1994). *Monitored Peril: Asian Americans and the Politics of TV Representation*. Minneapolis, MN: University of Minnesota Press.

India Today Web Desk (2017, November 14). Indian Twitter users roast New York Times for sari state of affairs. *India Today*. Retrieved February 9, 2020 from: https://www.indiatoday.in/fyi/story/new-york-times-sari-narendra-modi-bjp-fashion-nationalist-cause-1085979-2017-11-14

"Indian Population in." (2017). Indian population in the United States. *Pew Research Center*. Retrieved February 28, 2020 from: https://www.pewsocialtrends.org/chart/indian-population-in-the-u-s/

Juluri, V. (2006). How does California teach about Hinduism? State textbooks contribute to ignorance about Hinduism. *San Francisco Chronicle*. Retrieved October 13, 2019 from: https://www.sfgate.com/opinion/openforum/article/How-Does-California-Teach-about-Hinduism-State-2502554.php

Juluri, V. (2014). *Hinduism and Its Culture Wars*. New Delhi: Westland. (e-book)

Juluri, V. (2014, July 21). Nose-deep in their own… prejudice: Hinduism and the New York Times's sewage problem. *The Huffington Post*. Retrieved February 9, 2020 from: https://www.huffpost.com/entry/nose-deep-in-their-own-pr_b_5601260

Juluri, V. (2015a). *Rearming Hinduism: Nature, Hinduphobia and the Return of Indian Intelligence*. New Delhi: Westland.

Juluri, V. (2015b). Modi's civilizational moment. *Foreign Affairs*. Retrieved August 21, 2020: https://www.foreignaffairs.com/articles/india/2015-01-22/modis-civilizational-moment

Juluri, V. (2016). Framing the California history textbooks debate. *The Hoot*. Retrieved October 13, 2019 from: http://asu.thehoot.org/research/media-monitoring/framing-the-california-textbooks-debate-9432

Juluri, V. (2017). CNN's Believer is reckless, racist and dangerously anti-immigrant. *The Huffington Post*. Retrieved August 21, 2020: https://www.huffpost.com/entry/cannibals-and-corpses-cnns-believer-is-reckless-racist_b_58bbc5fee4b02eac8876cfad

Juluri, V. (2018, July 6). Can't take west's uneducated take on Swastika lying down. *My Nation*. Retrieved February 9, 2020 from: https://www.mynation.com/views/can-t-take-west-s-uneducated-take-on-swastika-lying-down-pbfjgk

Juluri, V. (2019, March 10). An analysis of the New York Times's coverage of the Pulwama attack and its aftermath. [*Medium* web log post] Retrieved February 9, 2020 from: https://medium.com/@vamseejuluri/an-analysis-of-the-new-york-timess-coverage-of-the-pulwama-attack-and-its-aftermath-how-8e675ac668bd

Juluri, V. (2019, May 9). An analysis of the representation of Hindus in western news coverage during the 2019 Indian Elections. *Pragyata*. Retrieved February 9, 2020 from: http://www.pragyata.com/mag/analysis-of-the-representation-of-hindus-in-western-news-coverage-during-the-2019-indian-elections-742

Juluri, V. (2019, September 16). Today in Hinduphobia: An analysis of NPR's depiction of Hindus [*Medium* web log post] Retrieved October 13, 2019 from https://medium.com/@vamseejuluri/today-in-hinduphobia-september-16-2019-an-analysis-of-nprs-depiction-of-hindus-in-2019-69796f7620b

Juluri, V. (2019, October 28). Today in Hinduphobia: "Austere Religious Scholars" and how the New York Times covered terrorist attacks on India 1993–2008 [*Medium* web log post] Retrieved February 9, 2020 from https://medium.com/@vamseejuluri/today-in-hinduphobia-october-28-2019-austere-religious-scholars-and-how-the-new-york-times-e5a595b774c1

Khan, S. (2016, March 25). What's really behind India's rape crisis? *The Daily Beast*. Retrieved February 9, 2020 from: https://www.thedailybeast.com/whats-really-behind-indias-rape-crisis?ref=scroll

Kilpatrick, J. (1999). *Celluloid Indians: Native Americans and Film*. Lincoln, NE: University of Nebraska.

Lau, L. & Mendes, A. (2012). *Reorientalism and South Asian Identity Politics: The Oriental Other Within*. New York: Routledge.

Long, J. (2017, December). Reflections on Hinduphobia: A perspective from a scholar-practitioner. *Prabuddha Bharata*. 797–804.

Malini. (2020 February 12). Use of the term Hinduphobia: 1883–1997. *Hindu Human Rights*. Retrieved February 28, 2020 from: https://www.hinduhumanrights.info/use-of-the-term-hinduphobia-1914-1997/

Mankekar, P. (1999). *Screening Culture, Viewing Politics: An Ethnography of Television, Womanhood and Nation in Postcolonial India*. Durham, NC: Duke University Press.

Nair, M. (2014, October 3). Narendra Modi was speaking in code when he visited America: Here's what he was really saying to his Hindu Nationalist base. *The Washington Post*. Retrieved February 9, 2020 from: https://www.washingtonpost.com/posteverything/wp/2014/10/03/narendra-modi-was-speaking-in-code-when-he-visited-america-heres-what-he-was-really-saying-to-his-hindu-nationalist-base/

Pennington, R., & Kahn, H. (2018). *On Islam: Muslims and the Media*. Bloomington, IN: University of Indiana.

Prashad, V. (2000). *The Karma of Brown Folk*. Minneapolis, MN: University of Minnesota Press.

Prashad, V. (2012). *Uncle Swami: South Asians in America Today*. New York: Free Press.

Preiss, D. (2019, May 13) Why it's hard to ban the menstrual shed. *National Public Radio*. Retrieved February 9, 2020 from: https://www.npr.org/sections/goatsandsoda/2019/05/13/721450261/why-its-so-hard-to-stop-women-from-sleeping-in-a-menstrual-shed

"Priyanka Chopra Apologises" (2018, June 10). Priyanka Chopra apologises for "Indian Nationalists" terror plot in "Quantico." *The Hindu*. Retrieved February 9, 2020 from: https://www.thehindu.com/entertainment/priyanka-chopra-apologises-for-indian-nationalists-terror-plot-in-quantico/article24127642.ece

Rajagopal, A. (2001). *Politics after Television: Hindu Nationalism and the Reshaping of the Public in India*. Cambridge, UK: Cambridge University Press.

Rajghatta, C. (2019, September 12). US Radio producer forced to quit after anti-Hindu slur. *The Times of India*. Retrieved October 14, 2019 from: https://timesofindia.indiatimes.com/world/us/us-radio-producer-forced-to-quit-after-anti-hindu-slur/articleshow/71102210.cms

Rotter, A. (2000). *Comrades at Odds: The United States and India 1947–1964*. Ithaca, NY: Cornell University Press.

Safi, M. (2017, March 11). Reza Aslan outrages Hindus by eating human brains in CNN documentary. *The Guardian*. Retrieved from https://www.theguardian.com/world/2017/mar/10/reza-aslan-criticised-for-documentary-on-cannibalistic-hindus.

Said, E. (1978). *Orientalism*. New York: Vintage.

Said, E. (1981). *Covering Islam*. New York: Vintage.

Sen, A. (2005). *The Argumentative Indian: Writings on Indian History, Culture, and Identity*. New York: Farrar, Straus and Giroux.

Shaheen, J. (2012). *Reel Bad Arabs: How Hollywood Vilifies a People*. Northampton: Olive Branch Press.

Sharma, A. (2017). *The Ruler's Gaze: A Study of British Rule over India from a Saidian Perspective*. New Delhi: Harper Collins.

Sharma, J. (2003). *Hindutva: Exploring the Idea of Hindu Nationalism*. New Delhi: Penguin.

Shohat, E. & Stam, R. (1994). *Unthinking Eurocentrism*. New York: Routledge.

Singh, A. (2016 January 29). How Rajiv Gandhi blundered on Ayodhya: Baba said Bacha let it happen and Bacha did. *First Post*. Retrieved February 28, 2020 from: https://www.firstpost.com/politics/the-errors-that-rajiv-gandhi-made-by-unlocking-doors-to-the-ram-janmabhoomi-temple-in-ayodhya-2603582.html

Sinha, M. (ed.). (2000). *Mother India: Selections from the Controversial 1927 Text*. Michigan: University of Michigan.

Smith, D. L. (2011). *Less than Human: Why We Demean, Enslave, and Exterminate Others*. New York: St. Martin's.

Thakore, B. K. (2016). *South Asians on the U.S. Screen: Just Like Everyone Else?* New York: Lexington.

Thapar, R. & Witzel, M. (2006). How does California teach about Hinduism? A different agenda. *The San Francisco Chronicle*. Retrieved October 13, 2019 from: https://www.sfgate.com/opinion/openforum/article/How-Does-California-Teach-about-Hinduism-A-2502701.php

Tharoor, S. (2002, March 6). India's past becomes a weapon. *The New York Times*. Retrieved February 9, 2020 from: https://www.nytimes.com/2002/03/06/opinion/india-s-past-becomes-a-weapon.html

"The United States" (2017, March 1). Trump condemns Kansas City shooting, threats targeting Jewish community centers. *The Hindu.* Retrieved February 28, 2020 from: http://www.thehindu.com/news/international/trump-condemns-kansas-shooting-says-us-stands-united-against-hate/article17386550.ece

Viswanathan, I. (2019, May 28) The attempted epistemicide of Hinduism. *Medium.* Retrieved October 13, 2019 from: https://medium.com/@induv/the-attempted-epistemicide-of-70e5566bc788

Woerkens, M. (2002). *The Strangled Traveler: Colonial Imaginings and the Thugs of India* (Catherine Tihanyi, Trans.). Chicago, IL: University of Chicago.

Chapter 8

Performing intersectional reflexivity

Conducting ethical interviews with Muslim International and Muslim American students in the Trump era

Aneesa A. Baboolal

Introduction

This chapter addresses ethical concerns in terms of the impact of participants' assumptions about a researcher, safety, and sensitivity regarding specific types of vulnerable populations. An intersectional perspective provides insight into the unique dynamic of non-white outsider researchers and racialized minority subjects that exist at the center of anti-Muslim, anti-immigrant, and anti-Black racism. Specifically, the vulnerability of Muslim communities during tense sociopolitical times (the Trump era) also results in changing interview dynamics based on participants perceptions of researchers. Thus, the assumptions of a vulnerable group in a cross-cultural interview setting have implications for the researcher, the researched, and the overall process. Reaching across differences can both facilitate and hinder the research process and ultimately shapes who chooses to participate in specific types of studies and how this interaction is managed by both parties; thus, an intersectional reflexive approach requires critical examination and introspection.

Reflexivity while conducting an intersectional examination of the experiences of multiply marginalized populations provides an opportunity to extend methodological conversations regarding navigating emotion work and the complexity of reflexivity in qualitative research. This chapter examines the techniques utilized and lessons learned during the course of a qualitative study of a diverse subset of Muslim students, across various intersecting identities and statuses. It sheds light on the experiences of a subset Muslim sample during a complex sociopolitical era. This chapter draws on the researcher's experience while conducting interviews with 50 Muslim students at two universities in the Mid-Atlantic region. Given that the study was informed by intersectionality and the diversity of the sample, this lens has also been applied to the researcher and subject dynamic to examine ethics and reflexivity when both parties are marginalized.[1]

This chapter addresses the methodological approach and related issues pertinent to the study of a population that has been largely overlooked within existing research (Ali, 2016; Stewart & Lozano, 2009; Nasir & Al-Amin, 2006).

There are few studies that address Muslim student experiences in the US and even less that focus specifically on international/immigrant status, graduate, and religious minority status, and all focus on experiences after 9/11. Yet, the intersectional experiences of Muslim students across gender, racial/ethnic identity, national origin, and student status are rarely explored simultaneously and are increasingly relevant not only in a post-9/11 society but also during the Trump Era as a result of the evolving sociopolitical tension in the US that has impacted various minority groups, including Muslim communities[2].

The lack of research in this area, as well as the sensitive nature of the subject, including an examination of bias incidents and participants' distrust of outsiders to the community, subsequently contributed to respondents' hesitation to discuss violence, bullying, and discrimination, as well as cultural and language barriers. In accordance with the intersectional theoretical framework for this study, the methodological approach was rooted in feminist theory to support marginalized voices in a way that both centers while simultaneously producing rich data and reducing harm to participants (Shdaimah & Leon, 2018). Furthermore, this study is guided by the voice of the participants, and thus, recognizes the multidimensionality of the Muslim experience and also recognizes that the dominant narratives surrounding Muslim communities, immigrants, and women, including ideas of being oppressed and submissive, can be challenged through humanizing participants and centering their standpoint in the research process (Shdaimah & Leon, 2018). Therefore, this approach shifts from a perspective of "repressed others" to engage with participants' choices and lived experiences as a vulnerable population (Shdaimah & Leon, 2018). Reflections and observations in this article emerged from methodological issues related to obtaining entry into a population that experiences both invisibility and hypervisibility (Baboolal, 2019), thus utilizing insider/outsider identity, as well as a close examination of the complexity of the researcher's marginalized statuses to build trust and facilitate access examined. Ethical methodological concerns are also addressed with a specific focus on reflexivity with an examination of the researcher's attempts to obtain insider access.

The researcher's intersecting social identities and impact on the research process are examined as it simultaneously facilitated and hindered the study (Corbin and Strauss, 2008).[3] While strategies were utilized to specifically "get to know" participants instead of "speaking for" them (Tillmann-Healy, 2006), this resulted in various outcomes during data collection. For one, participants expected the researcher to possess cultural knowledge, felt a sense of unity with a fellow person of color, and thus, were more likely to confide incidents of victimization including gendered microaggressions and verbal and physical violence, as well as instances of overt racism. During post-interview debriefings, many female participants indicated feeling a sense of cathartic release as they were able to openly discuss traumatic experiences that they had not previously shared with others. In some ways, the researcher was, therefore, able to "pass as Muslim"[4] and participants expressed a sense of community because of perceived empathy and solidarity. Therefore, the emotional labor in this context resulted in a dynamic between researcher and researched beyond simply building rapport. The relationship-building process to conduct such a study further humanizes populations that may be perceived as socially excluded, particularly in public or political rhetoric, thus, acknowledging the invisibility of their core identities and addressing their lived experiences centers their voices and sheds light on understudied issues. Thus, the assumptions of a vulnerable group in a cross-cultural interview setting have implications for the researcher, the researched, and the overall process of conducting in-depth interviews. Furthermore, there are also ethical considerations to account for including the impact of participants' assumptions about researchers and their affiliations, as well as the personal safety of stigmatized groups that have experienced interpersonal and institutionalized Islamophobia (Beydoun, 2018).

Literature review

After 9/11, there was an increase in bias incidents against Muslims, including 1700 acts of hate violence such as verbal or physical assaults (Khan & Ecklund, 2013; Sekhon, 2003), including on college campuses (Karam, 2012). Similarly, continued intolerance both leading up to, and after the 2016 US presidential election has resulted in "hateful harassment" incidents across the nation with 1372 incidents up to four months after (Post-Election Bias Incidents up to 1,372, 2017; Eversley, 2016; Dearden, 2016). These included acts that were anti-immigrant, anti-Black, anti-LGBTQIA, anti-Semitic, Islamophobic, and gender-based (Miller & Werner-Winslow, 2016; Allen, 2015; Perry 2014; Finn, 2011; Mir, 2011; Eisenstein, 2006).[5] These incidents have also occurred on university campuses (Dickerson & Saul, 2016) and are similar to post-9/11 campus incidents, eliciting fears and concerns among students. Specifically, after 9/11, graduate and undergraduate students reported higher stress levels, while international students encountered new conflicts as a result of "national security" policies that restricted immigration (Heyman, Brennan, & Colarossi, 2010; MacGeorge, Samter, Feng, Gillihan, & Graves, 2004). These changing policies resulted in a decline in international student enrolment in the US, even among Black international students (Chandler, 2004), similar to decreases in international enrolment observed in 2017 (Redden, 2018).

In order to contextualize the contemporary Muslim experience during the Trump era, it is important to historically contextualize post 9/11 Islamophobia. Muslims and other racial/ethnic minority groups perceived as an "othered threat" in the US experienced an increase in hate violence after the events of September 11, 2001, including racial profiling (both on the streets and at airports), verbal/physical assaults, and even murder of those "appearing to be Muslim" (Khan & Ecklund, 2013; Sekhon, 2003). Gendered and racialized perceptions of Muslims resulted in various civil rights issues within American society. At the community level, Arab Detroit post-9/11 experienced a crisis of citizenship, similar to what has been documented in other predominantly Muslim enclaves across the US, as well as changing policies including restrictive immigration regulations (including mass deportations) and scrutiny by law enforcement via surveillance that contributed to notions of Muslims as national security threats in the US (Nessen, 2014; Serhan, 2013; Byng, 2007).

The backlash against Muslim people and communities has included South Asians, African Americans, Middle Easterners, and Africans, and people perceived to be Muslims such as Sikhs, Latinos, and other communities that are all lumped together and perceived as "outsiders" because of physical characteristics such as phenotype (Serhan, 2013; Mishra, 2013; Bhatia, 2008). This backlash highlights the impact of anti-Muslim rhetoric and collective discrimination that plays out in personal, political, and social spaces (Mir, 2011). Similar to post-9/11, hate crimes against marginalized groups, including incidents motivated by religious bias, increased leading up to, during, and after, the 2016 US presidential election, including reaching a five-year high in 2016 (7175 total reported hate incidents) (Barrouquere, 2016; Barrouquere, 2018).

Racialization of Islam

Racialization includes a variety of intersecting factors including, but not limited to, language, clothing, nation of origin, and religion that has shifted over time as a result of anti-Muslim sentiment (Selod, 2015). The racialization of religious identity, particularly after 9/11, has been observed as a process in which diverse groups of people were lumped together, in most cases, Muslim, Sikh, Arab, and South Asian people, resulting in a racial construction of "apparently Muslim" (Singh, 2013; Singh, 2015). Scholars argue that post-9/11 society requires an examination of Muslim experiences as racialized in order to adequately reflect political, cultural, economic, and social contexts, as well as to acknowledge the fluidity of race, yet, the racialization of Muslims and gendered processes of racialization continues to be understudied (Garner & Selod, 2015; Selod, 2015).

The impact of 9/11 on Muslim women

The experiences of Muslim men and women have been historically different, especially in relation to violence, visibility, deportations, and detainment. In the aftermath of 9/11, approximately 7000 men were deported and over 500 Muslim men (most of them Arab) were interviewed by law enforcement, with the FBI primarily targeting working-class men that were non-citizens, naturalized, and US-born citizens (Naber, 2006). While men were targeted by formal legal mechanisms, women were more often victimized by societal prejudice in public life, yet, their experiences were initially understudied. Gendered Muslim identity in the US has also resulted in hypervisibility and increased vulnerability for veiled women (Allen, 2015; Perry 2014; Finn, 2011; Mir, 2011;

Eisenstein, 2006). For example, the *hijab*, the headscarf traditionally worn by Muslim women that has symbolic meanings beyond religious connotations including cultural identity and gender norms, has been considered a trigger for discrimination, yet, the focus on ethnic hatred renders the impact of gendered violence against Muslim women as invisible, and thus, normalized (Eisentein, 2006). Thus, racial discrimination, merged with the hypervisibility of veiling altered the lived experiences of Muslim women who increasingly faced societal discrimination and violence after 9/11 (Macias, 2016; Salman, 2015; Perry, 2014; Karandish, 2014; Ameen, 2012; Mir, 2011; Maruoka, 2009).

The Black Muslim experience

It is estimated that 80 percent of Muslims in America are non-Arab, thus Black Muslims in the US have a unique experience as a result of both Islamophobia and anti-Black racism that impacts both African Americans and Black immigrants, which requires further contextualization (Ochieng, 2017). Few studies exist regarding Black Muslim students on college campuses and these include comparisons between Black immigrant and Black native (domestic) students (Massey, Mooney, Torres & Charles, 2007), African student experiences (Basford, 2009), and more recently, gendered Black Muslim identity in college (Harris, Haywood, & Mac an Ghaill, 2016; Black & Williams, 2013), however, the double bind of facing both anti-Black and anti-Muslim racism, along with other intersecting identities, such as immigrant status or gender, remain understudied.[6] Thus, the unique experiences of Black students constitute a diversity within the population that needs to be accounted for as this group continues to face a "double jeopardy" in terms of being racialized as Black *and* as Muslim (Etman, 2016).

Muslim students on campus in the US

Both domestic (US-based) and international students (recruited from foreign nations) continue to be an important part of diversity initiatives on college and university campuses. While there have been a plethora of studies surrounding the experiences of students on various campuses (including historically black college/universities [HBCU], Hispanic serving institutions [HSI], and predominantly white universities [PWI]), there are few studies that address international student experiences in the US and even less that focus specifically on Muslim student experiences on campus. Among these, the focus has centered on veiled Muslim women post-9/11 (Macias, 2016; Salman, 2015; Karandish, 2014; Ameen, 2012; Mir, 2011; Maruoka, 2009), international Middle Eastern students (Johnson, 2016; Abualkhair, 2013; Schatz, 2009; Pinkerton, 2006;), and most recently, one study focusing on multiple marginalization on campus (McGuire, Casanova & Davis, 2016)[7]. Thus, the intersecting experiences of Muslim students are rarely explored simultaneously while excluding others including Muslim women who do not veil, the difference in experiences between international and first-generation immigrant students, and across race, specifically, in regard to the Black Muslim student population.

While overall societal intolerance toward Muslims in the aftermath of the 2016 US presidential election resulted in an increase in bias crimes across the nation, along with higher incidents of hate across 30 colleges/universities within ten days of the election (SPLC, 2016; Eversley, 2016; Dearden, 2016; Jaschik, 2016; Karam, 2012). These acts on university campuses have also elicited fears and promoted concern among minority students (Dickerson & Saul, 2016), therefore, making it critical to examine the perspectives of students given the social and political context as universities work toward achieving inclusive diversity.

Additionally, racial microaggressions, both verbal and non-verbal insults that convey hostile and derogatory messages, impact the experiences of Muslims in the US (Cainkar, 2009; Nadal et. al. 2012). College campuses are no exception as universities continue to pursue diversity initiatives and enroll multicultural students from a variety of nations, and a multitude of racial/ethnic and religious backgrounds (Cerbo, 2010). Thus, Muslim students, and particularly immigrant and international Muslims, not only endure challenges associated with attending schools in a foreign country, but may also be unfamiliar with the post-9/11 climate of the US and more recently, the Trump effect, where racial/ethnic, religious, and immigrant minorities face increased violence (Miller & Werner-Winslow, 2016; Costello, 2016).

Intersectional feminism and a culturally sensitive research approach

Intersectionality demonstrates the complex effects of multiple axes of difference that intersect across time and contextual space as various social systems, such as gender, race/ethnicity, class, age, and citizenship status, interlock simultaneously to shape experiences and provide a framework to better understand the inequality among groups along multiple dimensions (Cho, Clarke & McCall, 2013; McCall, 2005; Brah & Phoenix, 2004; Crenshaw et al 1994; Collins, 2000; Crenshaw, 1989). Given the diversity of Muslim identity, a complex site where gender, race/ethnicity, and citizenship status, along with religion take center stage, an intersectional framework allowed for a closer examination of subtle differences within specific social categories of a particular group to be observed more closely.

While some intersectional studies in the US acknowledge structures of race, gender, religion, and citizenship in relation to state policies and everyday acts of violence, few focus specifically on anti-Muslim racism. Some studies construct a racial/ethnic categorization of Muslims as "Arab-Middle-Eastern-Muslim," and therefore, disregard other groups, including non-Muslim Arabs, South Asians, and others who have been mistaken for Muslims, including

Latinos and Sikhs (Naber, 2006). The specificity of attributing anti-Muslim violence to only visible Muslims or Arab Muslims excludes other Muslims, including women who do not veil, others across race, ethnicity, and national origin, as well as non-Muslims racialized as such, minimizes the combined racial and religious minority consequences behind the notion of the "Muslim threat" by rendering the broad-reaching impact of Islamophobia as invisible. Additionally, it marginalizes the experiences of diverse Muslim people and communities by excluding the victimization of non-Arab Muslims, and those perceived as invisible, even while subjected to discrimination. Because of this, it is critical to examine perspectives across axes of difference.

Within the student experience, it is important to note that domestic students, as the majority on American campuses, have been studied more extensively while international students have not, whereas the opposite is true within the Muslim student experience. Additionally, veiled Muslim women have been centered more so than invisible Muslim women – those who do not veil (Baboolal, 2019). Furthermore, international student experiences have been examined more so than immigrant Muslims, an important difference in experience across country of origin, generation, and social class. Conducting research with participants with complex intersecting marginalized statuses brings additional research challenges including cultural differences, heterogeneity, and processes of inclusion/exclusion but addressing this marginalization aids in understanding how unique social locations impact student experiences. Ultimately, centering marginalized voices (Collins, 1992; Smith, 1974) of those invisible or absent from the literature enhances understandings of gendered and racialized violence that religious minorities are subjected to.

Overview of the data collection

The research question and methodological framework for the study this chapter is based on grew from an exploratory pilot study at Mid-Atlantic State University (PWI) conducted in November 2016. The pilot study addressed how Muslim students make sense of their identities and experiences on campus and informed the creation of the interview guide that was used for data collection between September 2017 and May 2018. The research design for the in-depth interviews (n=50) utilized a demographic questionnaire and semi-structured interviews guided by approximately 65 questions. Interviews were conducted at two research sites, a PWI (predominantly white institution) and an HBCU (historically Black college/university).

The local setting for the study was a Mid-Atlantic state where there were an estimated 10,000 Muslim households. In 2016, members of the Muslim community in the state voiced concerns related to policies that threatened to bring back a Muslim registry and visa restrictions, as well as spreading misinformation about Islam that resulted in harassment, discrimination, and even hate crimes. An article in a regional newspaper featured commentary by the Muslim Student Organization at Mid-Atlantic State University (PWI) where members highlighted the fear and hostility Muslims in this region were facing that aligned with national concerns. Students noted that blanket hostility toward Muslims misplaced the personalized nature of verbal assaults. While local newspapers documented previous bias incidents on campus, the Crime Statistics reports from Mid-Atlantic State University between 2013 and 2015 indicated no hate crimes occurred on campus, campus residences, or public property. The Muslim population at Mid-Atlantic State University (MASU-PWI) may appear small but is commensurate with various colleges and universities across the US, thus the study can offer generalizability beyond this single case, however, this can also be limited by the diversity of the sample.[8]

Sample and recruitment strategy for interviews at PWI

From the pilot study (n=7), it was clear that there was a diverse population of Muslim students on the PWI campus across various statuses, including undergraduates and graduates, and international and domestic students, as well as across a plethora of racial, ethnic, and national backgrounds. The 50 interview participants included 25 undergraduates and 25 graduate students. This included 27 women and 23 men who identified predominantly as Middle Eastern (24), Asian (14), or Black (11). Only one participant identified as a white Muslim convert. Within the sample, 24 participants had international student status, while 26 were domestic Muslim Americans. Participants were from various different states (mostly the northeast) and countries (these included the US, Canada, Afghanistan, Bangladesh, Iran, Pakistan, Saudi Arabia, India, Morocco, Turkey, Lebanon, Egypt, Oman, Jordan, Ivory Coast, Sierra Leone, Guinea, and Ghana).

Interviews

Interviews were conducted to produce a thick description of participants' accounts of their experiences and understandings. Flexibility in the sequence and content of questions allowed for obtaining detailed information from participants but also allowed for the interpretation of the data as it was collected (Schwandt, 2007; Rubin & Rubin, 2005; Denzin 1989/2001; Geertz, 1973). Thus, the validity and reliability of emerging themes were better assessed when data was collected and analyzed simultaneously (Corbin and Strauss, 2008). Engaging in this process, along with keeping detailed memos, ultimately aided in identifying preliminary themes related to participant experiences, perceptions, and protocol improvement.

Limitations

Because of the exploratory nature of this study, the research has some limitations. Participants in this study had moved to the Mid-Atlantic region from across the US and other countries, thus, the location may have influenced the generalizability of participant experiences. Nationally, universities largely recruit international students from India, Saudi Arabia, Iran, and Turkey, therefore, there is more representation from these countries in the sample. Though there was diversity in age (19–39), race/ethnicity, gender, immigrant status, and country of origin, it is important to note that larger cities and Muslim ethnic enclave communities with long-standing Muslim American populations, as well as more recently settled Muslim refugees, were not represented. This study was also conducted at universities in the Mid-Atlantic region, one in the northern liberal part of the state and the other in the southern, more conservative part of the state that alluded to some of these potential differences.

This study design centered the experiences of young Muslim men and women and cannot adequately capture the intergenerational effect of those who have lived through both 9/11 and are also experiencing further trauma as a result of Trump era violence. Furthermore, international students were largely in STEM disciplines where anti-Muslim prejudice seemed to be more overt, and participants more silenced regarding their experiences, thus, having further implications regarding inclusive diversity in higher education. Finally, the researcher's status as an outsider to the Muslim community, combined with the sociopolitical climate, may have impacted participants in various ways that are further examined in the next section (Ryan, Kofman & Aaron, 2011)

Researcher reflexivity

Researcher impact on research processes

Scholars of qualitative methodology support that it is imperative for researchers to engage in reflexivity to acknowledge their influence on the research process (Corbin & Strauss, 2008). As a non-Muslim, immigrant, and doctoral candidate during the time the study was conducted (2017–2018), who had resided in communities impacted by bias incidents against Muslims and those perceived to be as such (including Sikhs) in the aftermath of 9/11, I entered the study with socially normalized worldviews of the topic. Furthermore, my experience of working on diversity and inclusion projects in higher education, specifically as a mentor to international students and historically underrepresented groups influenced the approach to this study.

Insider assumptions, access, and obtaining entry

As stated, there was some social distance between the researcher and subject, as a non-Muslim however, my immigrant status and personal experiences with marginalized groups, including international students and Muslim communities, as well as racial/ethnic minority students, informed ideas surrounding the population. Furthermore, in some ways, I was able to "pass as Muslim" due to my perceived ambiguity (for example, having an Arabic name and sometimes being mistaken as South Asian/Middle Eastern), thus, obtaining access to insider moments where connection surpassed racial matching as both researcher and subject had shared experiences (Buford, 2014). The recruitment and interview process may also have been influenced by the preconceived notions about my social locations including gender, country of origin, status as a domestic student, immigrant, accent (or lack thereof), and doctoral candidate status.[9] To address concerns regarding cultural hesitations, I spoke with faculty and staff who worked with minority students, as well as met with Muslim student organization members to obtain a better sense of cultural sensitivity.[10] In regard to gender sensitivity, I made sure to greet both men and women equally.[11] Nor did I greet participants with any specific cultural greeting. Notably, some participants insisted that I had "given the salaam" upon the initial meeting. Participants' perception that I was an insider (a fellow Muslim) influenced interactions in person and via email. Some participants were certain that I had greeted them via email or in person with the traditional Muslim *salaam*.[12] Neither in person nor via email were participants greeted with these salutations, however, their racialized perceptions of the researcher and assumptions that only a Muslim researcher would be conducting such a study influenced how they experienced and interpreted researcher-subject interactions. Overall, with all participants, I utilized my intersecting social identities specifically, as an immigrant woman of color to navigate interactions with participants that may have facilitated the process.

Perception of friendship

My interactions with various diverse student organizations certainly aided in gaining access to some subset groups within the population, thus, resulting in a uniquely diverse sample. Participants were usually asked where they had heard about the study, and generally, they had either received an email directly from me, received the flyer from their friends (who had already participated), or received word of mouth via international student group chats. For example, one Iranian woman noted that her husband and many other Iranian students had a WhatsApp chat specifically for their volleyball team which she later sent a message to about my study. During the course of the study, board members of both the Muslim Graduate and Undergraduate Student Organizations, the Turkish Students Association, and the Indian Graduate Student Group were also interviewed, and subsequently, helpful in encouraging their friends to participate, thus resulting in a successful snowball sample. The participants' sense of trust in the researcher as an ally further facilitated access to this population.[13] Although some participants relayed their feelings of gratitude related to the study and finally having their voice heard, a handful also expressed trepidation about participating in such a study during a time in which they felt their personal information could be used against them. Some participants admitted that they had volunteered as a result of curiosity (some asked if the university had compiled lists of Muslim students while others were concerned because their parents had instructed them to not participate), while others were active in student organizations and wanted to voice specific concerns.[14] While at times I had concerns about participants' personal connections to me based on their assumptions that I was Muslim or a friend of the person who recommended the study to them, almost all of the participants indicated that their responses were more open as a result of my individual identity; as a person of color and my understanding nature regarding the issues we discussed. Overall, my involvement, including solidarity efforts and building relationships with participants, fostered a sense of friendship that aided access, data collection, and ultimately contributed to a more nuanced understanding of the diversity of experience within this population.

Power, authority, and representation

With younger participants, specifically Muslim men and women between the ages of 18 and 22, given that one of the interview locations was an on-campus adjunct or faculty office, I was concerned with whether or not I was seen as an authoritative figure and there could have been an invisible power dynamic at work during the interviews (Anyan, 2013).[15] To address this, I usually changed tone and demeanor, taking on a more casual, conversational stance, and encouraged the participant to talk more about their parents or high school experiences. In discussing dress, tone, interview location, seating arrangement, race/ethnicity, background, and other dynamics, multiple participants indicated that they were enthusiastic and spoke honestly because they felt comfortable. International students from predominantly Middle Eastern countries who had only recently moved to the US were usually the most resistant at first, usually, they became more open and responsive as the interview progressed. Thus, I determined that participants generally felt safe speaking with sensitive issues with me as a result of social factors that contributed to perceptions of my relatability but were specifically tied to my identities as an immigrant and fellow racial/ethnic minority. My perceived gender also played a role as women were more likely to disclose experiences of victimization while men seemed to either focus on women's issues or conveyed experiences of their mothers, wives, and sisters that they thought I would better understand. While I cannot determine with exhaustive certainty the influence it had on the data, multiple participants affirmed that had I been another race (specifically, white), they would have been more apprehensive to participate and careful about the information they disclosed. Therefore, access to the population, and ultimately, obtaining entry to this subset Muslim student community, could have been granted differently to a non-minority researcher or an insider Muslim researcher, thus, as a researcher, I captured different aspects of student experiences that perhaps enriched the data in unique ways.

It is important to note that throughout the research process, I remained aware of the effect personal beliefs could play in influencing the study (King & Horrocks, 2010). Approaching the research design, instrument, and interviews as centering the participants' narratives meant striving to encourage the participants' views and not what they thought I, as the interviewer, wanted to hear. Frequently, participants were encouraged to discuss how they felt, asked about their thoughts and reactions, asked if their friends or parents felt similarly, and how they thought people outside of their community or people in positions of power felt about the issues and perspectives discussed. Taking this into consideration for the transcripts, I reflected on certain comments to recall if they had any impact related to my personal feelings or beliefs, an important tenet of feminist epistemology (Harding, 1987). At times during the interviews, I was immediately aware of these processes because it did not support conclusions drawn based on an initial review of the literature, therefore, I documented these in post-interview notes. For example, I expected participants to be more aware of discrimination in various forms, however, considering that many were undergraduates (born between the years 1996 and 2000), they had essentially grown up in a country plagued by anti-Muslim sentiment (post-9/11) and did not recognize many prejudiced behaviors as outside of their norm. Therefore, it is critical to note that in circumstances when both the researcher and subject are multiply marginalized and aligned in various ways, there still remains unique aspects of social distance that can be attributed to worldviews and limits of scholarship on the experiences of understudied populations.

Emotional impact on the researcher and participants

Reflexivity can enable a more critical lens in regard to the impact of both the researcher and the political and personal context in which the research takes place (King & Horrocks, 2010). Thus, it is increasingly important to engage in reflexivity that examines the emotional aspects of the research process. Some scholars argue that both reasoning and emotions are critical to deciphering meaning, therefore, understanding researcher and participant emotions can aid in understanding this study.

Memos were utilized as a way to reflect on post-interview discussions and the participants' feelings/emotions, as well as the researcher's reflections on the experience and sensitive topics that emerged during the course of the discussion, and thus, were significant as one form of examining the personal and emotional aspects of the qualitative research experience (Lofland et al., 2006). While I expected the interviews to take some personal toll, I was surprised by my increased sense of risk given my immigrant status, as well as the long-term consequences of the legitimate concerns of participants. Overall, this part of the research process allowed me to separate personal perspectives from individual participants' experiences and ultimately contributed to the content of the interviews, including my ability to relate to being profiled, identifying with the precarious immigration status of the students, and sympathizing with their sense of vulnerability.

Furthermore, the interviews also elicited emotional responses from some participants. This usually occurred with women who relayed traumatic stories of violence but also emerged in the form of sympathy as they discussed the violent experiences of friends and family members in the Muslim community. Middle-aged participants, specifically those who were married or had children, displayed more physically emotional reactions when discussing their children's experiences at school or gendered harassment of their spouses in public places. Furthermore, for many, because it was the first time discussing these incidents, it elicited unexpected emotions. Some stated that while they had not thought about their experiences in some time or their reactions to it, they were surprised by how much it had shaped their perspectives and subsequent behaviors in social spaces. Many noted that discussing their experiences in the context of the interview was cathartic in nature because they had previously not discussed the incidents or the issues but noted that it weighed heavily on them. On the other hand, some participants conveyed anger toward others within the community such as "bad Muslims" (i.e., terrorists) or vented their frustration with even the perception of radicals as Muslim. Some women jokingly talked about their perceived oppressed status or engaged in dominant behavior during the interviews which seemed to be a way for them to process stereotypes and to gauge researcher responses related to notions of Muslim women as docile and passive. Men also engaged in similar tactics with some being very sympathetic and focusing their discussions on Muslim women's experiences, while others engaged in demeaning Islamophobic humor about fellow Muslims' choices, including the idea that Muslim women were actually oppressed and were not acculturating into Western (American) society. In some ways, I accepted this as part of the diverse perspectives but also as a mechanism that participants used to build trust with an outsider and to ascertain whether or not I was actually an undercover insider. These experiences indicate that affective responses and observations impacted the research process, including participant trust, and ultimately, willingness to reveal personal experiences.

Emotional labor and post-interview debriefing

Qualitative interviewing is an interactional project requiring emotion work by the researcher with participants before, during, and after interviews, therefore, researchers who study sensitive topics tend to engage in emotional labor in a variety of ways (Dickson-Swift, James, Kippen, & Liamputtong, 2007; Gubrium & Holstein, 2003; Hochschild, 1979). Emotional expressions during the interview process are not necessarily negative and it is possible that the participants did not fully understand the emotional benefits of their participation until the post-interview debriefing that included a more in-depth discussion of the current research and its potential impact. At the end of interviews, if participants inquired about their experience in relation to others, I systematically answered questions about patterns that had thus far emerged in the responses. For many participants, this seemed to affirm their experiences and sense of comradery with the Muslim community, but it also seemed to elicit more support and appreciation for the research, especially among those who were doubtful about participating. With international students in particular, I engaged in more overt emotion work both by openly conveying patience and supportive encouragement as they displayed insecurity about discussing experiences in English. Along with language barriers, demonstrating understanding when interviewees were unsure if they were being offensive and legitimizing their feelings by taking a non-judgmental stance also facilitated the interview process. In this way, emotion work via empathy and support during debriefings provided some sense of solidarity and closure for participants.

Additionally, as a researcher engaging in emotion work, I had to engage in specific tactics to build trust. For instance, some participants noted that they had done their research about me before reaching out about the study which included conducting a Google search of my name, title, and public university profile, thus legitimizing my researcher status, while others indicated that they looked for images of me online to determine my racial/ethnic background. Therefore, my physical appearance and publicly available information sometimes facilitated trust but in many other cases required additional repertoire building for those who immediately recognized me as outside of their racial/ethnic, religious, or national background. Where trust was initially withheld, I found myself using the literature or my background experience (as an immigrant, a student, and living in the US post-9/11) to validate and encourage the participants to share more of their stories with me.

In terms of utilizing intersecting identities in this process, I frequently switched between my master identities to better connect with participants. With some participants, I related to them as graduate students; with international students, I referred to my immigrant status to secure a sense of reliability; and with younger participants, I conveyed a more casual demeanor so that the interview did not come off as too formal, and thus, intimidating. During the post-interview debriefing, many participants conveyed that they felt that I had become their friend. One participant, a woman from Saudi Arabia who was very assertive about which questions she would answer and when she felt a question was answered, reflected later that she was surprised that she had shared such private information so openly to a stranger, as though I was her friend, thus, highlighting the fine line between emotion work and friendship between researcher and subject. Participants also engaged in behavior that solidified their perceptions of friendship such as asking for hugs after interviews, requesting to have friends/siblings contact me for advice on graduate school or careers. These experiences speak to the participants' sense of relatability to the researcher based on shared marginalized statuses, and thus, potentially closing some social distance between researcher and subject.

Recommendations for qualitative interviews with marginalized populations

Given the intersectional design of the study, as well as participant interactions to the researcher, there was a frequent assessment of the impact of social identities on the research process. As a woman, an ambiguous person of color, and an immigrant from a lesser-known country (Trinidad), and central to the study, my religious affiliation as an outsider (non-Muslim), were critical in facilitating access to different subset populations within this diverse sample. Beyond recognizing privilege, it is also important to reconsider how any researcher's worldviews are shaped and reshaped in relation to the standpoint knowledge of others; specifically, research subjects who are also marginalized in ways that are similar and different to the researcher. In some ways, my intersecting identities facilitated the research process, and in other ways, hindered it. In this case, my identity was at the core of how and why students chose to participate in the study, as they themselves openly noted. My status as a person of color and an immigrant aided in this process as participants expressed distrust of outsiders, thus, it is increasingly necessary to be transparent about data that may be influenced by not just who the researcher is, but how he/she is perceived to be. For this study, I observed participants' reactions upon initial meetings and at the close of the interviews, but also followed up with participants on their perceptions of my racial/ethnic, religious, and immigrant identity. This follow-up was critical to document how interviewees' ideas of the researcher changed throughout the interview, and specifically, how their perceptions of the researcher impacted their responses during the interview. Trepidation to participate was rooted in fears of being publicly identified as Muslim, and subsequently, retaliation from the university (including faculty and peers), as well as revealing their identity to outsiders (many women did not veil, and thus, were not perceived as Muslim). Graduate students explicitly noted that their trust in me encouraged their participation as they feared a backlash for engaging in research related to their own identities. Given that many of these students had lived in the US post-9/11 and were wary of the current sociopolitical climate, rife with Islamophobia, anti-immigrant, and anti-Black sentiment, they also expressed gratitude to be heard and made more visible through the study.

The participants' sense of being listened to and seen resulted in an outsider obtaining entry into the Muslim student community, and subsequently, insider insight into many issues. For one, students insisted that the researcher was "Muslim too" and questioned my lack of *hijab* or indicated they had been greeted with a *salaam* (which did not occur). Thus, participants racialized the researcher in similar ways to which they had been racialized as Muslim or "foreign" in mainstream society. Many generally assumed that the interviewer was of South Asian (usually Pakistani or Indian) or Middle Eastern (specifically, Saudi Arabian) descent. As noted in this chapter, these perceptions aided in respondent openness, thus, facilitating rapport between researcher and subject and speaks to having obtained "insider moments" as an outsider (Buford, 2014). The vulnerability of Muslim communities during tense sociopolitical times thus results in changing interview dynamics based on participant perception of the researcher as an insider. Given this, it is increasingly important for minority researchers to be more transparent with fellow marginalized subjects as power dynamics exist and persist in different ways even across close social distances.

While strategies were utilized to specifically "get to know" participants instead of "speaking for" them (Tillmann-Healy, 2006), this resulted in various outcomes during data collection. For one, participants expected me to possess cultural knowledge, felt a sense of solidarity, confided both covert microaggressions, and overt victimization including street harassment, slurs, and threats, as well as physical violence. During emotional post-interview debriefings, many participants indicated feeling a sense of therapeutic release as they could unburden themselves of traumatic stories they had not previously shared with others. Thus, the assumptions of a vulnerable group in a cross-cultural interview setting have implications for the researcher, the researched, and the overall ethical process.

Open, supportive, and culturally sensitive interview tactics utilized in the research process can result in enriched data. While participants were made aware of identities, they also conveyed a sense of comfort because of my non-white status, therefore, indicating that race/ethnicity, and perhaps perceptions of white researchers, mattered to vulnerable participants' sense of trust, more than gender, immigrant status, or shared religious identity. Furthermore, being non-Muslim facilitated connections with participants who saw themselves as "born Muslims" because of their family ancestry and traditions but were not necessarily faithful practitioners but rather those who abided by cultural norms of their upbringing. In this way, researcher identity impacted and shaped participant responses, and ultimately, honesty, as students noted that they would have been more careful with how they phrased certain incidents, and specifically, what they reported to a researcher of a different race or one who shared their religious background.

Overall, while there are ethical concerns to consider in terms of the impact of participants' assumptions about a researcher during tense sociopolitical periods that affect marginalized communities, the issues in this chapter provide further insight into the unique dynamic of researchers who are outsiders in various intersecting ways (across race/ethnicity, nationality, or religious status) but engage in research with vulnerable populations that may perceive them as insiders.

Notes

1 A total of 50 interviews were conducted at Mid-Atlantic State (PWI) and Mid-Atlantic State (HBCU), however, the majority of the interviews were conducted at PWI, thus, this chapter focuses on the experiences of the students who attended the larger institution.

2 This study was informed by the specific time period in which data was collected, colloquially known as the Trump era. The Trump effect could be observed nationwide with the surge of discriminatory rhetoric and a spike in bias incidents against marginalized people, including Muslims (Crandall, Miller, & White, 2018; South Asian Americans Leading Together, 2018; Ayoub & Beydoun, 2017).

3 Given that many of the research participants had either lived in the US immediately after 9/11, were the children of parents who experienced trauma in the US post-9/11, or were recent immigrants experiencing anti-immigrant and anti-Muslim Trump era policies such as the Travel Ban, many were apprehensive to discuss their experiences given the sociopolitical climate and narratives around Muslim people and communities. However, this also prompted ethical concerns, as well as a more reflexive approach throughout data collection and analysis.

4 Almost all of the participants in the sample (n=50) portrayed the researcher as a fellow Muslim that was trying to bring awareness to issues the community faced. This was largely in part to the researcher's Arabic first name, racial/ethnic appearance, research topic, and familiarity with social and cultural issues impacting the community.

5 Islamic dress code (Haddad, 2007) symbolizes modesty and identifies veiled Muslim women from non-Muslims, thereby creating an easily recognizable target for hate crimes, discrimination, harassment, and violence against women. Therefore, the intersectional subjectivity of gender, religion, and race/ethnicity, along with perceptions of "foreignness," complicates patterns of violence (Perry, 2014).

6 Black Muslim students have reported exclusion from Muslim student organizations and document the pressure to choose between "being Muslim or being Black."

7 Only a handful of studies specifically examine international Muslim graduate students, the mental health impact of Islamophobia after 9/11 on a small sample (n=5) (Saedi, 2012), and Iranian women in higher education in Canada (Hojati, 2011).

8 At MASU, the International Student Office (ISO) 2015 Report indicates that while students at the university hail from 97 countries, China accounts for 60 percent of the international student population, followed by Saudi Arabia (8.5 percent) and India (5.2 percent). There were also a growing number of students from Kuwait.

9 Early on in data collection, I decided not to address my religious affiliation and racial/ethnic or national origin background until after the interview. Participants engaged in racialization as they made assumptions about me as a result of my name, appearance, and the study: they assumed that I was Muslim, an international student, Asian, or Middle Eastern. On rare occasions, participants assumed I was African American ("Black"), Latina ("Mexican"), or African ("Libyan").

10 I am originally from Trinidad and Tobago, a country with a small Muslim population. I have Muslim family members and friends, and lived in an ethnic immigrant enclave with mosques, halal restaurants, and a visible Muslim presence. Therefore, efforts made to access the Muslim population at the research sites were done with the intention of cultural sensitivity.

11 Early interactions with participants allowed me to understand basic gender dynamics. For one, it was understood that it was inappropriate for men and women to shake hands.

12 *As-salamu alaykum* which roughly translates to "peace be upon you" and is returned with "waʿalaykumu as-salām" which means "and upon you, peace" and is the traditional way that Muslims across the world greet each other.

13 One Iranian participant insisted after the interview that the researcher was Muslim because of the subject of the interviews; another, an Indian graduate student, indicated that she was too fearful to do this type of research and appreciated that someone was.

14 Many participants admitted they were part of the study primarily for the Amazon gift card while some outright refused to accept "payment" for the "good work" they perceived that I was doing by conducting this research.

15 I engaged in several techniques to address this, including typing up a first draft of my notes related to the interviews in a memo format with emergent themes to begin to make comparisons and inferences from the interview data. This was especially useful during weeks where I had multiple interviews scheduled and was unable to have transcriptions done immediately.

References

1,094 Bias-Related Incidents in the Month Following the Election. *SPLC Hatewatch*. Retrieved from https://www.splcenter.org/hatewatch/2016/12/16/update-1094-bias-related-incidents month-following-election

Abualkhair, M. E. (2013). *Arab Muslim International Students' Lived Experiences in a U.S. Higher Education Institution*. Retrieved from ProQuest Theses and Dissertations Database.

Ali, A. I. (2016). Citizens under Suspicion: Responsive Research with Community under Surveillance. *Anthropology & Education Quarterly*, *47*(1), 78–95.

Allen, C. (2015). 'People Hate You Because of the Way You Dress'. Understanding the Invisible Experiences of Veiled British Muslim Women Victims of Islamophobia. *International Review of Victimology*, 21(3), 287–301.

Ameen, U. (2012). Social and Political Climates 'Influence on Muslim American Students' Intersectional Identity. (Publication No.1223498280) [Doctoral Dissertation, California State University. Proquest Dissertations and Theses Global. Retrieved from http://search.proquest.com.udel.idm.oclc.org/docview/1223498280?accountid=10457

Anyan, F. (2013). The Influence of Power Shifts in Data Collection and Analysis Stages : A Focus on Qualitative Research Interview. *The Qualitative Report*, *18*(18), 1–9.

Ayoub, A., and Beydoun, K. (2017). Executive Disorder: The Muslim Ban, Emergency Advocacy, and the Fires Next Time. *Michigan Journal of Race and Law*, *22*.(2), 215–241.

Baboolal, A. A. (2019). *Diversity and Exclusion: An Intersectional Analysis of the Experiences of Muslim Students after the 2016 US Presidential Election*. Retrieved from Proquest Theses and Dissertations.

Barrouquere, B. (2016). FBI: Hate Crimes Reach 5-Year High in 2016, Jumped as Trump Rolled Toward Presidency. Southern Poverty Law Center. Retrieved from https://www.splcenter.org/hatewatch/2017/11/13/fbi-hate-crimes-reach-5-year-high2016-jumped-trump-rolled-toward-presidency-0

Barrouquere, B. (2018). FBI: Hate Crime Numbers Soar to 7,106 in 2017; Third Worst Year Since Start of Data Collection. Southern Poverty Law Center. Retrieved from https://www.splcenter.org/hatewatch/2018/11/16/fbi-hate-crime-numbers-soar-71062017-third-worst-year-start-data-collection

Basford, L. E. (2009). *From Mainstream to Ast African Charter: East African Muslim Students' Experiences in U.S. Schools*. Retrieved from ProQuest Theses and Dissertations Database.

Beydoun, K. (2018). *American Islamophobia: Understanding the Roots and Rise of Fear*. Oakland, CA: University of California Press.

Bhatia, S. (2008). 9/11 and the Indian Diaspora: Narratives of Race, Place and Immigrant Identity. *Journal of Intercultural Studies*, 29(1), 21–39.

Black, L., and Williams, J. (2013). Contradiction and Conflict between "Leading Identities": Becoming an Engineer versus Becoming a "Good Muslim" Woman. *Educational Studies in Mathematics*, *84*(1), 1–14.

Brah, A., and Phoenix, A. (2004). Ain't I a Woman? Revisiting Intersectionality. *Journal of International Women's Studies*, *5*, 3.

Buford, M. R. A. (2014). When the Methodological Shoe is on the Other Foot: African American Interviewer and White Interviewees. *Qualitative Sociology*, *37*(1), 117–136.

Byng, M. (2007). When Religion Matters: The Impact of 9/11 on Muslim American Identity. *Conference Papers-- American Sociological Association*.

Cainkar, L. (2009). *Homeland Insecurity: The Arab American and Muslim American Experience after 9/11*. New York: Russell Sage Foundation.

Cerbo, T. (2010). *Muslim Undergraduate Women: A Phenomenological Inquiry into the Lived Experience of Identity Development*. Retrieved from ProQuest Theses and Dissertations Database.

Chandler, D. (2004). Reversing the Tide: A Complex Visa Process Has Contributed to a Decline in the Number of International Students Coming to the Country since 9/11. *Black Issues in Higher Education*, *21*, 19–20.

Cho, S., Crenshaw, K. W., and McCall, L. (2013). Toward a field of intersectionality studies: Theory, applications, and praxis. *Signs: Journal of Women in Culture and Society*, *38*(4), 785–810.

Clarke, A. Y., and McCall, L. (2013). Intersectionality and social explanation in social science research. *Du Bois Review: Social Science Research on Race*, *10*(02), 349–363.

Collins, P. (1992). Transforming the Inner Circle: Dorothy Smith's Challenge to Sociological Theory. *Sociological Theory*, *10*(1), 73–80.

Collins, P. H. (2000). *Black Feminist Thought: Knowledge, Consciousness, and the Politics of Empowerment*. New York: Routledge.

Corbin, J., and Strauss, A. (2008). *Basics of Qualitative Research: Techniques and Procedures for Developing Grounded Theory*. 3rd ed. Thousand Oaks, CA: SAGE Publication, Inc.

Costello, M. B. (2016). Teaching the 2016 Election: The Trump Effect. Southern Poverty Law Center. Retrieved from https://www.splcenter.org/sites/default/files/splc_the_trump_effect.pdf

Crandall, C. S., Miller, J. M., and White, M. H. (2018). Changing Norms Following the 2016 U.S. Presidential Election: The Trump Effect on Prejudice. *Social Psychological and Personality Science*, *9*, 2, 186–192.

Crenshaw, K. (1989). Demarginalizing the Intersection of Race and Sex: A Black Feminist Critique of Antidiscrimination Doctrine, Feminist Theory, and Antiracist Politics. *University of Chicago Legal Forum*, *14*, 538–54.

Crenshaw, K. (1991). Mapping the Margins: Intersectionality, Identity Politics, and Violence Against Women of Color. *Stanford Law Review*, *43*, 1241–1299.

Crenshaw, K. (1994). Mapping the margins: Intersectionality, identity and violence against women of color. In M. Fineman and R. Mykitiuk (Eds.), *The Public Nature Of Private Violence* (pp. 93–118). New York, NY: Routledge.

Dearden, L. (2016, November). Donald Trump's Victory Followed by Wave of Hate Crime Attacks against Minorities Across US – Led by His Supporters. *UK Independent*. Retrieved from http://www.independent.co.uk/news/world/americas/us

Denzin, N. K. (1989/2001). *Interpretive Interactionism*. Newbury Park, CA: SAGE.

Dickerson, C., and Saul, S. (2016, November 10). Campuses Confront Hostile Acts Against Minorities After Donald Trump's Election. *The New York Times*. Retrieved from https://www.nytimes.com/2016/11/11/us/police-investigate attacks-on-muslim studentsat-universities.html

Dickson-Swift, V., James, E. L., Kippen, S., and Liamputtong, P. (2007). Doing Sensitive Research: What Challenges Do Qualitative Researchers Face? *Qualitative Research*, 7(3), 327–353.

Eisenstein, Z. (2006). Hatred Written on the Body. In P. Rothenberg (Ed.), *Beyond Borders* (pp. 180–194). New York: Worth.

Etman, O. (2016, August 13). For Black muslim students, a two pronged fight for solidarity. PBS News Hour. https://www.pbs.org/newshour/nation/black-muslim-college-students-issue-call-allies

Eversley, M. (2016, November 12). Post-election Spate of Hate Crimes Worse than Post-9/11, Experts Say. *USA Today*. Retrieved from http://www.usatoday.com/story/news/2016/11/12/post-election-spate-hate-crimes worse than-post-911-experts-say/93681294/

Finn, R. L. (2011). Surveillant Staring: Race and the Everyday Surveillance of South Asian Women After 9/11. *Surveillance & Society*, *8*(4), 413–426.

Garner, S., and Selod, S. (2015). The Racialization of Muslims: Empirical Studies of Islamophobia. *Critical Sociology*, *41*(1), 9–19.

Geertz, C. (1973). Thick Description: Toward an Interpretive Theory of Culture. In *The Interpretation of Cultures: Selected Essays* (pp. 3–30). New York: Basic Books.

Gubrium, J., and Holstein, J. (2003). From the Individual to the Interview Society. In Jaber F. Gubrium and James A. Holstein (Eds.), *Postmodern Interviewing* (pp. 21–50). Thousand Oaks, CA: SAGE, Inc.

Haddad, Y. (2007). The Post-9/11 Hijab as Icon. *Sociology of Religion*, 68, 253–267.

Harding, S. G. (Ed.). (1987). *Feminism and Methodology: Social Science Issues*. Bloomington: Indiana University Press.

Harris, P., Haywood, C., and Mac, G. M. (2016). Higher Education, De-centered Subjectivities and the Emergence of a Pedagogical Self Among Black and Muslim Students. *Race, Ethnicity and Education*, 20 (3), 358–371.

Heyman, J. C., Brennan, M., and Colarossi, L. (2010). Event-Exposure Stress, Coping, and Psychological Distress among New York Students at Six Months after 9/11. *Anxiety, Stress and Coping*, *23*(2), 153–63.

Hochschild, A. R. (1979). Emotion Work, Feeling Rules, and Social Structure. *America Journal of Sociology*, 85(3), 551–575.

Hojati, Z. (2013). *Ironic Acceptance -- Present in Academia Discarded as Oriental: The Case of Iranian Female Graduate Student in Canadian Academia*. Retrieved from ProQuest Theses and Dissertations Database.

Jaschik, S. (2016, November 11). *Tensions, Protests, Incidents. Inside Higher Education*. https://www.insidehighered.com/news/2016/11/14/protests-and-incidents-spread-following-trump-election-victory

Johnson, K. A. (2016). *International Student Flows to the U.S. before and after 9/11*. Retrieved from ProQuest Theses and Dissertations Database.

Joshi, K. Y. (2006). The Racialization of Hinduism, Islam, and Sikhism in the United States. *Equity & Excellence in Education*, *39*(3), 211–226.

Karam, N. (2012). *The 9/11 Backlash: A Decade of U.S. Hate Crimes Targeting the Innocent*. Berkeley, CA: Beatitude Press.

Karandish, N. (2014). *Social Support and College Adjustment Among Muslim American Women.* Retrieved from ProQuest Theses and Dissertations Database.

Khan, M., and Ecklund, K. (2013). Attitudes toward Muslim Americans Post 9/11. *Journal of Muslim Mental Health*, 7(1). 1-16

King, N., and Horrocks, C. (2010). *Interviews in Qualitative Research.* Thousand Oaks, CA: SAGE Publication, Inc.

Lofland, J., Snow, D., Anderson, L., and Lofland, H. L. (2006). *Analyzing Social Settings: A Guide to Qualitative Observation and Analysis.* Belmont, CA: Wadsworth, Cengage Learning.

MacGeorge, E. L., Samter, W., Feng, B., Gillihan, S. J., and Graves, A. R. (2004). Stress, Social Support, and Health among College Students after September 11, 2001. *Journal of College Student Development*, *45*(6), 655–670.

Macias, T. (2016). *Saudi Women Studying in the United States: Understanding Their Experiences.* Retrieved from ProQuest Theses and Dissertations Database.

Maruoka, E. (2009). *Veiled Passion: Negotiation of Gender, Race and Religiosity among Young Muslim American Women.* Retrieved from ProQuest Theses and Dissertations Database.

Massey, D. S., Mooney, M., Torres, K. C., and Charles, C. Z. (2007). Black Immigrants and Black Natives Attending Selective Colleges and Universities in the United States. *American Journal of Education*, 113, 243–271.

McCall, L. (2005). The Complexity of Intersectionality. *Signs: Journal of Women and Culture in Society*, 30 (3), 1771–1800.

McCorkel, J., and Myers, A. (2003). What Difference Does Difference Make? Position and Privilege in the Field. *Qualitative Sociology*, *26*(2), 199–231.

McGuire, K. M., Casanova, S., and Davis III, C. H. (2016). "I'm a Black Female Who Happens to Be Muslim": Multiple Marginalities of an Immigrant Black Muslim Woman on a Predominantly White Campus. *The Journal of Negro Education*, *85*(3), 316–329.

Miller, C., and Werner-Winslow, A. (2016, November 29). Ten Days After: Harassment and Intimidation in the Aftermath of the Election. Southern Poverty Law Center. Retrieved from https://www.splcenter.org/20161129/ten-days-after harassment

Mir, S. (2011). "Just to Make Sure People Know I Was Born Here": Muslim Women Constructing American Selves. *Discourse: Studies in the Cultural Politics of Education*, *32*(4), 547–563.

Mishra, S. (2013). Race, Religion, and Political Mobilization: South Asians in the Post 9/11 United States. *Studies in Ethnicity and Nationalism*, *13*(2), 115–137.

Naber, N. (2006). Race, Gender and the Culture of Fear among Arab Immigrants in San Francisco Post 9/11. *Cultural Dynamics*, *18*(3), 235–267.

Nadal, K. L., Griffin, K. E., Hamit, S., Leon, J., Tobio, M., and Rivera, D. P. (2012). Subtle and Overt Forms of Islamophobia: Microaggressions Toward Muslim Americans. *Journal of Muslim Mental Health*, *6*, 16–37.

Nasir, N. S., and Al-Amin, J. (2006). Creating identity safe spaces on college campuses for Muslim students. *Change: The Magazine of Higher Learning*, *38*, 22–27.

Ochieng, A. (2017, February). Black Muslims Face Double Jeopardy, Anxiety in the Heartland. *KPBS.* Retrieved from https://www.kpbs.org/news/2017/feb/25/black-muslims-facedouble-jeopardy-anxiety-in-the/

Perry, B. (2014). Gendered Islamophobia: Hate Crimes against Muslim Women. *Social Identities*, *20*(1), 74–89.

Pinkerton, M. K. (2006). *United States Public Image: A Study of the Perceptions of International Students from Predominantly Muslim Nations.* Retrieved from ProQuest Theses and Dissertations Database.

Redden, E. (2018). New International Enrollments Decline Again. *Inside Higher Ed* https://www.insidehighered.com/news/2018/11/13/new-international-student enrollments-continue-decline-us-universities

Rubin, H. J., and Rubin, I. (2005). *Qualitative Interviewing: The Art of Hearing Data*. Thousand Oaks, CA: SAGE.

Ryan, L., Kofman, E., and Aaron, P. (2011). Insiders and Outsiders: Working with Peer Researchers in Researching Muslim Communities. *International Journal of Social Research Methodology*, *14*(1), 49–60.

Saedi, G. A. (2012). *A Qualitative Study of Islamophobia Post 9/11 in the United States: Building a Theoretical Model of Identity Development of Muslim American Youth Ten Years Following the Aftermath*. Retrieved from ProQuest Theses and Dissertations Database.

Salman, H. (2015). *Their Decision to Wear al Hijab: The Stories of U.S. Northeastern Muslim Women*. Retrieved from ProQuest Theses and Dissertations Database.

Schatz, V. G. (2009). *U.S. and Them: Communicating International Muslim Student Identity at U.S. Universities in the Post-9/11 Era*. Retrieved from ProQuest Theses and Dissertations Database.

Schwandt, T. A. (2007). *The SAGE Dictionary of Qualitative Inquiry* (3rd ed.). Thousand Oaks, CA: SAGE.

Sekhon, V. (2003). The Civil Rights of "Others": Antiterrorism, the Patriot Act, and Arab and South Asian American Rights in Post-9/11 American Society. *Texas Forum on Civil Liberties & Civil Rights*, *8*(1), 117–148.

Selod, S. (2015). Citizenship Denied: The Racialization of Muslim American Men and Women Post-9/11. *Critical Sociology*, 41(1), 77–95.

Selod, S. (2018). *Forever Suspect: Racialized Surveillance of Muslim Americans in the War on Terror*. New Brunswick: Rutgers University Press.

Selod, S., and Embrick, D. G. (2013), Racialization and Muslims: Situating the Muslim Experience in Race Scholarship. *Sociology Compass*, 7, 644–655.

Serhan, R (2013). Citizenship and Crisis: Arab Detroit after 9/11. *Arab Studies Quarterly*, *35*(1), 79–82.

Shdaimah, C., and Leon, C. S. (2018). Whose Knowledges? Moving Beyond Damage-Centred Research in Studies of Women in Street-Based Sex Work. *Criminological Encounters*, *1*(1), 19–29.

Singh, J. (2013). A New American Apartheid: Racialized, Religious Minorities in the Post 9/11 Era. *Sikh Formations*, *9*(2), 115–144.

Singh, S. J. (2015). Muslimophobia, Racialization, and Mistaken Identity: Understanding Anti Sikh Hate Violence in Post −9/11 America. In R. Y. Khan (Ed.), *Muhammad in the Digital Age* (pp. 158–174). Austin, TX: University of Texas Press.

Smith, D. E. (1974). Women's Perspective as a Radical Critique of Sociology. *Sociological Inquiry*, *44*(1), 7–13.

South Asian Americans Leading Together (SAALT). (2018). Communities on Fire Report. Retrieved from: http://saalt.org/report-communities-on-fire-confronting-hate-violence and-xenophobic-political-rhetoric/

Stewart, D. L., and Lozano, A. (2009). Difficult Dialogues at the Intersections of Race, Culture, and Religion. *New Directions for Student Services*, *125*, 23–31.

Tillmann-Healy, L. M. (2006). *Friendship as Method in S.N. Hesse-Biber and P. Leavy's Emergent Methods in Social Research*. Thousand Oaks: Sage Publications.

Chapter 9

"An explanation of each ceremony ... and on which occasion they are performed"

Red Jacket and the presentation of Native history in early American museums

Ryan Bachman

It was already dark by the time crowds began to file inside Rubens Peale's museum. As eight o'clock drew near, stragglers made their way along Broadway toward the brightly lit establishment. Inside, visitors paid the 25-cent entrance fee and strolled past cases of fossils and taxidermy animals before reaching the lecture hall. At the appointed time, an elderly Native American man stepped onto the stage. Sagoyewatha, better known as Red Jacket, began to address the crowd through an interpreter.[1] The Seneca orator was passing through New York City on his way home from Washington, DC, a city buzzing with activity surrounding Andrew Jackson's 1829 inauguration. Red Jacket was still days away from reaching his ultimate destination, the Seneca reservation near Buffalo. As a group of young warriors joined him onstage, Red Jacket explained that the crowd was about to witness a Haudenosaunee[2] war dance. The audience looked on as a drum began to play and the young men began to dance (*Commercial Advertiser*, April 2, 1829).

Museum exhibitions featuring Native people were increasingly common by the late 1820s. During these exhibitions, Native people demonstrated songs, dances, and other ceremonies for paying audiences. This chapter examines such demonstrations as rare instances when Native people were able to present their cultures within the confines of a museum. Although these exhibitions were found in a variety of other venues, such as theaters and taverns, this chapter focuses specifically on museums because of the unique ways that their content interacted with established museum interpretation. In the early nineteenth century, American museums presented their audiences with ethnocentric narratives of Native history and culture. These institutions, invariably owned and organized by white men, used Indigenous material culture to encourage popular notions of Indian primitiveness and racial inferiority. Public exhibitions allowed Native people to challenge these narratives. The 1829 exhibition featuring Red Jacket is used as a vehicle to explore this larger cultural phenomenon.

This chapter proceeds in three parts. The first section examines the general history of American museum culture, from its eighteenth-century origins up through the 1820s. By the time of Red Jacket's 1829 exhibition, museums had established themselves as sites that offered accessible public education and respectable entertainment. The second part is concerned with the history of museum collecting and Native people. Museums used their collections to provide the public with evidence of supposed Native primitiveness. Such prejudicial views permeated American popular culture but enjoyed a unique appearance of academic legitimacy through their presence in museums. The final section of this chapter looks at museum exhibitions featuring Native people and the ways in which their content provided audiences with an Indigenous perspective otherwise absent from museum interpretation.

Numerous scholars have studied Native American performance during the early national era. Philip J. Deloria's well-known 1998 work *Playing Indian* looked at various ways that whites coopted Native culture, but also examined how Native people influenced such depictions from "the margins" (Deloria, 1998, p. 8). Deloria's work was later expanded upon by literary scholar Laura L. Mielke who critically analyzed performances by Native people during this era. Mielke argued that Indigenous people used performances of their respective cultures to challenge the "grab bag" of justifications used to defend American colonial expansion (Mielke, 2011, p. 5). For example, the demonstration of a religious ceremony might challenge the belief that Native people lacked religion, while the reenactment of a harvest ritual could contradict the assumption that Native societies lacked agriculture. Performance scholars Marvin McAllister and Rosemarie K. Bank have also examined issues of Native performance and exhibitionism. In his study of theater culture and "ladies and gentlemen of colour," McAllister (2003) argued that Native people used public exhibitions as a way to demonstrate cultural vitality and thus challenge notions that Indigenous people were dying out in the face of American expansion. Bank (1997) similarly contended that exhibitions of Native history and culture served as a means for Native people to claim both a history and a place in the future of North America.

Because there is relatively little research specifically on the topic of Native exhibitions in the early nineteenth-century United States, this chapter also relies on scholarship related to contemporary developments in western Europe. Such works are used to contextualize similar events across the Atlantic. Historian Timothy J. Shannon (2011) identified connections between colonial expansion and the exhibitionism of Indigenous people in his contribution to the edited volume *Native Acts: Indian Performance, 1603–1832*. His observations on the British Empire can be applied to the rapidly expanding early American republic. Gilles Boëtsch and Pascal Blanchard (2008) similarly examined human exhibitionism in Europe. Their work on human zoos provided this study with contextual information on how exhibitions of Native peoples were used to encourage developing notions of race.

There is a growing body of scholarship on the ways in which Native cultures were presented in early American museums. In 2002, museum scholar

Ellen Fernandez-Sacco examined the ways that early American museums used Indigenous material culture to support the notion that Native people were a prehistoric race incapable of surviving alongside the modern, supposedly civilized American republic. In her 2006 article "(Un)disturbing Exhibitions: Indigenous Historical Memory at the NMAI," historian Myla Vicenti Carpio similarly traced how American museums have historically presented Indigenous people in ways that "benefit[ted] and justif[ied]" colonial expansion (Vicenti Carpio, 2008, p. 620). Most recently, historian Christine DeLucia (2018) looked at the ways in which Native people exerted control over how their cultures were presented in museums, whether through mediating what objects made their way into collections or through the presence of Native visitors themselves within such institutions. This chapter aims to expand upon this body of work by looking at museum exhibits that featured Native performance.

Early American museums

Rubens Peale's institution typified the nominally educational, profit-driven museum culture of the early national era. Officially known as Peale's Museum and Gallery of Fine Arts, it opened its doors in October 1825. The museum occupied the upper two floors of a three-story building at the corner of Murray Street and Broadway. Peale devoted the lower level to his extensive collection of "natural history." Its rooms were cluttered with glass cases full of taxidermy animals, seashells, fossils, and Native artifacts. The upper floor contained a portrait gallery, as well as the lecture hall in which Red Jacket and the anonymous Haudenosaunee warriors appeared in 1829 (*National Advocate*, October 26, 1825 & Peale, ca. 1831).

The New York press lauded the academic merits of Peale's museum. One reporter, after an exclusive behind-the-scenes tour, celebrated its "taste, neatness, and scientific accuracy" (*National Advocate*, October 26, 1825, p. 2). Another unnamed writer praised Peale for establishing a new "school of knowledge" along Broadway (*Evening Post*, October 22, 1825, p. 2). The sprawling collection, carefully organized and paired with hand-written exhibit labels, was described as the perfect means for creating "enlightened citizens" (*Spectator*, November 1, 1825, p. 2). Considering the anonymous nature of these newspaper articles, it is worth considering how involved Peale himself was in their creation. The equation of Peale's Museum and Gallery of Fine Arts with scientific accuracy and public education reflected its owner's marketing prowess, as well as larger cultural attitudes about the role of museums in American society.

Peale regularly advertised the academic merits of his institution. Shortly after opening, he instituted a policy geared toward attracting school groups; teachers got in free of charge, while students were admitted at a special discounted rate. In 1829 alone, Peale sent promotional materials to 350 schools in the New York area (Orosz, 1990). Julia Adams was one of the teachers targeted by Peale's marketing campaign. In a letter to her friend, Adams recounted her class' visit to the institution. Adams praised the educational value of the museum's collection and described it as "scientifically arranged for schools" (Adams, December 7, 1829). A young student echoed Adams' enthusiasm a few years later. The unnamed girl was especially impressed with a display of turtles and snakes, all living together within a "large glass box" (*Evening Post*, March 30, 1835, p. 3).

Peale's school discount program underscored the ways in which civic rhetoric was used to market American museums. Peale may have genuinely cared about providing people with accessible education, but the museum was also his livelihood. In a private letter to his brother, Peale boasted that the discount program provided a steady stream of school groups *and* effectively advertised his museum to students' parents (Orosz, 1990). Profit-driven museums that marketed themselves to the general public were primarily an American phenomenon during this era. Peer institutions in Europe typically restricted collections access to scholars and artists. The relatively broad outreach of museum proprietors like Peale reflected the unique history of American museum culture – a history dominated by Peale's father.

American museum accessibility resulted partly from wartime financial necessity. The nation's first publicly accessible museums sprung up in Philadelphia during the late eighteenth century.[3] It was mainly their public character that distinguished these institutions from their predecessors in Europe and the American colonies. Private "curio cabinets" affiliated with churches, monarchs, and well-off collectors had existed for centuries. These eclectic collections of natural and manmade objects catered to an exclusive clientele and essentially functioned as storehouses and trophy cases for their elite owners. The cultural climate of the Enlightenment caused some European collections to open their doors – but only to enlightened gentlemen interested in nature and history (Orosz, 1990).

Financial woes related to the American Revolution caused American collectors to open their cabinets to the paying public. Gentlemen artists and historians found little demand for their talents in cities wracked by military occupation and economic uncertainty. Charles Willson Peale, the father of Rubens, was one of the most influential people to transform their personal collection into a museum. In 1786, the financially strapped elder Peale opened his cabinet to the public (Brigham, 1995). For 25 cents, Philadelphians could gaze upon his collection of taxidermy birds, fossils, and Native artifacts (*Gazette of the United States*, February 5, 1794). Only a few years earlier, the Swiss artist and author Pierre Eugène du Simitière pioneered this strategy in Philadelphia. His museum only lasted for about two years, unceremoniously closing upon du Simitière's sudden death in 1784 (Orosz, 1990). Charles Willson Peale's institution proved to have a more lasting impact on American museum culture.

Unlike du Simitière, Peale was well-connected with Philadelphia's political and intellectual elites. Through their counsel, he designed an institution that would help shape a "virtuous" American citizenry. Peale promoted his collection of natural and manmade objects as a means for educating the body politic (Orosz, 1990). In order to consistently draw in crowds *and* maintain an appearance of Enlightenment-era respectability, Peale crafted a mission based on what he termed "rational amusement." This theory held that a visit to the museum should be both educational and entertaining; visitors would enjoy themselves as they wandered the rooms and learned about art, history, and nature. New acquisitions were constantly sought to keep the exhibits sufficiently novel and "amusing" (Brigham, 1995, pp. 20–21). Peale's model was emulated for decades. An early visitor to his son's museum similarly remarked that the institution had the power to "amuse while it instructs" (*Evening Post*, October 22, 1825, p. 2).

Early museums relied primarily on their spatial arrangements to instruct the public. The text-based interpretation was much less prominent than it is today.[4] Nineteenth-century institutions subscribed to what intellectual historian Steven Conn termed an "object-based epistemology." According to Conn, it was commonly believed that objects could, essentially, speak for themselves. Museumgoers were expected to discern their meanings through the close examination of artifacts on their own, as well as their placement within the larger museum (Conn, 1998, pp. 4–5). Museum guidebooks and exhibit labels provided the public with only a degree of interpretation. For example, the Columbian Museum in New Haven, Connecticut, contained a well-stocked gallery devoted to Chinese artifacts. Apart from noting the collection's Chinese origins, the museum presented visitors with little actual information (Mix, 1812).

Visitors relied on their own, ethnocentric preconceptions to make sense of exhibitions. With their lack of critical interpretation, museums oftentimes simply confirmed popular notions and prejudices. For example, the Chinese gallery at the Columbian Museum spoke to contemporary American attitudes toward China. As noted by John Rogers Haddad, citizens of the early American republic typically thought of China in abstract, romantic terms. China was envisioned as an ancient and mysterious land and recognized as the source of luxury consumer items, like porcelain. This popular mindset was shaped by the accounts of Yankee merchants who traded in the Chinese city of Canton (Haddad, 2008). The gallery at the Columbian Museum reflected and reinforced such romantic and materialist notions. The exhibit space was stocked with consumer products that would have been familiar to most visitors and complemented by sparsely written interpretation, such as a guidebook entry proclaiming that, although "heathenish and superstitious," China was "not exceeded, if equalled [sic], by any nation whatever in… workmanship and ingenuity" (Mix, 1812, p. 12).

Despite lofty rhetoric about accessible education, early American museums were ultimately business ventures. This reality helped determine the makeup of their audiences. David R. Brigham's exhaustive study of Charles Willson Peale's museum revealed that museum audiences of the early republic were overwhelmingly white and drawn from the middle and upper classes (Brigham, 1995). This was partly because Peale charged audiences 25 cents to view his collection. His price was deliberately exclusive; Peale reasoned that such an admission fee would protect his institution from being "over-run & abused" by the lower classes (Ward, 2004, pp. 103–104). Brigham's cross-referencing between admission records and city directories confirmed the general success of the strategy (Brigham, 1995). This policy was widely copied by subsequent museum proprietors. It was still a common admission fee in 1829 when Rubens Peale charged the same amount for Red Jacket's exhibition (*Commercial Advertiser*, April 2, 1829).

Race-based exclusion took on a more overt form at many institutions. The New York museum run by John Scudder, a rival of Rubens Peale, explicitly banned "coloured people" from visiting in the evening, unless they were "servants with their masters" (Scudder, 1823, p. 1). One New Haven museum took a more materially based approach toward exclusion. A wax model of an enslaved man was placed near the entrance to greet visitors – a less than welcoming sign for the city's African American population (*Connecticut Herald*, September 5, 1809). The same museum, which also posted a 25-cent entrance fee, ironically declared itself a "school for every class of people" in promotional literature (Mix, 1812, p. 9). Although American museums were more accessible than their European counterparts, with their more limited audience of scholars and artists, it is important to note that they were not fully inclusive spaces.

Museums occupied a unique niche within the culture of the early republic. By the early nineteenth century, their educational value was culturally ingrained, and their messages enjoyed an air of scientific authority. However, this perception was largely the result of marketing on the part of museum keepers. In the postwar climate of the newly independent United States, private collectors successfully pitched their cabinets as sites that could shape an educated, virtuous citizenry – for a price. The fact that early American museums operated as private businesses helped restrict who got to take part in their educating mission. Pricing practices and outright racism resulted in audiences that were typically white and members of the middle and upper classes. It was this section of the population that had their worldview – including their views on Native people – influenced by men like Rubens Peale.

Museums and Native material culture

Museums naturalized popular, racialized beliefs about Native people. Nominally scientific theories about "race" proliferated during the era in which American museum culture developed. In order to categorize humanity along with the rest of the natural world, Enlightenment-era theorists divided Earth's population into racial groups. Race was determined by a group's apparent level of "civilization," as well as physical and geographic characteristics. "Civilization" broadly referred to a society's political structures and technological achievements (Adas, 1989). Although specific racial hierarchies varied depending on their author, European theorists invariably placed themselves at the top and the rest of the world's people below. There was no single, unified theory on human difference at the time the first American museums opened – some observers believed that other "races" could eventually advance to levels of European "civilization," while others doubted the possibility – but a model of European supremacy based on supposed cultural and biological criteria was actively under construction (Hoquet, 2014).

The construction of race gave existing prejudice a nominally rational and scientific finish. Colonists had long discriminated against American Indians, but their justifications took on a new form in the wake of the Enlightenment. According to literary scholar Maureen Konkle, William Robertson's 1777 tome *The History of the Discovery and Settlement of North America* was one of the most influential works in shaping popular attitudes toward Native people in the early republic. The work argued that Native people were stuck in a primitive state and could never become as "civilized" as their Euro-American neighbors. Robertson, a Scottish clergyman and historian who never visited the Americas, theorized that Native people were inherently uncivilized because of an inability to form abstract thoughts and thus conceive of religion, governments, or agriculture. According to Robertson, this deficiency led to physiological differences between Native and European people, the former he described as physically and mentally feeble (Konkle, 2004).

Of course, Robertson's theories were based on prejudices rather than observable evidence. Religious beliefs, political structures, and cultivated fields were found throughout the Americas long before the arrival of any Europeans. In fact, maize cultivation was so ingrained in Haudenosaunee culture that settlement sites were selected based on their ability to support the crop (Mt. Pleasant, 2007). Regardless of its gross inaccuracies, Robertson's book remained popular well into the nineteenth century. The same week that Red Jacket appeared at Rubens Peale's museum, a print shop several blocks away announced a new run of the text (*Commercial Advertiser*, April 7, 1829).

Museums reified the ideas spread by theorists like Robertson. In keeping with Enlightenment rhetoric, early American museums organized their collections hierarchically. Charles Willson Peale's main exhibition space, known as the Long Room, served as a template for this type of spatial arrangement. The Long Room was organized to show the "ascending life forms" of the natural world; cases of supposedly lower life forms were located near the floor while images of prominent men were hung near the ceiling (Kelly, 2016, p. 180). Through analyzing images of the Long Room and surviving records of the museum's overall layout, Ellen Fernandez-Sacco found that Native artifacts were either held in cases near floor-level or stored in an adjacent room with prehistoric fossils. This interpretation reflected and reinforced the racialized belief that Native people were lower forms of humanity and apparently frozen in a type of prehistoric "temporal stasis" (Fernandez-Sacco, 2002, p. 601). Rubens Peale followed his father's example when organizing his own museum: Native artifacts were exhibited alongside his collection of American fossils (Peale, ca. 1831).

Written interpretation, however limited, complemented the messages conveyed through spatial arrangements. For instance, Charles Willson Peale advertised that the Native stone tools in his collection could teach museumgoers how "uninformed wild people" apparently made do without knowledge of metallurgy (*Gazette of the United States*, February 5, 1794, p. 5). John Mix, a museum keeper in Connecticut, was even more explicit with his interpretation. Mix's museum catalog urged visitors to compare their modern ways of life against his collection of artifacts showing the "savage genius and savage cruelty" of various "uncivilized nations" (Mix, 1812, p. 10). Early American museum interpretation was clear: Native people were members of a lower order of humanity, one that was apparently fixed in a permanent, primitive state.

Apart from spatial arrangements and written interpretation, the very act of collecting Indigenous material culture helped cast Native people as a racialized Other. All museum collecting relied on some degree of decontextualization. Native artifacts were removed from their cultural contexts and displayed in new settings as determined by their collector. As stated by Beth Fowkes Tobin (1999), such practices exoticized Native culture in Euro-American eyes. An object that had a well-known function within Haudenosaunee society became a curious relic once removed to a museum on Broadway. Crucially, decontextualized artifacts not only lost their original meanings but were also given new significance through their display. Wampum belts that served important cultural functions in Seneca society – such items played integral roles in trade, diplomacy, and record-keeping – often became souvenirs of military conquest when displayed in early American museums (DeLucia, 2018).

Objects seized through military action were foundational to many American museums. This trend began with the nation's first collecting institutions and was ongoing at the time of Red Jacket's exhibition. Du Simitière's museum was full of artifacts taken during the 1779 Sullivan Expedition. The expedition, commanded by General John Sullivan, saw the Continental Army wage a scorched-earth campaign against Native allies of the British. Countless settlements, orchards, and cornfields throughout present-day western New York were razed as thousands of refugees made their way toward the safety of British fortifications near the Niagara River (Mt. Pleasant, 2007). In addition to its widespread destruction, the campaign was also characterized by the theft of Native material culture. Du Simitière, long interested in the history of his adopted country's Indigenous people, sought out "plunder" from the expedition almost as soon as it ended (Fernandez-Sacco, 2002, p. 584). Of particular interest to du Simitière were Haudenosaunee weapons, clothing, and ceremonial masks. It should also be noted that the Swiss collector was eager for scalps, a trend that continued with later museum keepers of the early national era.

The display of body parts effectively dehumanized Native people in the eyes of the museum-going public. Scalps and tanned pieces of human skin were common in early collections, largely because of donors who had taken part in campaigns like the one led by Sullivan. In addition to the theft of material culture, Sullivan's soldiers also routinely mutilated Native bodies in order to collect the scalp bounties offered by various states or to keep as macabre souvenirs (Anishanslin, 2016). In 1790, a Philadelphia museum proudly listed a piece of "DRESSED skin" taken from a corpse during the "march of General Sullivan" among its recent acquisitions (Fernandez-Sacco, 2002, p. 591). The display of body parts literally objectified Native people within the walls of American museums. The fact that such treatment was typically reserved for non-white bodies reinforced the notion that Native people were inferior to the audiences who gazed at their remains under glass. Such exhibition practices endured for generations. Days after Red Jacket departed Rubens Peale's museum, Peale received a shipment of scalps from an army base in Kansas (*American*, April 13, 1829).

It is important to note that not all Native items found in early American museums were seized through such violent means. As noted by Christine DeLucia, Native people often had a degree of control over how their culture was represented in American museums. When the head of the Yale College museum explored a Niantic village, he noted that his fact-finding mission was closely supervised by members of the tribal community. Residents of the village were selective in the cultural knowledge that they shared with the museum keeper from New Haven (DeLucia, 2018). Collections of Native artifacts were often a mixture of items obtained through such negotiated means and those seized through outright violence. Trade goods occupied the same exhibition spaces as stolen items and tanned pieces of skin. All items impressed similar narratives upon their viewers.

Regardless of provenance, racialized displays of Native material culture carried with them significant political connotations. According to Myla Vicenti Carpio, exhibits that presented Indians as a primitive race that "never progressed" helped "benefit and justify" American colonial expansion (Vicenti Carpio, 2008, p. 620). Indeed, the early nineteenth century was a time of extraordinary and aggressive territorial and economic growth. Through land purchases and outright war, the borders of the United States crept increasingly west while new roads and canals cut through the land and ships fanned out around the globe. Within such a context, the belief that Indians were inferior, backward people helped justify the taking of more and more Native land.[5] After all, what use was such a bountiful country to people who, according to skewed Enlightenment rhetoric, lacked the ability to become adequately "civilized," especially when it could be used by the dynamic, growing republic to the east?

These types of perceptions fed into the popular belief that Native people were destined to disappear in the face of American expansion. Although early, eighteenth-century federal policies held that Native people could become "civilized" and coexist with their American neighbors, this notion was fading by the 1820s. Americans increasingly believed that such a "civilizing" change was impossible and predicted eventual extinction for the continent's native inhabitants (Konkle, 2004). Philip J. Deloria described this ideology, later known as the "myth of the vanishing Indian," as grounded in the conviction that "less advanced societies should disappear in the presence of those more advanced" (Deloria, 1998, p. 64). Museum collections provided a material component for this mindset. Displays of Native artifacts alongside prehistoric American fossils not only portrayed Native people as being stuck in a sort of stone-age state of development but also firmly associated them with the continent's distant past while questioning their place in its future.

The myth of the vanishing Indian enjoyed scientific authority through its presence in museums. Museums legitimized a "vanishing" message that was found in numerous types of popular culture. Nineteenth-century American audiences were fascinated with the topic of Native people and the belief that they were fading away. Poems, books, and plays all made liberal use of the trope. James Fenimore Cooper's 1826 work *The Last of the Mohicans* may be the best-remembered example of this phenomenon. The historical novel, set during the Seven Years' War, ends with the death of the titular "last" of the Mohicans and a speech by a Native elder declaring that "pale-faces are masters of the earth, and the time of the red-men has not yet come again" (Cooper, 1826, p. 295). The "last of" genre was immensely popular around the time of Red Jacket's exhibition (Deloria, 1998). In 1830, an advertisement for a Native exhibition at the New York Museum urged the public to come and see "the last of the Delawares" (*Commercial Advertiser*, June 18, 1830, p. 3). Museum exhibitions featuring Native people flourished within a cultural context that assumed their disappearance was inevitable.

Exhibitions of Native people

American museum exhibits featuring Native people arose during a period of intense national expansion. Historian Timothy J. Shannon explicitly linked the rise of human exhibitionism with colonialism. According to Shannon, as empire-building became more about subjugating territory and less about the strategic control of coastal entrepots during the late eighteenth century, Indigenous peoples were increasingly cast as resources under imperial control. As such, colonizers were less likely to view Indigenous peoples as diplomatic partners and more likely to exhibit them as souvenirs of "imperial conquests" (Shannon, 2011, p. 239). According to scholars Gilles Boëtsch and Pascal Blanchard (2008), exhibitions took on a starkly racialized tone by the nineteenth century. The presentation of non-Europeans, invariably described as "savage" or "primitive," provided scientific, corporeal justifications for colonial expansion in their homelands.

Although Shannon, Boëtsch, and Blanchard were concerned with European exhibitions, their observations can be applied to contemporary developments in the United States. The earliest known museum exhibits to feature Native people occurred around the time of the War of 1812.[6] This conflict saw the end of formal British support for Native American territorial sovereignty and intensified efforts at westward expansion in the United States (Turner, 2000). Within such a context, the "myth of the vanishing Indian" flourished. A fantastical essay on the "speculative future" of the United States published in 1818 captured this mindset. Written from the perspective of someone living in September 2000, the story told of flying carriages, the Nicaragua Canal, and the addition of three new states to the union: one was in present-day Alaska, the other two were in Siberia (*New England Galaxy*, March 27, 1818). Native Americans were conspicuously absent from the speculative future. By September 2000, as the speculative-United States expanded into Asia, the nation's Native population was presumably gone.

Museum owners likely arranged exhibitions featuring Native people in order to capitalize on public interest in their supposed disappearance. Before more-organized exhibitions gained ascendancy in the 1820s, proprietors simply invited traveling Native delegations to tour their institutions as they passed through town (DeLucia, 2018). In 1818, one Boston museum advertised an upcoming visit by several "Indian Chiefs" just in case curious city dwellers wanted to show up and watch the delegation walk through the museum (*Boston Patriot & Daily Chronicle*, December 8, 1818, p. 2). Christine DeLucia pointed out that the "very presence" of Native travelers in early American museums complicates the view that such institutions were the "sole preserves of colonial actors" (DeLucia, 2018, p. 111). Active demonstrations of Native history and culture by people like Red Jacket further challenge this perception.

Native exhibitions of history and culture were found in venues like theaters decades before their appearance in museums (McAllister, 2003). Performance historian Marvin McAllister (2003) and literary scholar Laura L. Mielke (2011) both argued that Native performers used such exhibitions to effectively demonstrate cultural survival to theater audiences. Performances functioned as a type of resistance against the belief that Native people were disappearing. Their observations build upon Philip Deloria's claim that Indigenous people were able to shape popular conceptions of Indianness from "the margins" of popular culture (Deloria, 1998, p. 8). Within the walls of a museum, where the disappearance of Native people was uniquely enshrined as scientific fact, such demonstrations of cultural vitality took on a particular type of significance.

Museum exhibits featuring Native people emerged as the museum experience underwent a period of increased commodification. By 1800, the efforts of first-generation museum keepers like Charles Willson Peale were routinely imitated by entrepreneurs who saw museums as a lucrative business opportunity.

Museums were still marketed as respectable, educational institutions, but proprietors expanded the bounds of what could be considered rational amusement in order to draw in paying customers (Orosz, 1990). Rubens Peale exemplified this trend through exhibiting a "Wise Dog" that could supposedly understand arithmetic and tell time, an exhibit he spun as a means of exploring whether animals had the capacity for "reason" (*American*, July 21, 1827, p. 3). As museums sprung up around the United States, especially in the nation's bustling cities, increasingly novel exhibitions were needed to compete within a crowded market (Wood, 2009). Days before he took the stage at Peale's institution, Red Jacket had demonstrated the same program at the rival American Museum (*Evening Post*, March 7, 1829). It was perhaps because of the desire to compete with one another that museums expanded their missions to include the types of spectacles that were previously found mostly in theaters and concert halls.

Haudenosaunee people took part in many of the earliest museum exhibitions of Native history and culture. For instance, 1829 was the third consecutive year that members of the Confederacy appeared at Rubens Peale's museum (*American*, November 2, 1827 & *American*, March 28, 1828). This situation was related to contemporary developments related to struggles over Haudenosaunee sovereignty. Following the American Revolution, in which four nations of the Confederacy sided with the British, the Haudenosaunee were treated as a conquered people by American policymakers (Anishanslin, 2016). Within a generation of the war's end, a series of controversial land deals had reduced Haudenosaunee territory, which once encompassed most of New York State as well as areas further west, to a fraction of its former size (Ganter, 2006). The construction of the Erie Canal, which began in 1817, threatened remaining Haudenosaunee territory as land speculators eyed valuable tribal property along the route of the waterway (Hauptman, 1998). Amid these circumstances, Haudenosaunee people began to increasingly travel to Washington, DC in order to protest encroachments on their sovereignty.

It is important to note that the rise of museum exhibitions featuring Native participants coincided with increased public debate over the westward removal of eastern Indigenous nations. According to James P. Ronda (2002), policies of Indian Removal were initially presented as humane solutions to the "myth of the vanishing Indian." Only through outright removal could such a supposedly "primitive" race be saved from devastating contact with the growing "civilized" nation to the east. In 1825, James Monroe became the first president to request that Congress codify removal as official federal policy (Mielke, 2008). Seven years earlier, the federal government had already advised the Seneca to consider removing to present-day Arkansas (Dennis, 2010). Exhibitions like the one including Red Jacket occurred at a time when such views were becoming more and more mainstream.

Red Jacket became a nationally known figure through his efforts to defend Haudenosaunee sovereignty during this era. Born around 1758 near Cayuga Lake in present-day western New York, he was given the name Otetiani at birth and renamed Sagoyewatha upon reaching adulthood. Sagoyewatha received his English name because of the red jacket he wore while serving with the British during the American Revolution (Ganter, 2006). By the early 1800s, Red Jacket was gaining recognition for his oratory skills. His speeches, delivered through an interpreter at treaty negotiations and councils, pointedly criticized American efforts to encroach upon Haudenosaunee territory and culture. Eventually, local newspaper editors began to attend his speeches and publish translated versions for their curious readers. Two of his best-known orations were published as a pamphlet titled *Native Eloquence* in 1811 (Ganter, 2006).

Although he was well-known as a speaker, Red Jacket's fame was the result of published speeches; few people outside of diplomatic meetings had ever actually heard him speak. Beginning in the 1820s, he began to regularly travel to Washington, DC to seek federal support for Haudenosaunee land claims. It was during these trips that some of the first paintings were made of the Seneca leader. A portrait by New York artist Robert W. Weir was especially popular. During the Christmas season of 1828, a print based on the painting was even marketed as the perfect gift (*New-York American*, January 2, 1829). Ironically, a poem that accompanied the image directly undercut Red Jacket's message of Haudenosaunee cultural vitality. The author, who misidentified his Seneca subject as a Tuscarora, expressed: "Sorrow – that *none are left* to inherit thy name, thy fame, thy passions, and thy throne" (Herbert, 1828, p. 157).

When Red Jacket appeared at Rubens Peale's museum in April 1829, he was on his way home from meeting with the recently inaugurated Andrew Jackson (*Commercial Advertiser*, March 4, 1829). The young warriors who took the stage alongside him were returning from a separate diplomatic mission to the American capital. Unfortunately, their names were not recorded by the New York press (*Commercial Advertiser*, April 2, 1829). According to an acquaintance, Red Jacket appeared at public venues, including museums, in order to finance his trips from the shores of Lake Erie to Washington (Ganter, 2006). Although much research remains to be done on the subject, it appears that many of the Native people who participated in museum exhibitions during the early nineteenth century were travelers, rather than professional performers.

Museum proprietors like Peale apparently sought out travelers upon hearing of their arrival in their respective cities.[7] Indigenous people would perform for a few nights, make some money, then resume their journey. A type of informal network even developed between museums on the route to Washington: the same diplomats who danced for audiences in New York often repeated their demonstrations in cities like Baltimore and vice versa. In one example, a group of Haudenosaunee chiefs staged an elaborate exhibition in Rubens Peale's brother's museum in Maryland before repeating the same spectacle on Broadway just days later as they traveled toward home (*Baltimore Gazette and Daily Advertiser*, March 18, 1828 & *American*, March 29, 1828).

The content of these museum exhibitions was fairly consistent, regardless of which institution hosted the event. The centerpiece of the spectacle was typically a war dance, as was the case at Rubens Peale's museum in April 1829. At eight o'clock in the evening, Red Jacket and a group of Haudenosaunee warriors took the stage in Peale's lecture hall. Red Jacket addressed the young men in his "native tongue," and they broke into the dance. A series of "other ceremonies" followed this introductory display. Throughout the exhibition, Red Jacket spoke to the audience through an interpreter. The elderly chief gave "an explanation of each ceremony… and on what occasion they [were] performed" (*Commercial Advertiser*, April 2, 1829, p. 3). Although the "other ceremonies" demonstrated at the exhibition went unrecorded, an examination of contemporary exhibitions reveals what they may well have been.

A year before Red Jacket arrived at Peale's museum, another exhibition with Haudenosaunee participants was held at the institution. Two Onondaga men agreed to demonstrate a series of dances in the museum's lecture hall. In addition to the war dance, the travelers also demonstrated a dance held to commemorate the election of a new chief and a dance used in the "worship of the Great Spirit" (*American*, March 31, 1828, p. 3). In January 1829, just months before the arrival of Red Jacket, Peale hosted an almost identical program, this time featuring Seneca participants (*American*, January 9, 1829). The "other ceremonies" shown at the Red Jacket exhibition likely included the political and religious dances commonly found in contemporary exhibitions of the early nineteenth century.

Public exhibitions by Native travelers were not necessarily popular with their countrymen back home. In fact, a group of Seneca leaders once condemned Red Jacket's participation in such events as "bad and disgraceful" (Ganter, 2006, p.xxix). On the one hand, this criticism may have been driven by factionalism. Red Jacket was an outspoken critic of Christianity at a time when other Seneca leaders were turning toward that religion (Dennis, 2010). On the other hand, he was also showing important cultural practices to non-Seneca audiences. In 1820, a group of white settlers in upstate New York was quickly rebuffed when they attempted to watch a nearby Haudenosaunee dance (*Orange Farmer*, March 13, 1820). Regardless of motive, Seneca criticisms of Red Jacket underscore the fact that Native performers did not necessarily speak on behalf of their respective nations. Some may well have used exhibitions to aid in the fight for their nations' interests, while others may have taken part for more personal reasons.

Demonstrations of political and religious dances had particular significance in a museum. As noted by Laura L. Mielke (2011), Native people used cultural presentations to challenge the popular notions that justified discrimination and colonialism. Through claiming political and religious identities, Native people refuted two key arguments that were used to cast their societies as primitive and uncivilized: namely, that Indians lacked religion and government. Both of these claims were presented as fact in William Robertson's aforementioned *History of the Discovery and Settlement of North America*, the "standard reference on Indians… in both Europe and the United States" during this era (Konkle, 2004, p. 9).

Exhibitions by Indigenous people provided views of Native history and culture that were otherwise lacking in American museums. Active demonstrations of Indigenous ceremonies clashed against the static and ethnocentric narratives enshrined within the glass cases of early national era institutions. Only yards away from Peale's lecture hall, Native artifacts sat among his collection of prehistoric fossils, spatially reinforcing notions of Indian primitiveness and extinction. Exhibitions held in American museums provided Native people with a unique opportunity to present their own histories and cultures within institutions that otherwise delivered audiences skewed and fatalistic narratives – narratives that lent scientific credence to the "myth of the vanishing Indian" and associated policies of national expansion.

At one point during Red Jacket's 1829 journey to Washington, DC, a venue urged the public to attend his exhibition, as it was likely his last trip outside of upstate New York (*United States' Telegraph*, February 17, 1829). The marketing ploy was correct. Red Jacket died in January 1830 after a bout of cholera (Ganter, 2006). Museum exhibitions featuring Native people continued well after his death. A year after he passed away, Red Jacket's wife and son took the stage at the New York Museum where they demonstrated Haudenosaunee rituals "in the style of ancient Chief Warriors" (*Evening Post*, July 11, 1831, p. 2). These types of exhibitions continued to inject stories of Native history and culture into institutions where those stories were often flattened and misrepresented.

Acknowledgments

The author would like to thank Dr. Dael Norwood and his cohort, as well as Dr. Divya Sharma and the reviewers, for their help in preparing this chapter.

Notes

1 He used both names during his adulthood. This chapter on museum culture uses the name Red Jacket because that was how he referred to himself when addressing museum audiences.

2 The Haudenosaunee Confederacy is composed of six nations: the Mohawk, Onondaga, Oneida, Cayuga, Seneca, and Tuscarora. The league is also commonly referred to as the Iroquois.

3 Although the Charleston Museum in South Carolina is sometimes described as the "first" American museum, it did not open to the public until the nineteenth century.

4 A surviving exhibit label from Charles Willson Peale's museum exemplifies this sparse text-based approach. The label for a "knife case" simply noted that it was "made by the Saukey nation" and named its American donor. David R. Brigham, *Public Culture in the Early Republic*, Fig. 23.

5 For more information on how territorial expansion influenced the racialized views of whites toward Native people, please see: Kariann Yokota, *Unbecoming British: How*

Revolutionary America Became a Postcolonial Nation (New York: Oxford University Press, 2011).

6 One of the first advertisements for a museum exhibition featuring Native people appeared in a Boston newspaper in 1812 (*Yankee,* March 4, 1812).

7 The language of exhibition advertisements suggests this arrangement. For example, Peale noted that Red Jacket "consented" to appear at his museum (*Commercial Advertiser,* April 2, 1829, p.3).

References

Primary Sources

Adams, J. (1829, December 7). *Julia Adams Letter Book.* The Joseph Downs Collection. (Document 131). Winterthur Library, Winterthur, DE.

(1827, July 21). Extraordinary Exhibition. *American.* Retrieved from www.genealogybank.com

(1827, November 2). Peale's Museum & Gallery of the Fine Arts. *American.* Retrieved from www.genealogybank.com

(1828, March 28). Unrivaled Musical Talents at Peale's Museum and Gallery of the Fine Arts. *American.* Retrieved from www.genealogybank.com

(1829, January 9). Peale's Museum and Gallery of the Fine Arts. *American.* Retrieved from www.genealogybank.com

(1829, April 13). Peale's Museum. *American.* Retrieved from www.genealogybank.com

(1828, March 18). Positively the Last Night of the Indians at Peale's Museum. *Baltimore Gazette & Daily Advertiser.* Retrieved from www.genealogybank.com

(1818, December 8). Advertisement. *Boston Patriot & Daily Chronicle.* Retrieved from www.genealogybank.com

(1829, March 4). Grand Celebration of the Inauguration of Our New President. *Commercial Advertiser.* Retrieved from www.genealogybank.com

(1829, April 2). Grand War Dance. *Commercial Advertiser.* Retrieved from www.genealogybank.com

(1829, April 7). Standard Works. *Commercial Advertiser.* Retrieved from www.genealogybank.com

(1809, September 5). Mix's Museum. *Connecticut Herald.* Retrieved from www.genealogybank.com

Cooper, J.F. (1826). *The Last of the Mohicans: A Narrative of 1757,* vol. 2. London: John Miller.

(1825, October 22). The New Museum. *Evening Post.* Retrieved from www.genealogybank.com

(1828, March 29). Peale's Museum and Gallery of the Fine Arts. Retrieved from www.genealogybank.com

(1828, March 31). Unrivaled Musical Talents at Peale's Museum and Gallery of the Fine Arts. Retrieved from www.genealogybank.com

(1829, January 2). The Talisman. *New-York American.* Retrieved from www.genealogybank.com

(1829, March 7). Last Night of the Great Attraction. *Evening Post.* Retrieved from www.genealogybank.com

(1830, June 18). Grand Indian War Dance. *Commercial Advertiser.* Retrieved from www.genealogybank.com

(1831, July 11). For the Benefit of the Indians. *Evening Post*. Retrieved from www.genealogybank.com

(1835, March 30). Visit to Peale's Museum. *Evening Post*. Retrieved from www.genealogybank.com

(1794, February 5). Peale's Museum. *Gazette of the United States*. Retrieved from www.genealogybank.com

Herbert, F. (1828). Red Jacket. *The Talisman*, 157.

Mix, J. (1812). *A Catalog of Part of the Curiosities, Both Natural and Artificial, Contained in the Museum in New-Haven, Collected, Preserved, and Arranged by John Mix*. Early American Imprints, Second Series (No. 26106). Morris Library, University of Delaware, Newark, DE.

(1825, October 26). Peale's New Museum. *National Advocate*. Retrieved from www.genealogybank.com

(1818, March 27). Anno Domini 2000, Anticipated. *New England Galaxy*. Retrieved from www.genealogybank.com

(1820, March 13). Native Amusement. *Orange Farmer*. Retrieved from www.genealogybank.com

Peale, R. (ca. 1831). *Guide Through Peale's New-York Museum, and Gallery of the Fine Arts* (Y.1825.Peale). Patricia D. Klingenstein Library, The New-York Historical Society, New York.

Scudder, J. (1823). *A Companion to the American Museum*. New York: G.F. Hopkins.

(1825, November 1). Peale's Museum. *Spectator*. Retrieved from www.genealogybank.com

(1829, February 17). Red Jacket. United States' *Telegraph*. Retrieved from www.genealogybank.com

(1812, March 4). Indian War Dance. *Yankee*. Retrieved from www.genealogybank.com

Secondary Sources

Adas, M. (1989). *Machines as the Measure of Men: Science, Technology, and Ideologies of Western Dominance*. Ithaca, NY: Cornell University Press.

Anishanslin, Z. (2016). "This is the Skin of a Whit[e] Man": Material Memories of Violence in Sullivan's Campaign. In P. Spero & M. Zuckerman (Eds.), *The American Revolution Reborn* (pp. 187–204). Philadelphia, PA: University of Pennsylvania Press.

Bank, R.K. (1997). *Theatre Culture in America, 1825–1860*. New York: Cambridge University Press.

Boëtsch, G. & Blanchard, P. (2008). The Hottentot Venus: Birth of a "Freak" (1815). In P. Blanchard, N. Bancel, G. Boëtsch, E. Deroo, & S. Lemaire (Eds.), *Human Zoos: Science and Spectacle in the Age of Empire* (pp. 62–72). Liverpool: Liverpool University Press.

Brigham, D.R. (1995). *Public Culture in the Early Republic: Peale's Museum and its Audience*. Washington, DC: Smithsonian Institution Press.

Carpio, M.V. (2008). (Un)disturbing Exhibitions: Indigenous Historical Memory at the NMAI. *The American Indian Quarterly*, *30*, 619–631.

Conn, S. (1998). *Museums and American Intellectual Life, 1876–1926*. Chicago, IL: University of Chicago Press.

Deloria, P.J. (1998). *Playing Indian*. New Haven, CT: Yale University Press.

DeLucia, C. (2018). Fugitive Collections in New England Indian Country: Indigenous Material Culture and Early American History Making at Ezra Stiles's Yale Museum. *The William and Mary Quarterly, 75*, 109–150.

Dennis, M. (2010). *Seneca Possessed: Indians, Witchcraft, and Power in the Early American Republic*. Philadelphia, PA: University of Pennsylvania Press.

Fernandez-Sacco, E. (2002). Framing "The Indian": The Visual Culture of Conquest in the Museums of Pierre Eugene Du Simitiere and Charles Willson Peale, 1779–96. *Social Identities: Journal for the Study of Race, Nation and Culture, 8*, 571–618.

Ganter, G. (2006). *The Collected Speeches of Sagoyewatha, or Red Jacket*. Syracuse, NY: Syracuse University Press.

Haddad, J.R. (2008). *The Romance of China: Excursions to China in U.S. Culture, 1776–1876*. New York: Columbia University Press.

Hauptman, L.M. (1998). The Iroquois Indians and the Rise of the Empire State: Ditches, Defense, and Dispossession. *New York History, 79*, 325–358.

Hoquet, T. (2014). Biologization of Race and Racialization of the Human: Bernier, Buffon, Linnaeus. In N. Bancel, T. David, & D. Thomas (Eds.), *The Invention of Race: Scientific and Popular Representations* (pp. 17–32). New York: Routledge.

Kelly, C.E. (2016). *Republic of Taste: Art, Politics, and Everyday Life in Early America*. Philadelphia, PA: University of Pennsylvania Press.

Konkle, M. (2004). *Writing Indian Nations: Native Intellectuals and the Politics of Historiography, 1827–1863*. Chapel Hill, NC: University of North Carolina Press.

McAllister, M. (2003). *"White People Do Not Know How to Behave at Entertainments Designed for Ladies & Gentlemen of Colour": William Brown's African American Theater*. Chapel Hill, NC: University of North Carolina Press.

Mielke, L.L. (2008). *Moving Encounters: Sympathy and the Indian Question in Antebellum Literature*. Amherst, MA: University of Massachusetts Press.

Mielke, L.L. (2011). Introduction. In J.D. Bellin & L.L. Mielke (Eds.), *Native Acts: Indian Performance, 1603–1832* (pp. 1–26). Lincoln, NE: University of Nebraska Press.

Mt. Pleasant, A. (2007). *After the Whirlwind: Maintaining a Haudenosaunee Place at Buffalo Creek, 1780–1825* (Doctoral dissertation, Cornell University, Ithaca, NY).

Orosz, J.J. (1990). *Curators and Culture: The Museum Movement in America, 1740–1870*. Tuscaloosa, AL: University of Alabama Press.

Ronda, J.P. (2002). "We Have a Country": Race, Geography, and the Invention of Indian Territory. In M.A. Morrison & J.B. Stewart (Eds.), *Race and the Early Republic: Racial Consciousness and Nation-Building in the Early Republic* (pp. 159–176). New York: Rowman & Littlefield Publishing Group, Inc.

Shannon, T.J. (2011). "This Wretched Scene of British Curiosity and Savage Debauchery": Performing Indian Kingship in Eighteenth-Century Britain. In J.D. Bellin & L.L. Mielke (Eds.), *Native Acts: Indian Performance, 1603–1832* (pp. 221–248). Lincoln, NE: University of Nebraska Press.

Tobin, B.F. (1999). *Picturing Imperial Power: Colonial Subjects in Eighteenth-Century British Painting*. Durham, NC: Duke University Press.

Turner, W.B. (2000). *The War of 1812: The War that Both Sides Won*. Toronto, ON: Dundrum Press.

Ward, D.C. (2004). *Charles Willson Peale: Art and Selfhood in the Early Republic*. Berkeley, CA: University of California Press.

Wood, G.S. (2009). *Empire of Liberty: A History of the Early Republic, 1789–1815*. New York: Oxford University Press.

Glossary

ABCD: An abbreviation for **Asset-Based-Community-Development** – a model designed to assess the potential and gifting of local communities.

Afrocentric: It is an approach to the research study of world history that centralizes and prioritizes the history of people of African descent in terms of its focus, design, orientation, philosophical outlook, approach, and presentation.

Afro-sensed: It is a research approach that is based on the African worldview as the foundation for understanding African people. In this case, African beliefs, values, and traditions are observed when conducting research with local indigenous communities.

Anonymization: It is a procedure to offer some protection of privacy and confidentiality for research partners, but it cannot guarantee that harm may not occur.

April Fools' Day hoaxes: On April 1 journalists trick the public with news stories often too outrageous or implausible to be believed. These stories both entertain and highlight the importance of thinking critically about media.

Attack fantasies: Factually undocumented but widely circulated cultural narratives and imagery that project black men as preying on white women and children (e.g., bushy or shaggy-haired stranger).

***Baghdad Burning*:** An award-winning blog written by a young Iraqi computer programmer (pseudonym Riverbend) during the US occupation of Iraq from 2003 onwards. Journalists relied upon her blog for an insight into Iraqi culture during the occupation. It is held as a high standard of citizen journalism by many while some critics still question Riverbend's authenticity.

Below Poverty Line (BPL) certificates: A certificate issued by the Government of India that indicates economic disadvantage and helps to identify people (individuals and households) in need of government assistance for subsidized food, education, healthcare, etc.

Belmont Report: The Belmont Report prepared by the National Commission for the Protection of Human Subjects of Biomedical and

Behavioral Research in 1979 is a statement of basic ethical principles and guidelines that provide an analytical framework to guide the resolution of ethical problems that arise from research with human subjects.

Bias by omission: The bias reflected in the omission of certain information including victimization of individuals or groups. It is commonly called selective observation in social science research.

Bonded labor: Also known as peonage, it is a form of slavery where people give themselves as security in return for debt or loan that they are not able to pay back.

Bushy or shaggy-haired stranger: A mythical figure in American culture that is scapegoated for violent crimes. This figure is often attributed to be black because of his stereotypical defining feature of bushy or shaggy hair. For example, Diane Downs in 1983 and Susan Smith ten years later, accused such individuals of murdering their children, crimes of which they were both later convicted. When the race is not explicitly stated it can be a coded racial reference by connoting race with hair type.

Central prison: In India, a central prison is a type of prison with larger capacity to accommodate prisoners, mostly convicted prisoners.

Child labor: Exploitation of children through any work that deprives them of their childhood, education, playtime, etc. It is morally and socially harmful, physically and emotionally exploitative, and a violation of basic human rights.

Children of prisoners: This group would include children between the age of 0 to 4 years who can be with the mothers inside the prison; and children above the age of 5 to 18 years who are outside the prison with their families or abandoned or in State custody.

Citizen journalism: When people who are not journalists by profession participate in the process of collecting and disseminating and/or commentating on newsworthy content, often by way of digital technology and social media.

Civilization: An evaluation of a given group based primarily on cultural criteria, such as religion, political structures, and technology. European and American observers placed their respective societies atop a hierarchy of civilization, with the rest of the world's people below.

Collective conscience: It is a concept defined by Émile Durkheim as 'the body of beliefs and sentiments common to the average of members of a society'.

Colonial tropes (reference Hinduphobia): Depicting Hindu suffering or deaths as unimportant and erasing the mention of Hindu victimhood. Depicting Hindus as a danger even in reports where they have been victims. It also includes erasing a Hindu view of history and depicting them as sexualized characters lacking in self-control and ethics.

Community-engaged research: Research in communities conducted by focusing on indigenous approaches and theories and including partnerships with the people who live in the communities.

Confidentiality: It is a principle that allows people not only to talk in confidence, but also to refuse to allow the publication of any material that they think might harm them in any way.

Consent note: It is a note that is signed or orally agreed to, in which the research participant understands the research and its risk. It is a tool to obtain informed consent.

co-opt: Majority cultural group members who use or claim the culture, identity, or perspectives, of minority cultures.

Countertransference: It is a concept in psychoanalysis in which the counsellor projects his or her feelings unconsciously onto the client.

Criminology: The scientific study of crime and criminals, including why individuals commit a crime, why groups of people come together to commit a crime, and why certain locations attract, sustain, and generate crime.

Cultural relativism: An understanding that certain behaviors, customs, attitudes, and values can only be explained within the context of the culture in which they originate and develop. It is aimed at sensitizing people to a different culture, however, it has also been criticized for being in conflict with certain universal rights.

Death penalty or Capital punishment: It is an ultimate or capital form of punishment in which the state sanctions the execution of a person who is convicted of capital crimes that are punishable by death in the legal codes of particular States.

Death row: It is a particular section isolated from the rest of the prison that houses prisoners convicted of death penalty either awaiting their execution or the ones who have appealed to higher courts or are waiting for a decision of their mercy petition to the governor of the federal state or President.

Decolonize/Decolonization: Decolonization of higher education refers to the process of native populations reclaiming their histories, voices, and stories, and narrating and documenting them from their lived experience and perspective. It also refers to questioning, challenging, and even undoing colonial interpretations, stereotypes, and perceptions of native cultures, peoples, and practices.

District prison: District prisons serve as the main prisons in states and union territories where there are no Central Prisons.

Epistemology: is a to a theory of knowledge, especially with regards to methods, validity, and scope, and the distinction between justified belief and opinion.

Ethnocentrism: Evaluating and drawing inferences about other cultures based on values, customs, and norms in one's own culture; rooted in a sense of superiority about one's own culture, values, etc.

Eurocentric: It is an approach that is overtly biased towards European history and civilization while undermining the contribution to global history by other civilizations such as African and Asian civilizations etc.

Exploratory research: Research that probes hidden meanings that people attach to social phenomena. It helps explain the framework within which various behaviors, attitudes, causal relations, and perceptions are shaped.

Facts by repetition: These are created when one piece of information is picked up by multiple sources and disseminated across all forums, without checking the veracity, authenticity, or context of the information.

Gatekeepers: They are individuals who are mediators or in-charge for granting permissions to access research settings and participants within social research.

Generalizability: It is the ability to generalize findings or observations based on a sample to the larger population or a group.

Germinal: A gender neutral to describe a body of knowledge or text as foundational, influential, or groundbreaking.

Hawala: It is a type of informal banking system that allows people to transfer money either without going through formal banks, without following formal procedures, or both. Many researchers and policymakers see Hawala only as an Islamic banking system, but in many countries including India, many non-Muslims also use it.

Helicopter researcher: Researchers who fly in and out of settings, take data and leave, and give nothing back.

Hinduphobia: It is the anti-Hindu sentiment or negative perception of Hindus based on their religious beliefs. It refers to negative stereotyping, loathing, insulting, and hate for Hindu symbols, practices, and values. It also involves willful distortion of Hindus in historical, cultural, religious, and sociopolitical contexts.

Hundi: It was a Bill of Exchange and an integral part of the indigenous banking system in India. In India, the terms Hundi and Hawala are often used interchangeably as they serve the same purpose.

Hyperpersonal communication: The experience of feeling more emotionally connected and/or bonded with someone more quickly when we connect with them via mediated versus face-to-face communication. It might be engagement with the videos, writings, and/or images of a person, versus the actual live person, that prompts this hyperpersonal connection.

Indigenous knowledge: It refers to knowledge that is located in various local communities used for survival. Every community has its own history of indigenous knowledge either recorded or orally transmitted.

Indigenous knowledge systems: It refers to systems that are located at various local communities used collectively or by local experts for livelihood and sustainability. Some of the examples of these systems include local knowledge about fisheries, mining, farming, oral history, medicine, local legal knowledge, etc.

Informed consent: It provides information to the participants to take part or refuse in a study after having received full information about the nature, risk and purpose of the study.

Institutional Review Boards/Ethics Committees: Boards/ committees set up to evaluate, approve, and monitor research involving human subjects.

Intertextuality: Every text that is created both interconnects and owes its origins to several other texts. Texts can be created by formal cultural industries (i.e., film, television), informally by individuals (i.e., a blog post) or cultural groups (i.e., a cultural story passed down orally).

Kali Beri settlement: It is government-owned land Ethics and generalizability 17 located approximately 18 kilometers (11 miles) from Jodhpur in the state of Rajasthan, India. About 200 Hindu families displaced from Pakistan have made it their home approximately since 1999/2000.

Liberal Orientalism: A perspective that views itself as an educated and open-minded Western perspective on the East/Middle East, however, like Orientalism, it has unexamined blind spots when it comes to representing the diverse region and its peoples in a problematic way (i.e., generalized, simplified) and/or by attempting to speak for this region and its peoples.

Male gaze: Viewing women, and indeed the world, from a perspective that sexualizes and objectifies women as objects for male sexual pleasure and or dominance.

Measurement reliability: When the researcher selects the method that adequately measures what is being studied.

Mid-Day Meal Scheme: Under the Government of India's Midday Meal Scheme, children in school receive free lunch on weekdays. It is aimed at improving the nutritional standing of school-age children. It has also attracted children from disadvantaged sections who may otherwise skip school.

Mistranslations (reference, Hinduphobia): Many words associated with Hinduism have specific meanings and contexts that Sanskrit and Indian languages experts would know, but the Western media often make up their own versions.

Museum: In an early American context, these institutions provided paying audiences with entertaining and nominally educational content. They were typically operated by entrepreneurs rather than academics.

Muslim boogeyman: A mythical figure meant to represent a Muslim man in the Western imagination who is capable of violence and tyranny both in his own family and within wider society. It is the product of an Orientalist perspective.

National Crime Records Bureau (NCRB): The NCRB is an Indian government agency responsible for collecting and analysing crime data. This Office also produces the Prison Statistics India among other data.

Naxalites: Naxalites are a group of far-left radical communists, supportive of Maoist political sentiment and ideology. The term Naxalites comes from Naxalbari, a small village in West Bengal.

Neo-colonial Hinduphobic tropes: Mistranslations of Hindu meanings and appropriation of Hindu symbols to equate Hinduism or Hindu nationalism with Nazis-ness; denial of Hindu indigeneity to India.

Non-probability methods: Sampling methods that are generally used when the sampling frame is not available; not every element in the population gets an equal and unbiased chance of getting selected in the sample.

Orientalisma: Western point of view that relies heavily on stereotypes that situate the West as the dominant culture and the East as its inferior counterpart to serve Western viewpoints, desires, and interests. It also refers to the tendency to portray Asia (or scholarly works by Asians) in stereotypical ways that embody a colonial view of native culture, language, religion, values, attitudes, and larger social and political systems and behaviors.

Overgeneralization: Studying a handful of cases and drawing conclusions about the settings, groups, or cultures that they do not fully represent.

Overidentification: It is a concept in social psychology when an individual identifies oneself to an excessive degree with someone or something else, especially to the detriment of one's individuality or objectivity.

Participatory research: It offer ways to identify and promote indigenous approaches and methods that bridge gaps between African people and African scholars from outside the local community and those who come to Africa from other parts of the world to conduct research.

Paternalistic benevolence: A privileged male perspective whereby an individual believes he knows more and/or better than a less powerful or less knowledgeable who must be educated, elevated, or saved. It is akin to white male privilege.

Penology: The study of punishment for crime and how society responds to crime and criminals.

Photo essay: A set of photos that creates a unified story about the subject, people, and setting. It may include brief comments and captions or full-length essays explained with photographs.

Postcolonial scholarship: An examination of colonial relationships, structures of power, ideologies, and cultural impact that occurred when formerly colonized countries gained their political independence. For some scholars, the term postcolonial is controversial because it suggests that we can draw clear boundaries around and separate periods in history who suggest that the lived experience of colonization is not so easily delineated or ended.

Primitive: From a European and American perspective, the belief that a given group was lacking in civilization.

Qualitative research: Research methods that require a semi structured and unstructured (not haphazard) approach, in which a criminologist may not be able to predetermine every aspect or step of research and may face unanticipated circumstances.

Race: A socially constructed, white supremacist understanding of human differences based on supposed physiological characteristics. In the early American republic, primitive traits were increasingly understood as biologically determined and permanent.

Recidivist: It is a category of criminal who re-offend even after being convicted for a similar crime before.

Religious persecution: Systematic mistreatment of people (individuals or groups) due to their religious beliefs. The mistreatment may entail bias, discrimination, and violence including kidnapping, rape, and murder, and so on.

Researching back: A term coined by Mogomme A. Masoga (28 June 2018) to capture the collective and community participatory mandate to deeply understand-the-work-together as equal partners to ensure the research process is meaningful to the community and honors indigenous knowledge systems.

Rotherham scandal: Predominantly British-Pakistani men (Kurdish and Kosovan men were also involved [Jay, 2014]) targeted teenagers for sexual grooming and raped them, but the sexual victimization was ignored for years as a) the police did not want to come across as xenophobic, racist, or Islamophobic when the victims where white teens; and b) though most of the victims were white girls, the police were accused of normalizing these acts of sexual abuse and violence as part of "their culture" when the victims were South Asian teens.

Sample: Subset or part of the population that is studied to make generalizations about the population.

Selective observation: The practice of selectively looking at only the information that is in line with what the researcher expects or prefers to find and conclude.

Self-reported data: This kind of data is obtained about one's behaviour, attitude or believes provided especially by one who is a subject of research. Self-reported data is limited by the fact that it rarely can be independently verified while conducting a qualitative research study and gathering the data on one's own.

Sex slave/sexual slavery: Enslavement that restricts a person's movement and autonomy, and s/he is used as a slave for sexual purposes by an individual or a group.

Social capital: The status, networks, or social relations that one has in a society; these improve an individual's stature, create a feeling of self-worth, and encourage others (individuals and institutions) to trust the individual.

Social institutions: A way of assisting people to identify shared values and goals so they can work toward a common interest.

Stand your ground: A cultural theme seen in hero narratives whereby the protagonist does not flee when confronted with violence, terror, and/or a more dominant, though villainous, opponent.

Telescoping: It is the tendency to have inaccurate memories concerning how recent and frequently events occurred.

Textual power: A method proposed by English literature scholar Robert Scholes that seeks to uncover the ideologies, structures of power, and intertextual origins of texts produced by a culture through the textual analysis skills of reading, interpretation, and criticism.

Total institution: Ervin Goffman (1961) describes five types of 'total institutions' of which one is the prison. This characteristic of this institution is to protect the community against what are thought to be intentional dangers to it.

Ubuntu: Implies a sense of humanness, recognizing, and caring about the human dignity of others, which should be adhered to in all research involving local indigenous communities.

Undiyal: It is a type of informal banking system used mainly in Sri Lanka; in Tamil, it means a piggy-bank, and in Sinhala, it means black-market or "kalu kadey".

Universal Just Action Society (UJAS): It organizes assistance for Hindu refugees and forced migrants from Pakistan. It helps them with food, shelter, jobs, legal advice, medical assistance, and so on. It was formerly known as the Seemant Lok Sangthan and formally founded as UJAS in 1999. It carries out social and legal advocacy work.

United Nations Rapporteur on Torture: A Special Rapporteur is an independent expert appointed by the Human Rights Council to examine and report back on a country situation or a specific human rights theme, in this context, torture.

Victimology: The study of victims of crime, factors contributing to victimization, and the impact of victimization.

Warder: Warder is a trusted convicted prisoner with duties that s/he carries in the prison as part of rehabilitation process.

Western epistemology: Refers to a theory of knowledge that is influenced and dictated by Western methods, validities, and scoping.

Index

Page numbers in **bold** denote tables

For Product Safety Concerns and Information please contact our EU
representative GPSR@taylorandfrancis.com
Taylor & Francis Verlag GmbH, Kaufingerstraße 24, 80331 München, Germany

www.ingramcontent.com/pod-product-compliance
Ingram Content Group UK Ltd.
Pitfield, Milton Keynes, MK11 3LW, UK
UKHW021301190926
475701UK00009B/529

* 9 7 8 0 3 6 7 6 4 4 4 7 5 *